to Ted
in struggle for social justice
Venceremos,
Cliff
Jan 2013

RECREATING DEMOCRACY
IN A GLOBALIZED STATE

D0946093

RECREATING DEMOCRACY IN A GLOBALIZED STATE

EDITED BY

Cliff DuRand and Steve Martinot

CLARITY PRESS, INC.

© 2012 CENTER FOR GLOBAL JUSTICE

ISBN: 0-9852710-3-5
978-0-9852710-3-9
EBOOK: 978-0-9852710-5-3
In-house editor: Diana G. Collier
Cover: R. Jordan P. Santos

Credit for cover photos:

"Day 60 Occupy Wall Street November 15, 2011" by David Shankbone
http://commons.wikimedia.org/wiki/File:Day_60_Occupy_Wall_Street_
November_15_2011_Shankbone_16.JPG

"Wall Street: A New Era" by Henry Han
http://en.wikipedia.org/wiki/File:A_New_Era.jpg

"Capitol Hill: Washington, DC" by Vinoth Chandar
http://commons.wikimedia.org/wiki/File:Capitol_Hill_-_Washington,_
DC.jpg

ALL RIGHTS RESERVED: Except for purposes of review, this book may not
be copied, or stored in any information retrieval system, in whole or in part,
without permission in writing from the publishers.

Library of Congress Cataloging-in-Publication Data

Recreating democracy in a globalized state / edited by Cliff DuRand and Steve
Martinot.
     p. cm.
  Includes bibliographical references and index.
  ISBN 978-0-9852710-3-9 (alk. paper) -- ISBN 0-9852710-3-5 (alk. paper)
  1. Nation-state. 2. Nation-state and globalization. 3. Globalization--Political
aspects. 4. Transnationalism. 5. Sovereignty. 6. Democratization. I. DuRand,
Cliff. II. Martinot, Steve.

  JC311.R317 2012
  320.1--dc23

                              2012006881
                          Clarity Press, Inc.
                    Ste. 469, 3277 Roswell Rd. NE
                       Atlanta, GA. 30305 , USA
                       http://www.claritypress.com

TO ALL THOSE WHO STRUGGLE
FOR SOCIAL JUSTICE

TABLE OF CONTENTS

INTRODUCTION

Cliff DuRand and Steve Martinot

"We have about 50% of the world's wealth, but only 6.3% of its population.... In this situation, we cannot fail to be the object of envy and resentment. Our real task in the coming period is to devise a pattern of relationships which will permit us to maintain this position of disparity.... To do so, we will have to dispense with all sentimentality and day-dreaming; and our attention will have to be concentrated everywhere on our immediate national objectives.... We should cease to talk about vague and ... unreal objectives such as human rights, the raising of the living standards, and democratization. The day is not far off when we are going to have to deal in straight power concepts. The less we are hampered by idealistic slogans, the better."

George Kennan
Policy Planning Study 23
written for the State Department planning staff in 1948[1]

The Development of Underdevelopment

At the time Kennan was writing, the US was embarking on an effort to reconstruct capitalist economic systems that had been devastated by World War II and the decade of depression that had preceded it. This included preventing countries of what would come to be called the Third World from escaping from the capitalist orbit. The fear was that they would turn to socialism as a way of overcoming their legacy of underdevelopment, joining the Soviet Union, which had already done so. China soon did and together they constituted an alternative Second World. What would become a four decade long Cold War ensued, a war that became very hot in various countries of the Third World. Korea, Vietnam, the Dominican Republic, Nicaragua were battlefields where the US sought to prevent socialism. This was deemed essential to accomplish the objective Kennan had articulated—keeping the world's wealth in the control of the capitalist First World.

Behind the mask of the Cold War armies marched in the name of freedom and capitalist corporations expanded in the name of development. And through it all, the gap between rich and poor countries continued and even widened. The foundations for a new world order called globalization were being constructed bit by bit.

In one sense we might say globalization began in 1492. That date symbolizes European expansion into what was for them a New World. That began a process that was to raise Europe from an obscure peninsula on the western fringe of Asia to a center of world power. And more significantly that process fueled the development of a new kind of economic system—capitalism—that was to become global in its scope. Colonialism was of particular importance in the development of capitalism because it was an initial stage in the process of combined and unequal development. The colonization of much of the Americas, Africa and Asia underdeveloped the societies of those continents into dependent appendages of Europe, impoverishing them in the process and enriching the 'Mother countries.' It was this 'primitive accumulation' that jump started capitalist development in the West. As has often been pointed out, when the British came to India, it was a land of immense wealth and Britain was poor. When the British left, India was poor and Britain wealthy. Britain had developed by dispossessing India.

The present division between rich industrialized countries and poor underdeveloped (or often today euphemistically called "developing") countries had its historical origin in an imperialism that entailed military conquest, European settlements and the cultural derogation of the colonized people. While the era of colonialism has largely passed, the resulting development of underdevelopment has led to what has been called neocolonial imperialism. Those countries subjected to dependent development are still afflicted by the process of combined and unequal development. Now when transnational corporations invest in the global South it is said they contribute to "economic development." But rather than contributing to development of the national economies of the South, foreign investment increases their dependency. The gap between rich and poor countries increases. Only slowly have people learned to call this imperialism as well, an imperialism characterized by the invasion of private corporations rather than armies marching across borders.

The focus of this volume is an analysis of what has emerged in our contemporary era from that process. Corporate investment has stretched its tentacles over the world, globalizing itself. But it also morphed its own structure, from nationally based corporations (exploiting local labor in their own name) to multinational corporations (exploiting local labor through local subsidiaries) to transnational corporations, which have become a new form of capitalist control over local economies and their politics, a networked structure of economic processes that has come to be known as corporate globalization. With the notable exception of Cuba, few countries have escaped it.

Inequality is inherent in capitalism. As an economic system capitalism rests on a class division between those who own the means whereby society produces the goods it needs, and those who do not, and must sell (or alienate) their labor power to the former group. That commodification of labor enables the owners of capital to appropriate the surplus value that labor produces resulting in an accumulation of wealth in the hands of capital. The creation and replication of such a division is a necessary condition for constituting capitalism (and in the case of Russia and China, reconstituting it).

That relation of exploitation between unequal classes within a capitalist society is replicated in the relations between rich and poor countries. The globalization of capitalism has resulted in a similar relation between the corporations of the core capitalist countries and the underdeveloped, dependent countries of the global South (formerly called the Third World). The advanced stage of globalization that we have witnessed over the last third of a century has entailed a growing incorporation of the economies of the South into an integrated system of capital accumulation under the aegis of transnational corporations (TNCs).

This can be illustrated concretely with the global production chains that have become a signature feature of contemporary capitalism. Components may be manufactured in Singapore, transported to China for subassembly and then shipped to Mexico for final assembly before sale in the United States. What we have here is a global assembly line presided over by transnational corporations. Although such assembly lines are geographically dispersed, they overcome the limitations of the fixed assembly lines of the Fordist era in that they no longer have to rely on a fixed labor force that can organize itself to effectively claim a share of the surplus they create. Instead, the global assembly line gives capital the flexibility to seek out the lowest wage workforce and friendliest business environment available anywhere in the world. This has been made possible by the development of a global computerized network of instant communications via satellite. That and the computerization of banking have made money transfers and the movement of capital both easy and instantaneous. The communications network also allows the decentralization of technological development and design. Technicians can work at points distant from the processes of production to which they address themselves. And the entire process can be coordinated by management located anywhere on the globe. The limitations of space and time have been overcome by digital communications and cheap energy for transporting goods to their ultimate consumers.

For such globalized production to be possible, capital must be mobile, flowing freely across national borders. And at the same time products have to be able to move with minimum friction across those borders, unhampered by tariffs or quotas or nonuniform standards. In other words, there must be free trade in order for transnational capital to optimize accumulation.

Neoliberalism and the State

The policy prescriptions that have guided corporate globalization have been derived from neoliberalism. This ideology is dissected by Cliff DuRand in the opening essay. Although the term 'neoliberalism' is not as familiar in the US as it is elsewhere in the world, this has been the dominant public ideology since the 1980s. It is familiar in the call for deregulation, privatization, free markets and less government. It is 'neo' in the sense that it is a resurrection of 19th century liberalism as distinct from the social or welfare liberalism associated with the New Deal. While its ancestor asserted the primacy of the individual (to sink or swim on his own), neoliberalism asserts the primacy of the corporation over the interests of individuals.

As David Harvey has pointed out, neoliberalism is a class project of capital designed to regain a larger share of the social surplus than had been possible under welfare liberalism.[2] Through an internal critique of neoliberalism, DuRand shows how it accomplishes that while purporting to advance freedom and equality. Corporate-led globalization is an extension of the same class project on a global scale.

With assistance from the state, corporate capital adopted neoliberal globalization as a fix for the crisis of overaccumulation that afflicted it in the last quarter of the 20th century. A tendency endemic to capitalism, a crisis of accumulation occurs when there is too much capital and not enough places to invest it profitably. A stagnation (i.e. lack of growth) in the economy results. When such limits are reached, there are ways of fixing the problem.[3] Neoliberal globalization was one such fix. The post WW II class compromise between capital and labor had enabled organized labor in large corporations to claim a share of rising productivity in the form of higher wages and benefits. But with a declining rate of profit setting in, incentives for further capital investment weakened. The problem was set forth in a 1984 policy address by IMF Director Jacques de Larosière:

> Over the last four years the rate of return on capital investment in manufacturing in the six largest industrial countries averaged only half the rate earned during the late 1960s.... Even allowing for cyclical factors, a clear pattern emerges of a substantial and progressive long-term *decline in rates of return on capital.* There may be many reasons for this. But there is no doubt that an important contributing factor is to be found in the significant increase over the past twenty years or so in *the share of income being*

> *absorbed by compensation of employees*.... This
> points to the need for a gradual reduction in the
> rate increase in real wages over the medium
> term if we are to *restore adequate investment
> incentives*.[4]

Finding insufficient places within developed national economies for profitable investment, capital looked abroad for lower wage labor. Corporations roamed the globe in search of cheap, compliant labor and used the all too real threat of "leaving home" to force down the wages and benefits of their traditional workforces. Expensive regulations were relaxed or circumvented. Public services (like trash collection, water, education, etc.) were privatized so as to become available for profitable investment. Both at home and abroad, capital was freed up to continue to heighten the process of accumulation.[5]

It is important to recognize that these openings for corporate capital required action by the state despite the tenets of neoliberalism which call for a minimalist state. While claiming to give priority to the market, neoliberalism actually seeks an active role for the state in two areas: defense and the creation and maintenance of the conditions necessary for a market to operate. It is precisely the latter that states have undertaken in initiatives to constitute a global market. The US in particular has championed neoliberal policies throughout the South. In the name of free trade, it established trade agreements with Canada and Mexico, opening the entire continent of North America to corporate capital, and attempting to extend it to the entire hemisphere. Operating through the World Bank and the International Monetary Fund, structural adjustment programs (SAPs) transformed economies of the South along neoliberal principles, thereby opening them to transnational corporations. What is called privatization might more aptly be called corporatization, since the process takes public assets formerly used to promote a common good and turns them over to corporations for private profit. Further, the US government led in establishing the World Trade Organization (WTO) to decide trade disputes according to neoliberal rules written by the technocrats of the transnational corporations. Clearly globalization has been a class project to benefit capital that could only be constructed by a state acting on its behalf.

The result has been a growing inequality in the global economy. Under the operations of neoliberalism, the globalized corporate economy has produced an enormous concentration of wealth, unprecedented in the history of the world, while at the same time it has also produced an unprecedented degree of impoverishment. Nowhere is this seen more starkly than in the inequality between the global North and the global South.

The countries of the South have been largely peasant societies. There the bulk of the population had sustained itself through small scale agriculture, with the surplus that was produced circulating in local and, to a lesser degree, national markets. Frequently peasant access to land was ensured by tradition and law. In the case of Mexico, for instance, the traditional access to land that had been destroyed by the *conquistadors* was restored through the 1910 revolution that gave land to the tiller and codified that in the 1917 constitution as *ejido* land, i.e. community held land that could not be sold. Among the neoliberal conditions the U.S. required of Mexico for admission into NAFTA was a new legal framework that allowed for the privatization of the communal *ejido* land—a modern day enclosure of the commons. This has had two consequences favorable to transnational capital: 1) the replacement of small scale peasant agriculture by agribusiness producing for export, and 2) the proletarianization of the peasantry, freeing vast quantities of labor power from the land and communities, making it available as wage labor for capital or as a reserve army of labor that would keep wages low. All of this opened new opportunities for profitable investment and renewed capital accumulation.[6]

In this and other SAPs we can see the close relationship between corporate capital and the state. Historically corporations and nation-states grew up together, as Steve Martinot suggests. It was the monarchy that chartered corporations for the purposes of exploration, exploitation and colonization of the New World. Recall that the Hudson's Bay Company and the Virginia Company were corporations that brought the settlers to North America. It was such corporations that settled the continent and the revolution of 1776 was not only against the King but also against his corporations. The new nation-state of the United States was initially very wary of corporations. But as industrial capital found the corporate form convenient and necessary for large scale undertakings, this limited liability joint ownership form grew in the post Civil War years until in 1886 the Supreme Court awarded a privileged legal position to corporations by declaring them fictitious persons under the 14th amendment. It was these protected corporate bodies of capital that went on to build the national market so instrumental in the creation of the nation-state we call the United States. Corporate capital and the nation-state grew up together, each nourishing the other.

However, in the present epoch of globalization, the national corporations have morphed into transnational corporations. In effect, they have leaped (or are leaping) over the borders of the states that gave them birth. And they are doing this with the assistance of those very states themselves, even though this limits popular sovereignty. It is this historical transformation that is the central focus of this book.

Imperialism and Sovereignty

While states play a key role in constituting globalized markets, is this necessarily an imperialist project? The word is popularly associated with the use of military force by one state to dominate another state. But what if it is not armies that march across borders but private foreign corporations entering under negotiated trade treaties? And even though these corporations from the North are able to soon dominate the markets of the South, isn't that only because the workers and consumers of those countries have freely accepted them? How can this be imperialism?

It is much easier to see imperialism in the militaristic foreign policies of the Bush administration. We might thank President George W. Bush and the neo-cons for stripping away the liberal glove that has so long concealed US imperialism. While it is only in the last few years that 'imperialism' has been restored to polite discourse, in fact, the US has been intervening throughout the Third World since at least the end of WWII to prevent democratic change and preserve US economic dominance, either covertly or overtly under the legitimating cover of multilateral support. This foreign policy has enjoyed bi-partisan Congressional support. It was only with Bush's "in your face" interventionism that US imperialism became visible to the public. While unilaterally invading other countries so as to bring about regime change is easily recognizable as imperialist, US economic dominance is a less recognizable form of imperialism. But Cuban philosopher Olga Fernandez argues that globalization, i.e. the economic dominance of transnational corporations over the global South, is also imperialism.

Setting aside US interventions, overt and covert, under whatever pretext or auspices, is it being imperialistic when it promotes globalization? Fernandez's answer is clear: *neoliberal globalization is imperialistic because it limits the sovereignty of the countries of the South economically, culturally, and politically.* It was the Treaty of Westphalia in 1648 that proclaimed the inviolability of national borders, thereby establishing the nation-state system. In practice this came to mean that a nation is entitled to determine its own internal affairs. It is precisely this corollary that globalization infringes. Neoliberal global markets' insertion into nations threatens to limit their sovereignty insofar as it weakens the nation's ability to control their own affairs. Among nation-states today, Cuba has been uniquely uncompromising in insisting on its sovereignty. Indeed, it was this that moved it towards socialism in the first place.

The concept of sovereignty is one of the central themes that threads its way through this volume. While the concept of sovereignty has a long history originating in Europe, and developing in Euro-American political thought, it has begun taking on a new and radical connotation in the last couple of decades.

Sovereignty began as an attribute of kingship during the Middle Ages, with the monarch as ultimate hierarch, the person whose word was law. But with the dissolution and overthrow of monarchy, that political space is characterized by a rejection of absolute power, or of top-down rule. The concept of a sovereign community, or a sovereign people became possible. It is this new sense of sovereignty that makes democracy possible. Early forms of constitutional government recognized the intimate connection between sovereignty and democracy. In the philosophical thinking of the time, a people had to see itself as sovereign in order to establish a democratic system of governance for itself. Today, we understand that the sovereignty of a people is the absolutely essential condition for democracy.

If democracy means that a group, a community, a people, or a nation collectively determine their own political destiny, they have to be sovereign in order to determine it. Any outside or foreign intervention, whether military, economic, political, or cultural that imposes conditions or influences that do not flow from the people themselves, disrupts or destroys their sovereignty and makes democracy impossible. Or, to state this in a different way, democracy means that the people who will be affected by a political decision have the means of participating in the determination of the issue in question, and in the formulation, articulation, and resolution of the decision.

This means that intervention in the affairs of another group, organization, people or nation in the name of democracy, or to bring democracy to another nation, is a contradiction in terms. Though the US claimed to intervene in Nicaragua in the name of democracy, or in Iraq, or in Indonesia (1965), and still attempts to intervene in Cuba, it is doing just the opposite. Its intervention is precisely what makes democracy impossible because it destroys or attempts to destroy the sovereignty of the people who suffer that intervention.

It is indeed ironic that today, in promoting or exporting what it calls democracy through its economic, political, and military interventions in other countries, the US in fact acts as the primary opponent of democracy in the world, because it disrupts the sovereignty that is the absolute condition for the existence of democracy.

This political relationship between intervention and sovereignty has become the primary domain of class and liberationist conflict in the world today. The story that each of the articles in this volume will tell, either in narrative or as the subtext for its concepts and thinking, will be similar struggles for sovereignty at the levels of social justice movements, nations, and the global economy.

The Globalized State

Popular struggles for sovereignty in the face of an encroaching globalization confront the transformation of their nation-states. The question that is associated with the state in the global South is how to survive the new structures of domination that appear to be assuming control of the global economy? How are peoples and nations to preserve themselves as peoples and nations if they face vast globalizing forces bent on the homogenization of their identities, while at the same time their own political structures are being whittled away to simply serve as administrative adjuncts to the management for global capital? Must the people of the relatively poor, underdeveloped countries accept their increasing impoverishment in order to participate in the global market, or can they participate while still raising their own overall wellbeing?

This is the issue that Cliff DuRand addresses in his article "State Against Nation" on the nation-state, by analyzing its components separately: the nation and the state. For DuRand, the separation between the two is something we have to take into account insofar as the nation, which is the people of a country, turns toward the pole of sovereignty, while the state, which governs the nation, and in some cases has been the midwife for the very birth of that nation (such as the US, or the decolonizing efforts of states such as Cuba or Vietnam) must necessarily confront and live with or against the character that the transnational corporations seek to give it in their own interest.

One of the claims that is often made about the transformation that nation-states are undergoing is that they are losing their role or purpose to globalization. But DuRand argues that in fact it is the *national* character of states that is weakened as they become transformed into globalized states. The nation-state, as a historical formation, corresponded to a specific era in which capital centered itself within a national society and a national market. At that time, political elites primarily served the interests of national capital, and used that to claim they also served the national interest. But now, to serve the interests of a transnationalized capital, those elites must abandon the nations over whose people they rule. Thus, devoid of real connection with or responsibility to the people they govern, while continuing to dominate them in the interests of the transnational corporations, they form what he calls globalized states. He suggests further that globalized states require polyarchic political systems. DuRand offers two concrete examples of globalized states: the U.S. and Mexico.

In a similar vein, Cuban political scientist Ármando Cristobal looks at the internal contradiction in the concept of a state as both the source or expression of an identity, and as the force of social structure and order in a society divided by class contradictions. He then looks at the transformation in the state's relation to both from the point of view of the global South, tracing the process of substituting a state of global capital for a state of national capital. He notes that the construction of the modern state still needs a collective identity to give cohesion to its subject population, which historically had been founded on the real ethno-social traditions that united it. Because globalizing capital needs states that collaborate in "a supra-state or transnational form" which actually supersedes their particular national identities, it seeks to bring about a certain uniformity of both state acculturation to the global economy and a suppression of the particularities of cultural identities it governs. Cuba has been able to resist this imposition not only because it has a long history of doing precisely that, but also because it has been uncompromising on its sense of national sovereignty. Thus, it has been able to integrate itself into the changing world economy without becoming subservient to it.

Popular resistance to neoliberal globalization comes from groups united as a collective entity. The members of national, ethnic, indigenous and other such groups share a collective identity. As Cuban philosopher Orlando Cruz points out, these collective identities are threatened by the homogenizing force of globalization. It is in reaction to that threat that they are mobilized into political action. He undertakes to theorize how this diversity can be unified in opposition to capitalism. This requires acknowledgment of the class character of anti-capitalist struggle.

Resistance to Neoliberal Globalization

The director-general of the World Trade Organization Renato Ruggiero observed in 1995 that "We are no longer writing the rules of interaction among separate national economies. We are writing the constitution of a single global economy."[7]

The remaining chapters in this volume focus on the nuts and bolts of neoliberal imperialism, its concrete strategies and histories, and how the peoples of the world have sought to circumvent or resist its onslaught. This history raises real political questions, from which future strategy aimed at autonomy and democracy will have to arise.

Steve Martinot looks at the attempt by the transnational corporations to construct a global state for themselves. In a world governed by such a global state, the corporations would be the citizens, while real humans would be reduced to subservience and irrelevance to the extent they did not work, consume, and participate in the military in some way. For such a global state, the various peoples of the world would constitute the work force, exploited and producing value for the corporations of the global state. He rehearses the recent spate of assaults by the US against other nations, from Grenada to Iraq and Afghanistan, and analyzes the way they form part of a process of state construction at the global level. If these military assaults, Martinot argues, have been an extension of the forms of economic hegemony that the US has reserved for itself as a state since WWII, with the consensual compliance of other states, they have also served to assure its domination and leadership in the building of forms of transnational governance. The institutions such as the IMF, World Bank, and World Trade Organization have been constructed to serve certain purposes within this overall project. They have held forth the promise of being able to govern international trade just as the UN sought to establish mechanisms to govern state-to-state relations to avoid the kind of inter-imperialist rivalries that led to two world wars.

Nevertheless, because of the variety of forces operating in the world, some of which having been described and analyzed in the preceding papers, Martinot suggests that the overall attempt by the US and the community of corporations to form a global state appears to be unraveling.

The next two papers deal with how Cuba has dealt with the emergence of this new system of economic and political hegemony in the world, both as a guardian of popular sovereignty against the onslaughts of corporate globalization, and as a nation that has decided not to fall prey to the weaknesses of the traditional form of nation-state that engender vulnerabilities to capitalist domination. The first is a description of Cuba's role as interstice in the global picture by Cuban sociologist Jose Bell Lara.

And the second is an analysis of Cuba's internal political structure by Steve Martinot. They begin to answer the question, what does a genuine nation-state, a state of the people (the nation) standing against the attempts of corporate globalization to undermine its sovereignty, look like in this globalizing world? How can a state effectively represent the interests of its people, the nation it governs, and yet participate in the corporate dominated globalized economy? Or can sovereignty be maintained only by withdrawing from that world, turning inward on oneself and being content with one's own narrower horizons?

The question becomes even more pressing in the case of a relatively poor, underdeveloped country. Are its people to accept continued poverty? Can its economic and social life be developed, raising the material, health, and cultural levels—the overall wellbeing of its people—without participating in the global market? And if it does participate, won't that subject it to exploitation by the transnational corporations with all of the inequality and social pathologies that follow in their wake?

That is the harsh dilemma that Cuba faced beginning in the 1990s after the disappearance of its trade relations with the former socialist countries. Facing the loss of 80% of its trade virtually overnight presented a major challenge to an island economy that had always needed international trade to live. Could Cuba insert itself into the capitalist global economy and hope to survive as a socialist country (the key to its sovereignty)? But if it stayed out of the capitalist world and turned inward, could it survive at all? Was there any way Cuba could hope to continue to overcome its historical legacy of underdevelopment?

Cuban sociologist Jose Bell Lara addresses this issue, outlining a development strategy for Cuba under these harsh conditions. The course he proposes (and which the Cuban state actually followed), combines endogenous development of its national economy along with a strategic insertion into the world economy by the state as guardian of the interests of the Cuban nation. While select foreign capitalist investment was welcomed, it was in joint enterprises with the state—a Revolutionary state strong and committed enough to protect the interests of its people. At the same time it was possible to venture into the world market offering high value-added scientific and technological goods and services in which it had a significant comparative advantage. The human capital that gave it this capacity had been developed endogenously over decades by the Revolution's emphasis on education and health.[8] The human endeavors of the Cuban people, seen not simply as human capital but the efflorescence of an autonomous human consciousness at work, has given it the capacity to resist devolving into a globalized state.

So what we see in Cuba is a nation-state—a socialist nation-state—that has been able to insert itself into the capitalist global economy while still able to represent the interests of its people in development and social justice. Being able to do this requires a state that is rooted in its people rather than wedded to the interests of an economically dominant class. It is just such a state that is theorized by Steve Martinot in his essay "The Nation-state and Cuba's Alternative State." He discusses the variety of levels of assembly in which the people have access to political expression and decision, as well as forms of direct participation in economic and political administration. He contrasts this participatory system with the representationalism of the modern republican nation-state. He argues that in pluralistic societies elected leaders cannot represent heterogeneous districts and so end up representing powerful corporate interests instead. Popular interests often are expressed through social movements precisely because they are outside the formal political system. In Cuba, however, those popular interests are organized in mass organizations that are themselves integral parts of the structure of the state.

Neoliberal globalized capitalism requires a republican political system through which it can force itself on nations. The World Bank in its 1997 report was refreshingly frank in its assessment of the kind of state necessary for structural adjustment programs to be implemented. These require "macroeconomic management by an insulated technocratic elite" able to carry out such unpopular reforms.[9] But at the same time, such a state needs a level of legitimacy. This is achieved through periodic contested elections so that there is a semblance of democracy. Such a system is what political scientists call polyarchy, of which the United States is the prototype. It is a low intensity democracy that veils rule by elites. This is the assessment of the political system of the US by Cliff DuRand in our closing chapter. He argues that such an elitist system was designed by the founders making it an ideal globalized state in the present era of capitalism.

This presents a challenge for popular forces dedicated to social justice. What kind of politics is possible in a polyarchic globalized state? DuRand's answer is that democratic politics is possible when it comes from social movements outside the state that promote universal social values of a nation against those of corporate capital. This is where democracy lies. To the extent that social movements can redirect the state toward those values, it can move it toward becoming a nation-state, i.e. a state that is an expression of the nation as a whole rather than the particular economic interests of capital. That is the challenge history presents to the popular classes in the era of corporate globalization.

Endnotes

1   Department of State, "Policy Planning Study 23," *Foreign Relations of the United States* (FRUS), 1948, vol. 1 (part 2), February 24, 1948, p. 23.

2   David Harvey, *A Brief History of Neoliberalism* (Oxford University Press, 2005).

3   The conceptual framework used here is that of David Harvey. Cf. *The Limits of Capital* (University of Chicago Press, 1982), and *The New Imperialism*, (Oxford University Press, 2003).

4   Quoted by William I. Robinson *A Theory of Global Capitalism: Production, Class, and State in a Transnational World,* (The Johns Hopkins University Press, 2004), p. 108.

5   For an early description of this, cf. Bennett Harrison and Barry Bluestone, *The Great U-Turn: Corporate Restructuring and the Polarizing of America* (Basic Books, 1988).

6   Cliff DuRand, "The Exhaustion of Neoliberalism in Mexico" in *Confronting Global Neoliberalism: Third World Resistance and Development Strategies*, Richard Westra, ed. (Clarity Press, 2010), pp. 235-243.

7   Quoted in Jeff Faux, *The Global Class War* (John Wiley, 2006), p.155.

8.   Cliff DuRand, "Humanitarianism and Solidarity Cuban Style," *Z Magazine* (November 2007) http://www.globaljusticecenter.org/2011/11/04/humanitarianism/

9   World Bank, *World Development Report 1997: The State in a Changing World* (Oxford University Press, 1997), p. 152.

Chapter 1

NEOLIBERALISM AND GLOBALIZATION

Cliff DuRand

'Neoliberalism' and 'globalization': these have been two of the key buzzwords of our times. What is neoliberalism and what is 'neo' about it? For that matter, we might also ask, "what is 'neo' about globalization?" for it too has often been claimed to be a new phenomenon.

In the United States neoliberalism has been the dominant public ideology of the last three decades, replacing the welfare liberal ideology that emerged out of the Roosevelt 'New Deal.' And thanks to the International Monetary Fund and the World Bank, neoliberalism has also become the dominant ideology in much of the Third World. In spite of that, the term 'neoliberalism' is less familiar to the U.S. public than it is elsewhere around the world. It refers to the resurgence of a 19th century liberalism –an ideology very different from the liberalism of the mid 20th century. When the older liberalism came back into vogue in the 1980s it was dubed *neo*liberalism. I want to analyze the basic claims of this ideology and offer a critique of it that exposes how it actually functions in social practice.

The core of neoliberalism is its insistence on the separation of the political sphere from the economic sphere. An autonomous economic sphere is envisioned in which the market is supreme. As neoliberals conceive of it, the market is made up of individual actors who freely engage in exchanges based on self-interest. Whether buyer or seller, each seeks to maximize their individual gain and enters into contractual agreements only if it is perceived to be to ones own advantage. The market is then the mechanism for summing up individual goods, producing the maximum good for the greatest number. This utilitarian calculus is performed through the invisible hand of the market *a la* Adam Smith. For neoliberalism there is no common good, there is only the sum of individual goods.

But in order for the market to work its magic, it must be free of social, i.e. collective interference. A 'free market', according to neoliberal theory, is one that is free of governmental action, which is seen as distorting the market and its outcomes. In a strict neoliberal view, the only economic actors that should be allowed are individuals who are guided not by altruism, conscience or compassion but only by their own individual self-interest—and not even enlightened self-interest, at that. Neoliberalism accepts the adage that the best government is the one that governs least, a minimalist state. The only legitimate role for the state is to establish the conditions necessary for a market to operate, and then maintain same—but only for as long as its participation is needed. This includes establishing a common currency and standard weights and measures as well as enacting laws and accompanying institutions to protect private property and enforce contracts. Permissible state action might even extend to the provision at public expense of necessary infrastructure like roads, ports, utilities and communications facilities that require large lumps of investment but where the benefits are long term and socially dispersed so that costs cannot be easily recaptured. But even here, the state should withdraw as much and as soon as possible so that these facilities can be privatized.

Throughout, the underlying assumption is that the market is the sole effective means for integrating society and making the decisions that can determine its development.

Neoliberalism is well represented in the game of Monopoly.[1] We have all spent many pleasant hours playing this popular Parker Brothers game with friends and family. It gives players the excitement of being a business tycoon with all of the risks and rewards of competition. It also offers children an initial socialization into the free market.

If we reflect on this game of Monopoly, it can tell us much about neoliberalism for it is a fair simulation of the operation of a neoliberal market, revealing its logic and its limits. First of all, what is the objective of the game? To win, of course, by buying up all the property around the board. You win by bankrupting the other players, forcing them to pay rent every time they land on your property. You win by driving them into destitution so they can no longer continue to play. It is a zero sum game; what one wins is at the expense of another. This is a game in which each is to be guided by self-interest alone. Compassion for another player who is not doing well can simply make you vulnerable to your competitors. This is not to say that you may not enter into alliances with others. But in the free competition of Monopoly there are no permanent friends, only permanent interests.

What makes this game of such interest is the fact that all the players begin at the same starting point. They all begin at the same place on the board with the same amount of money. In spite of this egalitarian initial position (cf. John Rawls), after a sufficiently long play of the game, they end up grossly unequal, with one player having it all and the others having nothing. The logic of the game inevitably, inexorably moves toward this outcome. The free market competition of Monopoly inevitably transforms a condition of perfect equality into one of maximum inequality. The only thing to be determined by the play of the game is who will be the winner and who will be destroyed in the process. The answer to this question is based on strategic skill and luck. One time it may be you, another time a different player. But what is certain is that every time the game is played, the perfect equality of the original position will be destroyed as wealth becomes increasingly concentrated.

And so the game ends. Indeed, it must end. Without money, the other players are forced out of the game one by one. The game *must* end because it breaks down when the winning player becomes the monopolist. No one else can continue; they must simply fold as economic actors. And curiously, the winner too can no longer continue to advance his own self-interest. He can no longer collect rents on his property; he no longer has income and so might just as well close up his hotels and board up his houses. It's game over for everybody.

Of course, in a game this is not a problem. You just clear the board, redistribute the money so as to restore the original position and begin a new play of the game. And those who lost last time can hope to be the successful monopolist next time. But in the real world free market the board game is intended to simulate, this does not happen. There is no Jubilee Year when all debts are forgiven and we can all start over again from a position of equality. Real world market exchanges continue to go on and on, and we all prefer that they do so. We don't want the game to break down into the utter destitution and mass starvation of almost everyone as wealth becomes so concentrated in the hands of a diminishing few that it becomes useless. As real life players in the economic game, we want life to go on.

How might this be accomplished? Returning to the Parker Brothers board game again, consider what it would take to keep the game of Monopoly going not just for hours, but for years and even generations. Within the neoliberal rules of the game it might be possible to prolong it, but it is not possible to keep it going indefinitely. For that to happen, the players would have to agree among themselves to modify the Parker Brothers rules.[2] They could decide to impose a graduated tax on property and use the funds collected from that to assist losing players so they could survive in the game even though they might be property poor. Or they might agree to put a cap on how much property a player can acquire. But whatever mechanism they might devise to sustain the game (and thus themselves), it would be a *political intervention* into the market. It would amount to a *democratic* decision to use the *collective* power of all in pursuit of a *common good*. And as such, it would represent an abandonment of neoliberalism engendered by a recognition that *neoliberalism is ultimately not just destructive but self-destructive*.

Returning again to the real world, this is basically what happened in the United States in the 1930s. The free market capitalism of the Roaring Twenties broke down, resulting in the Great Depression of the 1930s. Few could afford any longer to stay in expensive Boardwalk hotels and more and more couldn't even hold on to their humble homes on Mediterranean Avenue as they were driven from the economic game altogether. A massive social movement of the dispossessed formed and demanded a political intervention to change the rules of the economic system. The New Deal was the response of the political elite who responded to popular cries for social justice in order to save capitalism from itself. Thus was Welfare Liberalism born.

Before turning to this new public ideology that was to dominate US politics for the middle half of the 20th century, let me focus briefly on three criticisms of neoliberalism that have been implied in our discussion of the game of Monopoly.

First, neoliberalism is profoundly anti-democratic. Not just *un*democratic, but *anti*-democratic. By removing politics from the market, it denies the populous the possibility of any collective decision-making that might promote their common interests. But that is what democracy is all about. It is the possibility of collective decision making about collective action for the common good. The democratic use of the state makes government the instrument for such collective action. But neoliberalism envisions no common good except maintaining the conditions for markets and the common defense. Aside from that, there are only individual private goods. Indeed, Margaret Thatcher, who led Britain to neoliberalism, famously said that there is no such thing as society, there are only individuals. Thus the only collective entities neoliberalism can envision are private corporate bodies and special interest groups. This amounts to a negation of the very idea of democracy.

Consequently, individuals are rendered increasingly *powerless* in the face of the giant corporations that have come to dominate the market. In the real life market, it is not flesh and blood individuals like you and me who are winning in the game of Monopoly, it is those fictitious persons called corporations. We are not all equal players in the projected free market and consequently we are not effectively free. The neoliberal market had promised to promote individual liberty. In fact it has dwarfed the individual, leaving him defenseless against corporate giants. More on this in a moment.

A third critical point about neoliberalism is that it has widened immensely the income and wealth gap, as the rich get richer and the poor get poorer and the middle gets squeezed. This polarization grows not only within countries, but between countries as well. According to the U.S. Census Bureau studies, in 2009 the ratio between the earnings of the top 20% of the population and those below the poverty line was 14.5 to 1, up from 7.69 to 1 in 1968. The income gap between rich and poor in all OECD countries has reached its highest level in over 30 years. The average income of the richest 10% is now about nine times that of the poorest 10 %.

Statisticians measure inequality with what they call the gini coefficient. This is a number between 0 and 1 where 0 means perfect equality. Thus, the higher the gini coefficient for a country, the greater the inequality. If we look at the inequality of disposable incomes in the US, the gini coefficient was 0.37 by 2009, the highest of the world's industrialized countries. Only Turkey at 0.40 and Mexico at 0.47 was higher among the OECD countries. But if we look at the gini coefficient of all other countries, the most unequal of all is Chile with a gini coefficient of 0.50. It is no coincidence that Chile was the first country to have neoliberal policies forced on it under the brutal dictatorship of General Pinochet. Chile has had the longest run of the Monopoly game and as a result now has the greatest degree of inequality. Not surprisingly, the Scandinavian countries, with their strong social welfare programs are the most equal among OECD countries. Sweden, Finland and Norway have low gini coefficients of 0.26, with Denmark taking the equality prize at 0.24.

The Occupy Wall Street movement has called public attention to the growing inequality under neoliberal policies. It has raised out consciousness of this large and growing income disparity in the US. The more hotels you own on Boardwalk, the more income you receive. In 2008 the richest .01% (14,000 families) had 22.2% of the countries' wealth. The bottom 90% (over 133 million families) had just 4%. But it is not just ownership of capital that makes for high incomes. Managers of capital also make out like bandits too. If we look at the occupations of the top 1% of income "earners" we find an important phenomenon. The largest portion of that 1% list their occupation as managers. The managers of security, commodity brokerage and investment companies do especially well. These are people whose income comes not so much from capital they own, but from managing other people's capital. In the current financial stage of capitalism those at the peak of the income pyramid are not only the owners of hotels on Boardwalk, but also those who manage the investment funds that buy and sell those hotels. This conclusion is further supported if we look at lawyers. They are also heavily represented in the top 1%, especially those who are employed in security, commodity brokerage and investment companies. The big winners income-wise are not just the owners of capital, but the owners of the expertise to manage capital. What has been called the managerial revolution is an important part of advanced, financialized capitalism.[3]

Of all industrialized countries the U.S. has the largest income disparity.   Income is unequal because wealth is so unequally distributed. The more hotels you own on Boardwalk, the more income you receive. In 2008 the richest .01% (14,000 families) had 22.2% of the countries' wealth. The bottom 90% (over 133 million families) had just 4%.[4]

Just as in the board game Monopoly, so too in the actually existing neoliberal world of capitalism, inequality grows. This fact is celebrated by the institutions of capital accumulation such as Citibank who promote what it calls plutonomy – defined as "An economy that is driven by or that disproportionately benefits wealthy people, or one where the creation of wealth is the principal goal."   In a 2006 report to investors, Citibank shamelessly prognosticated, "we think that global capitalists are going to be getting an even greater share of the wealth pie over the next few years, as capitalists benefit disproportionately from globalization and the productivity boom, at the relative expense of labor."[5]

Neoliberalism is not altogether insensitive to this economic polarization, particularly as it affects the poor. But it views the remedy as lying in acts of private charity rather than through public provision, which might replace charity with an entitlement. Beyond that, the poor are told to help themselves through work and self-discipline—the Protestant work ethic of individual responsibility. What neoliberalism denies is that there is a social responsibility to ensure the well being of its members or a right of the individual to expect that from society.

On all these points, welfare liberalism (sometimes called social liberalism or even social democracy) contrasts with neoliberalism. As we have said, welfare liberalism arose as a response to the crisis brought on by a neoliberal economic order in collapse. To save monopoly capitalism from its breakdown, decisive state intervention into the market was necessary. This has taken place on a number of levels. First, welfare liberalism seeks to alleviate the plight of the poor through *public supports* such as unemployment benefits, direct aid to dependent families, social security for the elderly, etc. This is where the word 'welfare' enters into the term 'welfare liberalism'. Basically the state intervenes into the market, protecting individuals from the negative outcomes of market forces, by establishing a floor below which no one needs to fall. This public provision of a minimal level of material well-being is established not just out of a sense of compassion for the unfortunate, but in the interest of social harmony. Without such social insurance, an economic crisis might well develop Into a revolutionary situation. Thus welfare liberalism can be seen as a systemic response that seeks to protect the capitalist system from dangerous social turmoil.

This welfare liberal response is administered through governmental agencies staffed by experts from the 'helping professions' such as social workers. Rather than mobilizing the energies of communities or the dispossessed themselves, welfare liberalism bureaucratizes mechanisms for public provision. This bureaucratic feature of welfare liberalism has been the target of much attack by neoliberals for creating dependencies and stifling initiative—but more particularly because it strengthened labor's capacity to bargain by mediating its economic duress.

A second role of the welfare liberal state involves *regulation* of economic institutions. This is the most direct form of state intervention into the market. It involves more than just establishing the conditions for markets to operate. It involves regulating how they operate so as to ensure they will not break down. The Securities and Exchange Commission and the Food and Drug Administration are two familiar federal agencies that purport to serve this purpose and have failed miserably, particularly the SEC as we have seen from the 2008 financial crisis.

In addition to this, the welfare liberal state also seeks to promote economic growth by stimulating capitalist economic activities. Welfare liberalism embraces *Keynesian policies* of deficit spending so as to ensure corporate profitability and effective consumer demand. This approach was adopted by the New Deal to try to lift the economy out of the Great Depression and a kind of military Keynesianism was employed to sustain prosperity in the decades after World War II. Thus we can speak of a Keynesian welfare state.

On each of these levels welfare liberalism embraces an active state so as to ensure the survival of a capitalist economic system. In the words of Robert Bellah, "the public good is defined as national harmony achieved through sharing the benefits of economic growth."[6] While the welfare liberal state endeavors to ensure that individuals have equal opportunity and the means to pursue their private ends, it does not seek to empower citizens collectively to pursue a common good which they, themselves, determine. Instead it empowers an unaccountable bureaucratic administrative apparatus. While this has been a strength of welfare liberalism, it has also been a particularly vulnerable point in the ideological struggles of recent decades as welfare liberalism has been attacked from the Left in the name of a democratic collective empowerment and from the Right in the name of individual freedom.

The political basis for welfare liberalism lay in a certain balance of power between capital and labor. It reflected the existence of a working class sufficiently mobilized to be able to press its demands on the state and a capitalist class weakened by economic crisis. But at the same time, the working class was not strong enough to take full control of the state, nor was capital so weak that the state could not save it from itself. In other words, a revolutionary endgame had not been reached. Instead, a capital-labor accord was struck in the decades following World War II in which capital shared with labor some of the fruits of rising productivity in exchange for labor peace. This was the culmination of the Fordist regime of production that had evolved over the first half of the 20th century. It served to dampen class struggle and fostered a false consciousness in America's working class who self-identified as a 'middle class' and by the 1950s had come to identify their interests, indeed the interests of the nation, with those of capital. As articulated by former GM chairman and Defense Secretary Wilson, "What's good for GM is good for the U.S."

But in the mid 1970s capital broke this accord and launched a class war against labor. As capital moved toward a new regime of flexible accumulation, it carried out an offensive against unions and worker's standards of living. It sought flexibility through other forms of labor besides wage labor and the mobility to tap lower wage labor abroad. And the state weighed in on the side of capital in this transition to flexible accumulation—not only during periods of Republican governments like that of Ronald Reagan, but also during Democratic governments like that of Bill Clinton. This was made patently obvious by Clinton's pushing through the NAFTA negotiated by Republican Bush against the opposition of organized labor. Recycling old illusions, Clinton claimed that NAFTA was in the national interest. But workers came to understand that it was actually in the interest of the large corporations. No longer did they buy the illusion that the interest of capital is identical to the national interest.

With the Reagan administration, as with the Thatcher government in Britain, we saw a return to neoliberalism as the dominant public philosophy. The long process of weakening and dismantling the institutions of welfare liberalism began, a process that was politically enabled by a highly individualistic culture and mass consumerism that privatized daily life and led toward the collapse of the public sphere. Without a politically engaged populace, the state reverted to its natural neoliberal function of promoting the interests of capital by restoring the freedom of the market. Indeed we might think of neoliberalism as the default position of capitalism to which it reverts unless restrained by popular struggles.

Deregulation, privatization, and free trade became national policy as corporate capital sought a union-free environment, shedding its fixed relations with massive in-house, high wage workforces. This gave it the mobility to move production off shore into globalized assembly lines that could tap low wage Third World labor while still being able to access high income consumer markets with its commodities. Globalization came hand in glove with neoliberalism. They provided the fix for the fiscal crisis of the state, the stagflation of the economy and the declining profits of corporate capital in the 1970s. Such a solution would not have been possible if the popular classes had been socially conscious and politically mobilized. Without that willingness to struggle, capital's class war was fought by only one side. It is only with the emergence of Occupy Wall Street that we see the beginnings of a mass movement against neoliberal capitalism.

Neoliberal globalization is a class project. The neoliberal ideology has been a cover that conceals as much as it reveals. While neoliberalism purports to eschew state intervention into the market on behalf of labor, in practice it welcomes state intervention on behalf of capital. States have re-structured the rules of the world market in the name of 'free trade,' removing tariffs that protected domestic production, and assenting to trade agreements that impeded their capacity to address the needs of their own economies. Under claims of equal treatment for foreign and domestic capital, global neoliberalism in fact favors transnational corporate capital, which can mobilize extensive resources and enjoys huge economies of scale. It would hardly be a level playing field in the game of Monopoly if some players started with only a few dollars in their pocket and other players started with millions as well as hotels on Boardwalk. The developed states champion removing restraints on trade but maintain generous state subsidies to their agriculture while requiring poor states to remove theirs. About the only area where global trade rules treat all equally is when it comes to anti-labor policies.

Thus we can see how neoliberalism functions as an ideology, i.e. a body of ideas that legitimate certain social interests over others. Neoliberalism is the ideology of capitalists—the winners in the real life game of Monopoly now being played on the world stage—just as welfare liberalism was the ideology of that game's losers who nevertheless wanted to keep the game going in the illusory hope of one day themselves becoming winners.

Earlier we spoke of the possibility of popular political action to democratically change the rules of the game to favor the disadvantaged. Such democratic interventions are the exception. Ordinarily the rules the state establishes for the real world market prevail, just as the Parker Brother rules govern the players of Monopoly. These rules protect property and enforce contracts —they favor the winners in the "free market." But when from time to time those wealthy winners find themselves in trouble, they need and even may call for a different, undemocratic kind of political intervention in the market, an intervention to protect their interests. It is just such an intervention that we saw in the 2008-09 bail-out of the U.S. banks when they were faced with a financial crisis. Banks that were "too big to fail" held the rest of society hostage, requiring a change in the rules of the "free market" in order to save them. It was as if Parker Brothers not only established rules of the game of Monopoly so the winner takes all, but then also intervened to decide who would be the winner by protecting the favored player from his own strategic errors. In fact, the neoliberal ideology of "free markets" is a cover for a class project.

Neoliberalism on a Global Scale

Returning to the simulation of neoliberal capitalism in the board game Monopoly, consider how it reveals the realities of contemporary globalization. We have seen that it is a fair simulation of neoliberal markets when all actors start from an equal position and that in spite of this equality, the logic of the game tends toward growing *in*equality. This tendency can only be accelerated if some of the players enter the game already richer than the others. The poorer, more vulnerable players will then have little chance of prevailing—or even surviving. "But that wouldn't be fair!" you object. However that is exactly what happens in the real world when a relatively poorer country allows corporations from richer countries into their game. Even those national players who had been successful will find themselves at a competitive disadvantage. The logic of free markets will visit them with a vengeance. This is the real world of neoliberal globalization.

Why would a country accept a game in which it is so clearly disadvantaged? In practice there have been many factors. In the case of Mexico the elite was already ideologically committed to neoliberal principles and positioned to benefit by the privatization process that ensued, acquiring public properties or reaping huge commissions on their sale to foreign buyers. Most of the people saw no benefits. In the case of Argentina, the country was so heavily in debt that the IMF was able to make further loans conditional on accepting neoliberal structural adjustment programs.[7] In the case of Panama when its president refused to play the neoliberal game, he was simply assassinated. In other cases like Iraq, it took a military invasion to impose a "free market." The one case that stands out as an exception is Cuba. For a half century it has been able to resist neoliberal globalization even though all of the above measures have been brought to bear against it with great force.[8]

In all of those cases where the above stratagems were able to bring a country into the neoliberal game, what made this possible was the lack of democracy. Resisting the pressures to play a rigged game requires a state committed to the interests of its people and a politically engaged people to back it up. Without a nation-state to protect them, the citizens of the poorer countries will find themselves falling farther and farther behind. That is the inevitable outcome of combined and uneven development under global neoliberal principles.

Much of the ideological obfuscation of neoliberalism comes from its promotion of an antiquated image of the market that has little reality in advanced capitalist states. Constantly harking back to Adam Smith, contemporary ideologues promote free markets drawing on his imagery of peasant and handicraft markets of a pre-capitalist era, where vendors set up temporary stalls offering for sale everything imaginable from fresh produce to clothing, hardware, cassettes, birds, etc. The sellers were often also the producers and dealt directly with buyers who could negotiate prices in face-to-face interactions that were often as personal as they were commercial in character. The products are largely expressions of local culture and the revenues realized circulate back into the local community. These are the genuinely free markets of an earlier era.

It is the appealing memories of such entrepreneurial markets that neoliberalism congers up in its effort to legitimize the real markets of the present capitalist system. But in fact, they are very different. In many ways today's "markets" are the direct opposite of a free market. Buyers do not face producers but rather a middle man, the merchant capitalist, or actually his employees. Prices are fixed by the seller and generally not subject to bargaining. Products are mass produced at distant points, often across a chain of states and/or contracted out, by alienated wage labor unknown to either the buyer or the seller. Consumer demand is largely stimulated by advertising rather than the result of autonomous need. And the surplus value realized by sale goes to distant non-producing stockholders and corporate managers and thus does not recirculate in the local community. Such are the real national and global markets of today. They embody highly asymmetric relations between buyer and seller that are far from the fabled free markets of neoliberal lore. In fact individual consumers find themselves powerless against the corporate giants that dominate today's real markets,[9] where "the competition" may be just another trade-named division of a multinational giant.

Today's real neoliberal markets are increasingly tied into world markets that are structured by states in the interest of transnational corporations. These are the giants that condition our lives under rules established by neoliberal states. As William I. Robinson points out,

> Transnational capital requires that states perform three functions: (1) adopt fiscal and monetary policies which assure macroeconomic stability (2) provide the basic infrastructure necessary for global economic activity (air and sea ports, communication networks, educational systems which impart the specific skills among labor which capital requires in different spatial locations, etc.) and (3) provide social order, that is, stability, which requires sustaining instruments of direct coercion and ideological apparatuses.[10]

The governments of highly capitalist economies like the United States and Britain have long served these three requirements, although often tempered by the forceful demands of popular classes for social justice. But in recent decades, since the advent of Reaganism and Thatcherism, the dominant neoliberal states have sought to create similar neoliberal states throughout the world. The IMF, World Bank and the World Trade Organization have been primary instruments for imposing neoliberal rules on sometimes reluctant states. When these fail, the US Marines are called in to assure success.

What transnational capital requires are neoliberal states that are strong enough to serve these three functions, but not so strong as to be able to protect their nation's interests when that is inconsistent with the interests of transnational capital. The institutions of welfare liberalism have to be dismantled and a deaf ear turned to the weak cries for social justice by the subject populations. This is not always easy to do, if only because governments require some measure of legitimacy to be able to rule effectively. It is here that the global economic system is cited to quiet restless populations. In order to be effective competitors in global neoliberal markets, they are told, they must accept the discipline of those markets. In effect, popular sovereignty must give way to the interests of transnational capital as the neoliberal state claims it is powerless in the global market. Thus, we find ourselves victims of one market, under god, with liberty and profits for some. So it will be until popular social movements can win some measure of justice within this system, or create a new one in its place.

Endnotes

1   My discussion of Monopoly as a simulation of neoliberal markets draws from *The Good Society* by Robert N. Bellah, Richard Madsen, William M. Sullivan, Ann Swidler and Steven M. Tipton (Alfred Knopf, 1991), pp. 82 ff.

2   Note that Parker Brothers plays the role of the state in that it sets the rules for the market—rules that inevitably make some rich and impoverish the rest. As in the game, so too in the real world, the class character of the state is largely invisible. The rules of the market are accepted as "natural facts".

3   Jack A. Smith, "What Classless Society? The Growing Rich-poor Gap in 'Classless' America" (October 3, 2010) http://www.globalresearch. ca/index.php?context=va&aid=21284 ; James Crotty, "The Great Austerity War" (June 2011) G http://www.peri.umass.edu/fileadmin/ pdf/working_papers/working_papers_251-300/WP260.pdf ; ; OECD, "Divided We Stand: Why Inequality Keeps Rising" (December 2011) www.oecd.org/els/social/inequality Figure 9 OECD Income Inequality; *New York Times* graphic on occupations of the 1% http://www. nytimes.com/packages/html/newsgraphics/2012/0115-one-percent-occupations/index.html?nl=todaysheadlines&emc=thab1;James Burnham, *The Managerial Revolution* (John Day, 1941) and Donald Clark Hodges, *America's New Economic Order* (Avebury, 1996).

4   Jack A. Smith, "What Classless Society? The Growing Rich-poor Gap in 'Classless' America" (October 3, 2010) http://www.globalresearch. ca/index.php?context=va&aid=21284 ; OECD, "Divided We Stand: Why Inequality Keeps Rising" www.oecd.org/els/social/inequality

5   *Equity Strategy. Revisiting Plutonomy: The Rich Getting Richer,* Vol. 1 at http://tinyurl.com/y9qrqh6 and Vol. 2 at http://tinyurl.com/ ya486kf .

6   Robert Bellah, Richard Madsen, William M. Sullivan, Ann Swidler and Steven M. Tipton *Habits of the Heart* (University of California Press, 1985, 1996, 200) p. 264.

7   John Perkins tells the story of how such massive debt was brought about in his *Confessions of an Economic Hit Man* (Plume, 2005).

8   Antonio Carmona Báez, *State Resistance to Globalization in Cuba* (Pluto Press, 2004).

9   This contrast is well developed by John McMurtry, *The Cancer Stage of Capitalism* (Pluto Press, 1999) pp. 37-62; cf. also his *Value Wars: The Global Market Versus the Life Economy* (Pluto Press, 2002).

10   William I. Robinson, *Promoting Polyarchy: Globalization, US Intervention, and Hegemony* (Cambridge University Press, 1996) p.36.

Chapter 2

GLOBAL IMPERIALISM AND NATION-STATES*

Olga Fernández Ríos
Instituto de Filosofia, Habana, Cuba

We live in an era of rabid capitalist globalization in which the centers of world power try to minimize the role and the autonomy of the nation-states located in the South of the planet in order to consolidate the devastating advance of the capitalist market with its negative consequences for the majority of humanity and its survival, as statistics increasingly show us. At the same time neoliberal ideology has proliferated the thesis, among others, that the nation-state loses its importance to the supposed superiority of the private over the public and the "necessity" of domestic policies handed down by international regulatory agencies charged with designing them.

There are multiple contradictions that exist in the contemporary world, derived from capitalism and from the myth that considers it the only legitimate mode of production for the entire planet, this in spite of it having generalized social exclusion, poverty, the ruination of natural resources, violence, militarization and political corruption. These deformations caused by capitalist society have been joined by additional phenomena that affect the relations between countries, such as terrorism.

*Translation by Otto Begus and Lydia Carey

Supported by a huge international media machine, the control and interconnection of large transnationals and the military industrial complex, the United States and the other NATO countries concoct all kinds of excuses for military actions and interference around the globe. The acts of September 11th and the so-called war against terrorism have served to impose fear in citizens and to arm a "new interventionism" that springs from a cynical rhetoric of fear, fabricated scenarios, and supposed humanitarian justifications. These have become the fundamental pretexts that the principal imperialist power of the world wields in order to exercise its influence in any country under the supposedly objective pretext of liberating the world from this sore which is deliberately attributed only to less developed countries enslaved in the global south. The nation-states of the South are also affected by the North American interventionism in their internal affairs through a variety of means that include war, declared legitimate, when in fact it is an instrument of coercion and domination. They are also affected by the high rates of earnings of important oligarchic Yankee sectors. The military budget of the United States, already high, has grown in the last three years by more than 20%. The military rhetoric that exudes from the center of global imperialism becomes even more cynical when the new North American interventionism justifies itself—in the words of George Bush—in the name of civilization and as God's command.

In our judgment, the nation-states, inclusive of the less developed ones, have the right to seek their own solution to the existing situations. These states continue to have a cardinal importance which, in many instances, is reinforced by the fact that they are territorial and cultural places where important searches for alternatives to capitalism and struggles for a more just and equitable world are taking place.

The theme we analyze here is complex and impossible to exhaust in so few pages. We only propose to engage in some reflections—fundamentally from the Latin American and Caribbean perspective, which, we think, will make a contribution to the debate. For that purpose we are arranging our ideas in four fundamental categories:

- Some reflections on global imperialism and nation-states.
- The removal of national sovereignty from the so-

called peripheral states as an instrument of global imperialist domination.
- New North American formulas for justifying imperialist domination by global imperialism over the nation-states on the "periphery"
- Some alternatives to the reigning order.

Some Reflections on Global Imperialism and Nation-states

Actually existing capitalism maintains the logic of development analyzed by Karl Marx, which includes the expansionism of the bourgeoisie denounced with foresight in *The Communist Manifesto*: the bourgeoisie"forces all nations, if they do not want to succumb, to adopt the bourgeois mode of production, and to introduce the so-called civilization, that is to say, to become bourgeois. In a word, it forges a world in its image and likeness".

The expansionist and imperialist character of capitalism, denounced at the end of the 19th and at the beginning of the 20th centuries by Jose Marti and Vladimir Lenin, has been consolidated in our day by means of formulas that go beyond the export of capital, colonialism and neo-colonialism.

Like never before, capitalism has grown worldwide, or, expressed differently, there now exists a global imperialism that affects and involves the immense majority of humankind. This imperialism has become consolidated based upon the predominance of the market and the growing social exclusion that prejudices not only those human beings dispossessed of the "advantages" of private property, but also those countries that, being considered secondary, are hindered in reaching the development and strength of the imperialist powers .

In reality what is called globalization is really the switch from national to transnational concentration of property and political power, whose prevailing vehicle, the monopoly, has been transformed from a national to a transnational entity. Since the 1970s, a new phase of the development of capitalist societies has been a movement towards transnational monopoly capitalism resulting from an accumulation of factors that occurred in the Second World War. These factors include, among others, the development of productive forces, of telecommunications and of means of transportation; the interpenetration of capital in the United States, Western Europe, and Japan, and strategic alliances established amongst the imperial powers in opposition to the USSR and the socialist camp.[1]

Within this context the asymmetry and inequality among nations is further deepened in accordance with a dominant trinity integrated by the United States, Europe and Japan, but with a clear hegemony and domination by the former. The impressive economic dynamism that has emerged in some of the periphery countries such as China, India, Brazil and others, as well as the economic crisis affecting the central imperial powers, does not detract from the unipolarity that emerged due to the breakup of the USSR.

Let us not forget that the United States did not have a feudal development, but was born as a capitalist nation and grew in three steps to become an imperialist one by:

1. Conquering and usurping territories by force to enlarge considerably the settlements of the 13 English colonies which were the origin of the country. Without wasting time, they snatched up neighboring enclaves, taking the lands from the indigenous peoples that had settled in North America for centuries, as well as from other countries, while at the same time complementing this considerable "original accumulation" with successive waves of immigrants, ready and willing to support the country with their productive power;

2. Turning into an imperial power of the hemisphere during the 20th century, gaining control over Latin America and the Caribbean, and

3. Since the end of WWII until today the United States has been building itself up as the center of imperialism with a growing control of the world market, and finding support through interference in the internal affairs of other states.

Through usurpation, interventionism and a remarkable lack of political ethics the United States has succeeded in forming a transnational economic and political dominion. As the center of global imperialism, it has developed a network or system of multiple domination—which is not to imply a simple system from the exterior, but also a system that integrates different formulas, relationships, institutions and logistics of domination.[2] These are the various political and ideological mechanisms used to complement the overwhelming power of the market and affect the actual development of the countries of the South.

It is not an idle thought to recall that the nation-states are temporally and organically tightly connected with the rise and the expansion of the capitalist markets. There is an intimate connection between the rise of the nation-state and the unequal and imbalanced properties of original capitalism. At the same time, the nations were affected by the development of capitalism and by the interests that have guided its expansion.

Within the framework of this century-long conditioning, nation-states found their consolidation, different peoples of different geographical latitudes have come together, and in the lap of these geopolitical enclaves, historical and cultural values have affirmed themselves along with defining national identities and socio-political interests which legitimize the right to national sovereignty, the self-determination of different peoples, and the exercise of democracy. All these elements have been decisive in the struggles against colonialism and for independence, as well as in the definition of the international regulatory mechanisms in order to protect the integrity of the nations and world peace.

Nation-states are the spaces where the ties between the state, the market, the nation, classes and international elements flow together, and the framework within which important anti-capitalist struggles have been carried out in order to arrest the negative effects caused by global imperialism and neoliberalism experienced by two-thirds of humankind. Moreover, these spaces are of great importance where socio-political and revolutionary movements develop in order to achieve a better world.

The principal centers of the transnationalized market are situated in countries that are at the center of the political power of the world, headed by the United States of North America. At the same time the economically less developed nations are forced to involve themselves in the complex network of this market. Global expansion, the mobility of capital, the access of consumers and labor forces, both qualified and unqualified, has broken down traditional barriers to foreign penetration and considerably increased the power of negotiation, blackmail and domination, and enriched the transnationals[3] that set the worldwide standards of production, financing, and consumption through a network of labor, commercial and financial relations that mold society with a capitalist logic.

The new phase of the globalization of capital demands a re-configuring of spaces and sources of political power on a global scale, and a re-configuration of the basis that legitimizes the exercise of that power. Meanwhile today's institutions and dominant elites continue to circumscribe national parameters since the projection of capital has a global reach that extends beyond transnational politics. This is compounded by the lack of legitimate and concerted global institutional mechanisms that limit the exercise of power by capital. This situation results in an extra-legal default consensus on which the pseudo legitimacy of capital is based, insofar as many international institutions and organizations for dispute resolution are dominated by central imperial powers.[4]

Increasingly, in many countries, there is a continued imposition of the ideological program of "liberalizing the market" and the "adjustment" programs of the International Monetary Fund, World Trade Organization and other "regulatory" organisms of the international economy that call for privatization, government de-regulation and cuts in social spending that favor the large transnationals; at the same time, these are becoming extremely unpopular and leading to movements to combat the power of these companies. Against this panorama, The Economic Commission for Latin America and the Caribbean (ECLAC) has, on more than one occasion, called for more bona fide international policy coordination and economic stimulus measures—not merely fiscal adjustment.[5]

But the connections and inter-relations between the national and the trans-national become much more politically complex when the United States tries to impose a single model of development, while at the same time trying to ratify its hegemony over the nation-states, presenting itself as a model of regulatory mechanisms and of control. This is also what allows the United States to exercise its hegemony.

The United States designs the patterns of production, financing and consumption for the world through a network of productive, commercial and financial relations that serve to model the whole of society upon the logic of capitalism. It promotes a single orientation and consistently increases its actions to thwart the search for alternatives and diverse opinions designed to achieve economic development and social justice.

The Stripping of National Sovereignty
from the States of the So-called Periphery

It is without dispute that the conditions of global imperialism have changed and restructured the functions of the state. Although these do not alter its class nature, they do, however, imply changes in the correlation of its internal elements with negative consequences for society as a whole and the mutilation of its capacity for sovereignty. Both elements are directly related.

Increasingly, states on the periphery have been stripped of or have given away the essential rights of their own functionality, suffering an erosion of national sovereignty. This stems in part from the delegation of power on the part of neoliberal states themselves and, to a large extent, from the impact of globalization and power asymmetries exacerbated by the absence of legal mechanisms and protection against the crisis as well as the wars suffered by many countries.

Powerful international financial and economic actors continually affect the sovereignty of the least developed nations and confirm Christian de Brie's statement that "the dominant forces wear a mask of the right to destroy rights". When negotiating agreements with foreign investors, states can accept or refuse fiscal, social, and environmental policy and submit the different for eventual litigation by an arbitrator more given to promoting an agreement than to a rigorous application of the law. In this way states impotently and complicitly assist in the increase of inequality.[6]

It is not the first time that something like this has occurred, but it is the first time that it has manifested itself all over the planet as a whole and been regulated by a great power. Since the 1980s, in a very generalized manner and especially in Latin America and the Caribbean, the spread of neoliberalism has legitimized the process of transnational concentration of property, production, and political power along with the destruction and degradation of the environment.

Nation-states who obtained formal independence after the colonial period who, in good measure, formulated public policy in accordance with national interests, are increasingly characterized by placing resources and sovereign spaces in subordination to the interests of the great transnational companies, who have their territorial enclaves within the imperialist powers. Over the past twenty years, the role of the state and its powers over such things as monetary sovereignty, the military and its ability to regulate the economy, information and communication have been reductively redefined worldwide—all have been greatly diminished, if not totally reduced to a minimum.[7]

The same has occurred in the state's representation and credibility to its people; according to public opinion, the state has become increasingly weaker and more impotent in confronting global companies and "markets". An example of this is the liberalization measures legitimatized through the framework of the General Agreement on Tariffs and Trade (GATT) and the World Trade Organization (WTO). The WTO emerged in the course of the past 20 years as a global regulatory power submitting to the interests of large private enterprises, with the support and consent of the most powerful governments worldwide, primarily the United States. In a majority of countries, the waves of deregulation and privatization of entire sectors of the economy were the corollary to liberalization.[8]

It has produced an evident impact on peripheral countries where national sovereignty ceases to be an attribute of the state and a regulatory source of the common national interest. Instead, the state is turned into an instrumental puppet in the service of great capital and the globalized market, all aspects that some authors have considered as modifying the nature of the state. In this regard, the Egyptian political scientist Samir Amin introduces the concept of "market-states", in which all the functions, including the coercive power, are exercised in favor of transnational entities or local elites connected to large foreign enterprises.[9]

In our judgment, the loss of national sovereignty also noticeably changes democratic foundations and mechanisms, a situation that manifests itself in the high indices of discontent that exist in Latin America and other regions in relation to the reigning democracy, and the lack of credibility of this form of government. These indices have been demonstrated by the analysis of Latinobárómetro, especially the 2003 study.[10]

The "authority" to intervene militarily in peripheral countries has been established in defiance of international law with "humanitarian" pretexts and "preventive" justifications. The right of US intervention supercedes national sovereignty when, for example, the US justifies any invasion or illegal overthrow of a president, as recently happened in Honduras. This practice combines with others to alter three functions of the state in countries of the southern hemisphere that largely ensure national sovereignty:

1. The configuration of states' own policies: as part of neoliberal politics, with some exceptions, states do not design their own economic policies, not even of a bourgeois-capitalist kind, but are obligated to apply those developed by the World Bank, the International Monetary Fund, the World Trade Organization, and Latin American Trade Agreement (ALCA), among other mechanisms created for international economic design and control.

2. The definition of the forms of government: the nation-states do not design their mechanisms of government, but rather see themselves as forced to assume a democratic model that is entirely imported and emptied of the principle attributes that correspond to a democratic government and the political organization of society. In that regard we must remember the "policy of democracy promotion" imposed by Ronald Reagan at the beginning of the 1980s, whose formula was a dogmatic prescription of democratic components, in addition to an absurd identification with capitalism, to be adopted as a compulsory and binding model for all countries, regardless of their individual conditions or national interests. The policy of promoting liberal bourgeois democracy amounts to absurd reductionism and empties democracy of the values that have sustained it for the past 25 centuries. This was one of the instruments used to justify North America's interference in Cuba.

3. Also the ideological function of the state is affected by neoliberal ideology which structures an ideological-cultural model to be exported to countries in order to promote a culture favoring imperial domination, cultivating ideas involving the inevitability of capitalism, of North American superiority and the "advantages of the market."

What is even more serious is the fact that the concept of "people" is affected; it begins to become supplanted by the concept of multitude or population, where cultural interests and identities are substituted by extra-territorial macro-interests.

This is a theme which deserves to be addressed. One shall not forget that due to the influence and the interest of the United States, countries' cultural and national identities have become fragmented and this has promoted violent local wars.

On these three paths to loss of sovereignty and national independence, the importation of state attributes brings with it new patterns that increase the anti-populist nature of many subordinate states and limit the possibilities of rectifying social inequalities at the national level. Through a disdain for the public interest, societal interest, and the power of the popular sectors, public policies are privatized and are not even given a pretense of priority.

Linked to the loss of sovereignty, another area where these policies have significantly impacted the countries of the so-called periphery are some of the traditional functions of the state that have suffered modifications due to the major disequilibrium between states' repressive function, which is increasing exponentially, and the reduced generation of public policies due to growing privatization of the resources of the state. Among the sectors most affected by the wave of privatization are critical economic resources, educational entities, health, and social security.

What some authors consider to be the downsizing of the state in the countries of the periphery is nothing less than the absolute loss of the responsibility of the state in relation to education, public health, social security, the protection of the natural resources, and of everything that contributes to foment a minimal equilibrium that the state must achieve so that society can function with a certain normality.

The contradictions and negative consequences created by the loss of national sovereignity have been of great dimension. Even without changing the already analyzed correlation between global imperialism and nation-states, lately the public speech of those governments attached to the neoliberal model shows concern regarding the "shrinking of the state", which introduces different perspectives than those that were dominant in the initial period of implementation and creation of the economic and political neoliberal model.

The goal is to look for palliatives to the negative consequences derived from the neoliberal policies which are, among others: the significant increase in poverty, unemployment and social exclusion, united with a deeper inequality in income distribution, an increasing gap between the richest and the poorest, and increasing delinquency and citizen insecurity, including the high rates of violence and moral degradation that rule in many countries . Those are without doubt social problems that affect domestic stability.

But above all, the goal is to stop the increasing social protests against neoliberalism and the depredation of important natural resources by the big trasnational firms based out of the United States and other countries, and to counteract the electoral triumph of governments that oppose United States dominance and resist neoliberal policies.

Within North American circles as well as several right wing governments in Latin America, there is an increasing attempt to legitimize the neoliberal state by conferring it with an apparent neutrality and impartiality that stresses its function as a distributor of supposedly public wealth, presenting it as the institution of well being and appealing to a social dimension of the State that is nothing but *assistencialism* (handouts) focused on extreme poverty with the goal of eliminating social tensions and avoiding conditions that might lead to ungovernability or discourage foreign investment.

The prevailing demagogical speech presents the national interest as the governing force despite the maintenance of links with the International Monetary Fund, the World Bank and the World Trade Organization. With that intention, a very refined ideology is designed with political and cultural propaganda that promises to create the conditions to access the first world kind of development. Within that context, the emphasis is put on the intentions of achieving a better distribution of wealth, lowering unemployment and eliminating extreme poverty with the demagogic promise of a more responsible role of the state— adopting public policies that favor the people and those that have less, the excluded.

The truth is that without structural changes in capitalist society and with the current correlation between nation-states and global imperialism, the palliatives that can be introduced at the local level will not eliminate the large social disparities and the socio-economic differences between rich and poor states of the center and the periphery. Given the level of integration and interdependence that already exists in the global economy it would be very difficult for the state to recuperate all of its faculties and power, as is the demand of the "populist" or "nationalist" sectors. But even so, while we await a new, more harmonious and equitable international order, the state remains vital for global stability and the hope for democratic development, for nations to retain the capability of autonomy and sovereign self-management.

Even though the power of the nation-state does not itself guarantee freedom or social justice, territorial and cultural frameworks continue to be important keys to finding avenues out of the current situation, for searching for alternatives to capitalism, and in the fight for a more just and fair world.

New North American Formulas to Justify Imperialist Domination Over the Nation-states of the "Periphery"

In order to achieve world hegemony, the United States coordinates alliances and competitive relations; it represses in any part of the planet what it considers to be a threat to great capital. It favors inter-state agreements; it regulates the logic of capital from the point of view of its interests and pressures to connect internal markets to the global one.

The centers of developed capitalism maintain themselves through a global economic order that allows them to extract wealth and to feed the underdevelopment of the rest of the planet. The system works so that the market can be the principal regulatory element, and that preserving and favoring it is among the principal functions of the nation-states. One cannot ignore the logic of the market functions based upon the possibilities that the state creates for it, even at the cost of losing its sovereignty.

Although the nature of the sources of power have come to be changed in the direction of factors such as technology, education and economic growth, although the great capitalist powers draw the benefit from the economic world order and have succeeded in establishing international norms and institutions that are in tune with and are consistent with their interests, in the present epoch there is a dramatic increase in the use of military power.

With the end of the Cold War and the sharpening of the financial and structural crisis of capitalism, and with a certain loss of legitimacy for its policies, the United States, in a precarious alliance with its minor partners, has gone on to use more expensive coercive methods of power.

It is the United States that pressures and invades countries, and that designs mechanisms of political and military domination through its specialized agencies and regional organisms, especially directed towards the countries of the South. This context frames ALCA, Plan Colombia, Plan Puebla Panama, and the laws of Torricelli and Helms Burton that reenforced the embargo on Cuba, and more recently the attacks on Afghanistan, Iraq, and Libya among others.

In the last few years, and especially after the terrorist attacks of 9/11, 2001, the government of the United States has developed different plans with the pretext of protecting national security. In this regard, then president George W. Bush stressed the principles of foreign policy and government security and expressed the intention to act preventatively and with force against threats to US security before they materialized.[11] The so-called "Bush Doctrine" was an aggressive conception of foreign policy that ratified and amplified the hegemonic doctrine of US imperialism.

Among the highlights of this doctrine are the "legitimate" use of force, a combination of unilateralism and the involvement of allies—both in the theater of war and in the logistics and financing of operations—growing military power with sophisticated weapons and robots, the employment of mercenaries and subcontractors, and the promotion of preventative or anticipatory action in military strategy for achieving foreign policy objectives and security. These objectives stand in opposition to the most basic elements of International law and coexistence among nations that once prevailed, particularly since the end of the second World War.[12]

Stemming from a distinct ideological basis this doctrine supported the hegemonic expansion of United States imperialism and provided justification for its actions of interference.

The new strategy of national security made public in September 2002 follows this reasoning and self-authorizes unlimited powers to this country for the control of the world in the name of North American interests. This presupposes the assumption of the right to define which countries need American intervention, and to legitimize any interference in the internal affairs of many countries while at the same time using arguments to legitimize the role of international gendarmerie and global "Protector" that the United States has assigned itself, when the joint imperial aggressions are implemented under the guise of protecting collective security, joining with national defense as a guiding principle of armed intervention.[13]

Two new concepts stand out to identify countries of the periphery that "need to be tamed"—rogue states, and failed states—and at the same time the habit was established of making lists of countries that fall under this category.

The rogue states are those who are accused of having or trying to obtain weapons of mass destruction, or that constitute a threat to the interests of the United States by dissenting with the international policy that this country has designed. Rogue states are seen as capable of promoting terrorist actions. Failed states are those that have elements that cannot be governed by the state, high levels of organized crime, corruption, and chaos, whose condition could lead them to become rogue states, and as such they are also a threat that must be eliminated.

In accordance with this North American logic, the condition of "not being able to be governed" can derive from different causes, among which are the following: popular revolts or the existence of zones of turbulence against the state; or the breakdown of the power of the state or the deterioration of its institutions in sections of that country; or when international agents feel forced to abandon the country; or the absence of legitimacy or authority of the government to manage internal affairs, or the loss of monopoly over the national security services. It is also put forward that the absence of legitimate authority can happen because of the existence of corrupt ruling officials or because of an arbitrary definition of the national frontiers which would legitimize the reconfiguration of those states based on this reason.

Utilizing the rhetoric of "defense" and "humanitarian" pretexts, imperial powers' interest is to dominate regions and countries that retain large amounts of natural resources or have geopolitical importance. These arguments and justifications are the foundation the United States uses to grant itself the right to reconstruct these states after abolishing their regimes and to qualify those states as ungovernable that disagree with its policies, as it happens in the case of Cuba and Venezuela, among others.

A phenomenon related to the above is the exploitation of emergency situations and their ensuing confusion to permit global imperial offensives to gain access to "virgin territory" in the sense of the separating or re-partitioning of regions and the concurrent elimination of traces of state interventionism and protectionism in the areas of trade and investment. Naomi Klein's research in her book *The Shock Doctrine* has documented this phenomenon. With solid arguments and evidence, Klein shows that crises of all kinds and the aftermath of war are now favorable environments for organized attacks on institutions and public goods, with revenues in very precious publicly owned assets likely to be privatized, as has occurred over the past several decades in Eastern Europe, Latin America, the Far East, and the Middle East.[14]

The new concepts coined by the "Bush doctrine" are instruments that legitimize the new North American interventionism and interference in the internal affairs of other states, and the imposition of political rules that shall govern the entire planet. Although in the majority of cases this new interventionism presents itself as a "liberating mission", or a "humanitarian mission", it is not a way to eliminate the poverty and misery in which the majority of humanity lives, nor for braking the degradation of the environment caused by capitalism itself. On the contrary. It deepens social inequality and the gap that exists today between rich and poor countries.

Are There Alternatives?

Under the conditions of global imperialism, the inter-action between the question of class and the national question has deepened as never before. This is expressed in the unequal growth of the gap between rich and poor on two levels: in the interior of countries and among the countries considered as belonging to the center or the periphery. The predominant logic from the side of the imperialist vision is that of social and national exclusion as regulatory elements of the market and of international relations. It is for this reason the search for alternatives passes along those two levels.

This situation makes it so that today the class struggles are very much tied to anti-imperialist struggles, and happen for the rescue of national sovereignty. Any conquest that favors the anti-capitalist and anti-imperialist struggle within the framework of nation-states is at the same time a step towards the disconnection from the system of global imperialism. It is outdated and counterproductive to offer prescriptions for change or pretend to coin a predetermined societal model. At the same time one has to keep in mind that all anti-imperialist and anti-capitalist struggles contribute to the search for alternatives that might lead to a better world than the one we have now.

The political situation taking shape in Latin America and the Caribbean for a little over a decade has created conditions for taking a firm step in defending true sovereignty and independence. The promising movements in Venezuela, Nicaragua, Ecuador and Bolivia, along with a half a century of the Cuban Revolution serve as a basis for renewed effort.

We are interested in stressing some ideas in this regard:

1. To achieve a more just and equitable world that overcomes the conditions imposed by global imperialism, it is necessary to rescue national sovereignty and the self-determination of nations as a framework for a new economic world order demanded at various latitudes, of which Fidel Castro has offered many profound reflections and important analyses.[15] Regional agreements, which are increasingly being organized in many places, are an important step in the development of international relations based on cooperation and respect for the interests of each country. An important example is the Bolivarian Alliance for the Americas (ALBA), which set precedents for counteracting the imbalanced conditions for trade and commerce between the central and periphery countries while recovering the structures of production in each country and granting an important role to national economic space as a priority in any strategic framework.[16]

The demand for a new financial and monetary system worldwide and new rules for international trade translates into various proposals that are channeled into a search for more equitable international conditions. Among them you will find proponents of the Association for the Taxation of Financial Transactions and Aid to Citizens (Attac), the Committee for the Abolition of Third World Debt (CATDM), and the World Forum of Alternatives. This is compounded by the demand for an International Criminal Court (ICC) to promote the creation of planetary moral and political consciousness and a global "state" law to support widespread claims against the policies of the International Monetary Fund, the World Trade Organization and the World Bank, among others, and US interventionism.[17]

2. Today, popular resistance not only follows class or sectarian interests. It also seeks to reclaim the nation through a growing reaffirmation of national identity. One of the more interesting examples in that respect is that the notion of territoriality of the peasants and the indigenous peoples in a variety of Latin American countries goes hand in hand with the confrontation with extra-territorial mechanisms such as the ALCA or the Free Trade Agreement between Mexico, Canada and the United States. The same happens in the struggles against privatizations, an extension of the general rejection of the policies of the International Monetary Fund, the World Trade Organization and the World Bank, among others, and the opposition to North American interventionism.

3. Even if the classical configuration in relation to the earlier stages of capitalism and imperialism has changed, and the so-called social movements or new social agents occupy the first line in the struggles for a new society, the most important element is that today almost the entire world has great reasons for being discontented with capitalism, a discontent that before was centered fundamentally in the working class.

4. The examples of Cuba, Venezuela and other countries confirm the ties between the struggles for social justice and the elimination of the socio-economic differences within the framework of the nation-state, and the struggles for sovereignty and national independence. In these countries, the popular resistance is decisive and generalized, and it confronts actions promoted from Washington that pretend, in the first case, to subvert the disconnection of Cuba from the orbit of global imperialism, and in the second to put brakes to the anti-imperialist advance of the Bolivarian Revolution.

5. The struggles and protests of the progressive sectors of the imperialist countries, and especially of the United States, have an extraordinary importance, be it in order to confront the internal inequalities that exist in these countries, or to oppose an external policy based on aggression and the motive of global dominion. In particular the anti-war struggles, those directed towards achieving more just international policies, and those that promote solidarity with the countries of the South, and with governments or revolutionary movements interested in a society that is more just, are of incalculable value.

6. Alternative forums, be these worldwide or regional, alternative means of spreading information, informal networks, all these are important links in the anti-imperialist struggles and in the promotion of a necessary process of unity among the progressive forces. They also express new forms of internationalism in accordance with the actually existing conditions of proliferation of social actors interested in reaching a more just and equitable society.

The great social transformations derived from the capitalist model of production have reached limits above those analyzed by Marx and Engels more than 150 years ago. They envisioned the possibility of socialism as a social alternative to capitalism and they worked out interesting conclusions that still have extraordinary force and validity.

In my opinion, socialism continues to be the alternative to capitalism, and it has become necessary to rethink this option from its original sources, while keeping in mind the positive and negative experiences that have existed in the processes towards the establishment of such a society. The necessity to listen closely to the realities of each country and to interpret historical, social, cultural and international contexts constitute the decisive premises for socialism.

The strategic and tactical transformations will necessarily have a revolutionary character, generated in national and regional contexts that bring to bear on this process the originality and creativity deriving from the historical and cultural values of each scenario.

The contradictions capitalism has generated on the social and national level exist now in the entire world. Thus, the centers of resistance can be generalized, and increased in a kind of chain-reaction in which every link is of importance. Each movement that struggles within the confines of a nation-state against the order imposed by the world, plays an important role.

Today it is possible to envision a multiplication of national scenarios in the struggle against capitalism and imperialism. Thus the order of battle which Ernesto Che Guevara proclaimed in 1965 in his "Message to the Tricontinental" to "create two, three, many Viet Nams" seems to acquire force in a new historical context. The road is long, but it is a road that has already begun. It is not utopia, but even if it were, let us remember that many realities of today have at some moment been utopias.

Endnotes

1   Cf. Roberto Regalado "La teoría de la revolución y la izquierda latinoamericana en el siglo XIX: exámenes desde la filosofía política". Doctoral thesis, accessible at the library of the Instituto de Filosofía, Havana.

2   Gilberto Valdés Los movimientos sociales populares y el socialismo latinoamericano, Ocean Sur, Mexico, DF, 2011 pp.1-14.

3   A team of Swiss researchers and mathematicians led by S. Vitali of the Swiss Federal Institute of Technology in Zurich, using methods of analysis often applied to Internet connectivity and studying the control relationships between interconnected companies, showed that among more than 43,000 transnational corporations (TNCs), relatively few of them control nearly 80% of the global economy. The team identified a core of 1318 corporations (mainly financial services companies), with considerable control links between them, which represent only 0.7% of the TNCs receiving 18.7% of income for all multinationals. When you account for 59.8% of income earned by subordinate companies or controlled by the transnational giant core, it appears that they control almost 80% of the global economy. A "super-bank" of 147 companies, or 0.3% of all TNCs, has control over all transnational capital. Christine Lepisto, "The Network of Global Corporate Control", 24 Octubre 2001 at Treehugger, http://www.treehugger.com/corporate-responsibility/proof-of-global-domination-by-a-few-corporations.html.

4   Ulrich Beck, Poder y contra-poder en la era global - La nueva economía política mundial, Edit Paidos, Barcelona, 2005.

5   See the CEPAL website at http://www.eclac.cl.

6   Christian de Brie, "L´AMI nouveau est arrivé", *Le Monde Diplomatique*, May, 1999.

7   For further information about the idea of reductive redefinition of US power see Pierre de Senarclens, *Mondialisation, souveraineté et théories des relations internationales*, Armand Colin, París, 1998, cited by Riccardo Petrella, *La desposesión del Estado*, Edición Cono Sur, agosto 1999, Buenos Aires

8   For further reading see Riccardo Petrella, *La desposesión del Estado*, Edición Cono Sur, agosto 1999, Buenos Aires.

9   Samir Amin, "Capitalismo, imperialismo, mundialización", *Marx Ahora* 4-5, pp 185-194, Editorial de Ciencias Sociales, La Habana, 1998.

10   For information about democracy in Latin America see Latina, 2003, website http://latinobarómetro.org

11   To view the president of the United States speech, see the White House website at: http://www.whitehouse.gov/news/releases.

12   For further reading see Carlos Fernández de Cossío *La Doctrina Bush y la política exterior y de seguridad nacional de los Estados Unidos: Fundamentos ideológicos, continuidad y ruptura*. Unpublished doctoral thesis, Biblioteca del Instituto Superior de Relaciones Internacionales, Havana.

13   Claudio Katz, "Gestión Colectiva y Asociación Económica imperial", June 2011.

14   For further reading consult Naomi Klein's book, "La Doctrina del Shock. El Auge del Capitalismo del Desastre", Editorial Ciencias Sociales, La Habana 2009

15   Fidel Castro, "Globalización neoliberal y crisis económica global". Oficina de Publicaciones del Consejo de Estado, La Habana, 1999. También puede consultarse la entrevista concedida a La Jornada de México,

16   ALBA was created in 2004 by Venezuela and Cuba, and now includes Bolivia, Nicaragua, Antigua and Barbados, Dominica, Saint Vicente and Granadines and Ecuador. Honduras was a member until the coup d'etat overthrew President José Manuel Zelaya.

17   For further information consult the Attac website http://attac.org and Carlos Gabetta, "Multinacionales al poder", Trespuntos Nº 34, Buenos Aires.

Chapter 3

STATE
AGAINST NATION*

Cliff DuRand

Introduction

The hyphenated term 'nation-state' reflects a linking of two historically related but separable social phenomena. The term 'nation' refers to an interconnected population that has a sense of their common unity. A nation exists both objectively in its compatriots' interdependence and subjectively in the consciousness they share. There may be more than one nation or people within a state, but to the extent that the state is successful in nation-building, the non-dominant groups will also partake of the larger identity, becoming, e.g. French Canadians, Native Americans, African Americans, etc. The term 'state', on the other hand, refers to the political institutions that rule over the population of a certain territory or country where the members of one (or more) nations might live. For our purposes herein,

* I am indebted to Olga Fernandez Rios and Miguel Limia David for discussions that helped to sharpen the ideas developed in this essay. I also want to thank Mike McGuire, Bob Stone, Steve Martinot, and Jerry Harris for their thoughtful comments on an earlier draft of the essay.

the term "nation" is used to refer to the state-level identity of the internal peoples; the political institutions which govern these peoples, by whatever internal arrangements, constitute the state.

Historically, the rise of bourgeois society saw the linking of nation and state to the extent that in many minds the nation-state came to be thought of as a single (although complex) entity. To be a Canadian, for example, was thought of at once as being a citizen of a state and a member of a people—Canadians, composed of English and French "founding nations" along with a multitude of indigenous nations collectively termed First Nations. The resulting identification with such a nation-state as a single entity became an important source of identity. Who one *was* came in no small measure from the people with whom one shared a culture and a history. And in so far as the nation became linked to a state, subjection to its rule also became a part of one's identity. Thus, one's identity as a Canadian meant at one and the same time to *belong to* a *Canadian* nation and *live under* the politico-legal system ruled by a territorially defined state. Thus did the nation-state become an essential element in modern personal identities.

While a nation has its own interests, a state also has its own, often different, interests. The convergence of these two sets of interests lent credibility to their conflation into a single entity called the nation-state. However, in the present historical stage of capitalism known as globalization, the interests of nations and those of states are diverging and thus the two parts of this hyphenated term are becoming detached. Not only are they moving in different directions, but also *globalized states are often pitted against the nations over which they rule*. We will want to explore the possible implications of this for the social struggles of this era. But first, we need to look more closely at how a nation is constituted and its relation to the state that rules over it.

Nation Building

Objectively the members of a nation are economically and socially interdependent. Often complex institutions that they may not even be fully aware of link them to one another. While these institutions may have evolved for a variety of other reasons, sometimes they are deliberately constructed so as to build a nation. The construction of the United States is a case in point.

Originating as a confederation of thirteen relatively independent states, the central government created by their federation constructed a web of interconnections through the 19th century. The federal state saw to the construction of roads and canals and eventually railroads to link the people within its territory. The state also fostered means of communication: a postal system, telegraph, telephone, etc. put people in touch with one another across an increasingly vast area. This transportation and communication infrastructure facilitated the development of economic integration. Commerce (utilizing a common currency and standard weights and measures provided by the state as well as a supporting legal structure) expanded from a local base to a regional and eventually national scope, as distant people became more and more interdependent. For example, at the beginning of the 19th century the population of the city of Baltimore was fed by the wheat grown in rural Maryland. By century's end the grain that supplied this and other cities came from the farms of the Midwest, transported by rail to milling centers in Minneapolis and Chicago, and the flour was distributed from there to bakeries and kitchens throughout the country. In exchange, the steel industry in the East supplied the plows and other farm implements used to grow the wheat as well as the rails on which this trade road. And it was the state that promoted the development of this nationally integrated market; it was the state that fostered the objective interconnections necessary to build a nation.

However, nations exist not only objectively but also subjectively: objectively in the economic and social interdependence of a multiplicity of people, and subjectively in the conscious identification of those in that multitude with one another. Subjectively a nation is what Benedict Anderson called "an imagined community."[1] But unlike the real community of a village or small town, which is based on face-to-face personal knowledge, a nation is a community that exists in the imaginations of millions of people who are perfect strangers to one another.

How does such an image get into the minds of so many? Most often this comes about through war. It is when men and women go forth along with others to defend their home and community that they come to identify with others with whom they are objectively interdependent. It is then that they come to imagine themselves as all part of that single community called a "nation." That is why so many national anthems are about war (defending against the British bombardment of Fort McHenry in 1812, in the case of our nation) rather than about the land that a people call their country (as in "America the Beautiful" or "This Land is Our Land"). It is out of armed civic virtue that nations are born.[2]

It is important to understand the essential role of leadership in the creation of a nation. Nations don't just evolve by some natural process; they are created. The imagined community of a nation is born when a leadership succeeds in mobilizing an otherwise diverse multitude behind a common project. (It doesn't always have to be war. It can be putting a man on the moon.) But such national leadership always represents the interests of a class or group and is able to link that to the interests of other classes or groups so as to win their support for the common project. As Marx pointed out some time ago, a rising class always presents itself as representing a wider, more general sector of society. It is then through the experience of participating in such common projects that a multitude comes to imagine themselves as a nation and a people.

Modern nation-states are creations of the bourgeoisie and the political elites that serve their interests. These political elites, acting through the instruments of power that states provided, create the conditions needed for capitalist production and exchange. The *function* of the state is to maintain social order and cohesion. It does this not only by providing for the common defense, but also by its laws and social and economic policies. A crucial function of the bourgeois state is the protection of private property and enforcement of contracts. But capitalist society is divided by classes with different and even conflicting interests. Within it the interests of the capitalist class are dominant in so far as other classes are dependent on it. For example, the interests of wage labor within such a society lie in the wages and benefits they receive and the conditions under which they work. But within a capitalist system, their very employment depends on capital being able to realize a profit from its use of wage labor. Thus in maintaining the social order, the state invariably promotes the interests of capital because it is only if capital can profit that labor will be employed at all. In capitalism, as in all divided societies, the function of the state leads it to promote the interests of the dominant class within civil society. If that were not done, the existing system would not work. It is thus that the political elite serves the economically dominant class of capitalists.

We should always bear in mind that when we speak of the state as acting, when we say the state does this or that, we are using a shorthand expression. Strictly speaking it is the political elite that is acting through the structure of power of the institutions of the state. If we forget that, it is easy to reify the state. In reality, agency lies in the political elite; the state is its instrument.

However, in order to be able to govern effectively a state has to have some degree of legitimacy, i.e. its rule has to be accepted as right and good by the subject population. This means that the political elite that controls the instrumentality of the state has to have legitimacy. One way this is often achieved is through elections. By being able to elect which members of the elite will govern them, the state and its government is likely to be accepted as legitimate, even if the extent of popular political participation is limited to elections. Polyarchy can be a very effective political system for maintaining class domination.[3] However, as we will see shortly, this should not be confused with a genuine democracy.[4]

Beyond the mere formality of elections, in order to maintain legitimacy the state also has to be able to respond in some degree to the demands of the popular classes, even though that may mean limiting the benefits to the dominant class. That is, the state must adopt the *form* of justice in order to ensure governability.[5] From time to time the state may have to shift the benefits and losses of the economic system toward the favor of the popular classes in the name of justice. This *official justice* is not likely to go as far as the *radical justice* demanded by the popular classes, seeking greater say and benefits. How far it will go depends on the level of political activity of those classes. When they are organized and active, they can sometimes win significant concessions to their interests. Those are the democratic moments in a nation's history. The state can be turned to serve popular interests, although within limits. But when the popular classes are inactive, the state reverts to its default position that favors the economically dominant class and the gains previously won are gradually taken away. The state is democratic only to the extent that the popular classes force it to be so.

That is the pattern we can plainly see in the polyarchic political system of the United States over the last 75 years. The 1930s and the 1960s were two democratic moments in that nation's history. The social movements of those decades forced the state to adopt far-reaching measures in the interests of the popular classes, even when they were strongly opposed by the dominant class. But once popular forces were demobilized, as in the 1970s, the political elite could begin whittling away at those concessions. We have now seen four decades of class struggle by the dominant capitalist class, with little effective resistance from the popular classes until the emergence of the Occupy Movement in 2011. But as at this writing, what remains of the welfare liberal gains of the New Deal are in danger.

Perhaps we can see more clearly the relation between nation and state if we contrast the US and Cuba. The US struggle for independence late in the 18th century was led by a propertied class that projected its interests as those of the whole society. They succeeded in defining the nation in terms of their class project. The Cuban nation, by contrast, has been defined by a different class project. It was born in the 19th century in struggles for independence from Spain. However, the efforts of the Cuban nation to create its own state were thwarted by the intervention of the US. Under the resulting conditions of neo-colonialism the interests of the Cuban bourgeoisie were not identical to the interests of the nation as a whole and so any attempt to promote social justice was compromised. Official justice always fell far short of the more radical demands of the popular classes. Through the struggles of the 1950s and 60s the revolutionary leadership that captured the state was able to project a socialist vision that was embraced by most of the Cuban people. Thus the socialist project came to define the Cuban nation.[6] Through this project popular struggles for social justice found their realization. The state was restructured so that it could more closely reflect the interests of the popular classes. Social justice is ensured through collective means with the agency of the state. As a socialist society the well-being of each is a public affair within the concern of all. Accordingly, the scope of public affairs is far broader than in the US. The state thus becomes the legitimate institutional structure for participation in collective decisions that are far reaching. Official justice is informed by radical justice. It is for this reason that Cuba is more democratic than the US.

In the US, on the other hand, the nation accepted the capitalist project as its own. In the years after World War II, a capital-labor accord was fashioned. In exchange for labor peace, capital shared with labor the gains from rising productivity and US economic dominance in a war-ravaged world. In an accord mediated by the state, labor accepted the rule of capital, seeking only to increase its gains within the existing relations of production. For its part, capital accepted the right of workers to bargain collectively, particularly since their own union then became the enforcer of the contract over its members.

To a large extent the popular classes came to identify their interests with the interests of capital. As a result, few questioned the assertion of former General Motors C.E.O. Charles Wilson (later Secretary of Defense in the Eisenhower administration) that "What's good for GM is good for the US." Such an ideological obfuscation resulted in a trade unionism that saw itself as a partner with corporate capital and a working class that was rabidly anti-communist, accepting the definition of patriotism as opposition to the enemy of capitalism. Such was the unity of nation and state through the years of the Cold War; it was a unity under the leadership of a political elite that served the interests of national capital.

In sum, we have argued that a state is a *nation*-state in so far as it represents the interests of the peoples over which it rules. That nation includes both the dominant class of capitalists and the dependent popular classes. The constellation of class forces within the nation at any given time directs the nation-state. The state mediates class relations, as for instance in constructing the class compromise of the capital-labor accord represented in the Fordist regime of production. However, as we will see, with globalization, transnational corporate capital has leaped over the territorial and legal boundaries of the nation and the state is following it. In so doing, the nation-state is morphing into a globalized state that serves the interests of transnational capital rather than its own national population.

Globalization

In the closing decades of the 20th century, the development of capitalism reached a new stage. In one sense of the term, globalization is not a new phenomenon. Capital has been globalizing for the past 500 years. But in spite of its extension into new areas of the earth, it remained rooted in those nation-states that were its sponsors. There was British capital, and French capital, and German capital, and US capital. No matter how far it roamed, it remained *national* capital. Thus even popular classes who identified their nation with the interests of "their capitalists" could be tricked into supporting imperialist projects that were not in their own interests. Working class youth would fight and die for flag and country, even though it was their own exploiters who benefited from their sacrifice. It was this that has given nationalism a bad name.

Even though corporations had long entered into international trade and some had even set up production in other countries, capital remained national in the sense that it operated within a national economy that was externally linked to other national economies. Commodities were produced within the nation primarily for the domestic market and only secondarily for export. Each capitalist state fostered and protected the national circuits of accumulation within its territory.

What is new now is that capital is becoming not just *inter*national, but *trans*national. As William I. Robinson has argued, capital is becoming globalized in the sense that what were previously national circuits are being broken down and functionally integrated into new global circuits of accumulation.[7] This is reflected in the emergence of global production chains linking the production and assembly of components in various parts of the world under the centralized command and control of transnational corporations. This decentralized and fragmented production is a feature of the new regime of flexible accumulation. Capital is no longer bound by the vertically integrated mass production model of the Fordist regime of accumulation. Capital is no longer confined to a national economy where better wages for workers means better consumers, thereby enabling it to realize profit. With the advent of what David Harvey has called "space-time compression"[8] due to low cost transportation and global communications, goods and services can be produced across borders. Now capital has been set free to roam the globe in search of cheap and compliant labor, lax environmental regulations, low taxes, a business-friendly legal system and states that will protect its interests, while still able to sell commodities in segmented markets where there is effective consumer demand.

In effect, transnational capital is now able to take advantage in new ways of the combined and unequal development that the era of colonialism has left us. The countries of the North were enriched by the industrialization made possible through the exploitation of the South. At the same time, this impoverished the countries of the South (many of which had been far wealthier than Europe prior to their colonization) and underdeveloped their societies into dependent appendages of the North. When England arrived in India it was an obscure poor island off the western coast of Asia and India was a land of great wealth. When England was finally forced to leave, it was wealthy and India was poor. Now transnational capital is undertaking to complete the proletarianization of the South, tapping its low wage labor force to produce goods for high-income consumers in the North as well as privileged enclaves in the South. The conquest continues[9] to dismantle the remaining local non-capitalist social relations in the South, uprooting populations from their traditional communities, thereby swelling the multitudes of low wage superfluous laborers, while at the same time appropriating their resources and traditional knowledge. This renewed accumulation by dispossession enables transnational capital to realize immense profits.

William I. Robinson has argued that this process of globalization is creating a single economic system, global in reach, comparable to the national economies that national capital constructed in the 19th century. The neoliberal policies of the "Washington Consensus" promote a worldwide market liberalization and

> the internal restructuring and global integration of each national economy. The combination of the two is intended to create ... an open global economy and a global policy regime that breaks down all national barriers to the free movement of transnational capital *between* borders and the free operation of capital *within* borders.... This process parallels the nation-building stage of early capitalism in which an integrated national

market was constructed with a single set of
laws, taxes, currency, and political consolidation
around a common state. Globalization is
repeating this process, but on a world scale.[10]

Just as nation-building took place under the leadership of a
class and the political elite that represented it, so too with the
building of a global capitalist economic system. Hypermobile
capital has become detached from the particular nations that
once nourished it. As a result, the captains of global industry and
finance are emerging as a *transnational* capitalist class. These
owners and managers of transnational corporations, along with
the bureaucratic staffs of transnational agencies like the Bank for
International Settlements, the International Monetary Fund, the
World Bank and the World Trade Organization, and in concert
with the political elites of core states of the G-8, comprise a global
ruling bloc that has been fashioning this new global order. In the
meetings of the World Economic Forum and other such conclaves,
this global ruling bloc has operated largely out of public view
and without even the charade of the democratic participation
of the nations of the world whose peoples are being profoundly
transformed. It is only through the militant opposition of an
evolving global justice movement that this globalist conspiracy
has become publicly visible. More on that shortly.

The Globalized State

Just as capital is becoming detached from nations, so too
are the states that once nurtured capital within those nations.
National political elites that have long served the interests of
capitalism as a system have become globalist political elites in
service to transnational capital. In so doing, they have bent
states away from purely national interests (although the rhetoric
of "national interest" is still commonly used as camouflage) in
favor of transnational capital and the emerging globalized system.
Consequently states have become less nation-states and more
globalized states.[11] Many observers have claimed that states are
becoming obsolete. To the contrary, we want to argue that in
their globalized form, states are still essential to capitalism. It
is only in their willingness and ability to serve their nation that

they are being weakened. For example, in response to the 2008 financial crisis, the US government bailed out the banks, but not the homeowners. How has this come about?

As a result of the last terminal crisis of capitalism—the worldwide depression of the 1930s—core states had adopted welfare liberal policies. Responding to the popular demands of their nations and the need to save capitalism from itself, they had sought to protect their peoples from the negative effects of the market and to promote human development measures through support of education and culture. They had undertaken to regulate markets to ensure they would not break down; and they had adopted Keynesian policies to promote corporate profitability and effective consumer demand through deficit spending and taxation.

Similarly, many states in the periphery, responding to popular pressures from their peoples, had adopted similar welfare liberal policies. Employing an import substitution strategy, they sought to escape underdevelopment by promoting domestic industry, just as core countries had done earlier in their history. Such developmentalist states were responding to the interests of their nations, often against the opposition of core states that hoped to continue to benefit from the uneven development they had long promoted and maintained.

However, the process of globalization has involved the transformation of nation-states into globalized states. States are becoming globalized not in the sense that their rule is becoming global in scope (with the single exception of the United States), but in the sense that *they serve the interests of global transnational capital more than the nation over which they rule*. This transformation of states can be seen in the shift away from developmentalist, welfare policies to neoliberal policies over the last few decades.[12] This shift has taken place in the global South and the North alike.

In the countries of the South the shift was facilitated by the external debt crisis of the early 1980s. Then as a condition for refinancing debt, the IMF imposed structural adjustment policies that involved dismantling social welfare programs, privatizing the economy and opening it up to foreign, i.e. transnational, investment. The reorientation of a state's economy toward exports was designed so that it could earn the hard currency needed to service the debt—not to stimulate growth with a view to increasing public well being. It meant production was less for domestic consumption. It was the population of the nation that suffered.

In order to be able to impose these harsh conditions on the people, the state had to be insulated from popular pressures. This is one of the fundamental political requirements for an effective globalized state. The political elite has to be able to serve the interests of transnational capital even at the expense of the people it rules over and whom it nominally serves. This is to be done by what the World Bank has called "macroeconomic management by an insulated technocratic elite"[13] willing to carry out unpopular reforms and able to withstand the resulting "IMF riots" (as former WB chief economist Joseph Stiglitz has called them). There can be no clearer instance of such a phenomenon as that now playing out in Europe with the replacement of democratic governments in Italy and Greece by unelected technocrats brought in to manage and further impose austerity.

National barriers to the mobility of capital were battered down by IMF structural adjustment programs (SAPs) based on neoliberal policies. While acting for corporate capital, states were crucial agents in implementing this transformation. The US state led the way, acting through the instrumentalities of the IMF, the World Bank, and later the World Trade Organization as well as free trade treaties. Within the countries of the global South, the transformations were made by the client states of the periphery and imposed on the national populations. The states of both North and South alike played an essential role. And in so doing they were representing the interests of transnational capital rather than their own nations. They were acting as globalized states.

The following chart may help make clear the chain of actors.

CAPITAL ⸱⸱⸱→ TNC⸱⸱⸱→ US STATE ⸱⸱⸱→ GGI ⸱⸱⸱→ T.W. STATES ⸱⸱⸱→ T.W. NATIONS

Capital acted through transnational corporations (TNC) represented by the government of the US which controls the global governance institutions (GGI) of the IMF, WB, WTO, etc. These were the instruments that imposed on the elites controlling the states in the Third World the standard SAP package of privatization, deregulation, trade liberalization, and opening to foreign direct investment (FDI) by the TNCs. It then rested with the states of the periphery to impose this transformation on the national populations, usually against popular opposition.

What emerged under neoliberal globalization is a new regime of capital-labor relations based on a post-Fordist flexible accumulation and the disempowerment of the popular classes. Corporate capital moved "off shore" to tap low wage workers in the global South where governments could ensure a compliant workforce. Unionization was prevented or company unions created (sometimes called ghost or signboard unions), legal labor protections were minimized or not enforced. The massive displacement of peasants from the land ensured an endless supply of labor to keep wages low. A vast reserve of superfluous labor built up in slums on the fringes of major cities, eking out a living in a growing informal economy.[14] Many emigrated to El Norte to find work. There, capital used them to displace unionized workers with undocumented immigrants with few if any legal rights. In many ways these workers, stripped of other social relations, without legal protections, isolated disempowered individuals embodied the capitalist ideal of alienated labor power, a mere commodity that exists only to create value for capital.

With globalization the state's historical function of preserving the social order is increasingly accomplished with no more than a passing glance at the form of justice that had once ensured governability. The governance exercised by globalized states amounts to providing infrastructure for export oriented development, macroeconomic norms required by transnational capital, and political and social stability.

Mexico provides a notable example of the transformation of a nation-state into a globalized state. As a result of NAFTA, Mexico now has one of the economies most thoroughly integrated into the global system, exporting 40% of everything it produces. This was accomplished in spite of the revolutionary heritage from the early 20th century that had produced a strong developmentalist state legitimated through extensive social welfare programs. A kind of nationalist patrimonial state had been consolidated in the 1930s during the presidency of Lázaro Cárdenas and continued under the political organization that evolved into Partido Revolucionario Institucional or PRI. As an official party, PRI, in the words of Mexican historian Elisa Servin, "functioned as a state apparatus, utilizing a powerful corporate structure and a thickly woven network of interests and relationships to operate as a privileged space for mediation and negotiation between state and society."[15] PRI political dominance continued unchecked until the end of the century through a combination of cooptation of popular forces (campesinos, workers, and the middle classes), patronage, election rigging, and, when all else failed, assassination and violent repression. For seven decades Mexico experienced political stability under the rule of an insulated elite—just the political conditions needed to achieve a state-directed integration into the globalizing capitalist system.

The drive to use this political power to globalize the state came from within the state-party bureaucracy. Under the external impetus of the debt crisis, Harvard trained technocrats succeeded in capturing PRI and through it the presidency. Neoliberal reforms were pushed through, beginning under President Miguel de la Madrid (1982-88) and then consolidated under President Carlos Salinas de Gortari (1988-94), culminating in the incorporation of Mexico into a North American Free Trade zone, NAFTA. Salinas built a political base independent of those PRI leaders still committed to the Revolution's heritage by co-opting local campesino groups and neutralizing or co-opting PRI unions—all this in order to make way for the neoliberalization of the Mexican state that De la Madrid had begun. As the head of Ford Motor Company in Mexico, Nicholas Scheele, observed, "is there any other country in the world where the working class... took a hit in their purchasing power in excess of 50% over an eight-year period and you didn't have a social revolution?"[16] It was quite a political feat, comparable to the undoing of Roosevelt's New Deal in the US, begun during the Reagan presidency and continued up through the presidency of George W. Bush.

The methods Salinas used in the campo through PRONASOL or Programa Nacional de Solidaridad, co-opted previously autonomous, oppositional civil society groups, even linking with local Maoist leaders by promoting programs based on the "maximum feasible participation of the poor," bringing them into his camp politically so he could carry through national policies

(NAFTA) that were contrary to their interests. The strategy Salinas used in the campo is well summed up in the slogan that LaBotz suggests for him: "where civil society is—there the state shall be."[17]

This tying of civil society to state elites whose hegemony is then accepted is the essence of what political scientists call polyarchy. As a political system of elite rule based on competitive elections that masquerade as democracy, the US has promoted polyarchy throughout the global South.[18] Salinas's rule is a textbook case of such elite rule and it succeeded in transforming the Mexican state from a nation-state into a globalized state. However, this transformation and its effects undermined PRI's legitimacy and weakened the system of *presidentialismo*, the twin pillars of the political system that President Ernesto Zedillo (1994-2000) was unable to repair. Although PRI lost the presidency in 2000, the Partido Acción Nacional or PAN government of Vicente Fox followed by Felipe Calderon enthusiastically continued the neoliberal policies of their PRI predecessors. The Mexican state seems to have been successfully locked in to serving the interests of transnational capital above those of the nation. It is doubtful that even a Lopes Obrador presidency (the populist PRD candidate in 2006) could have detached the economy from transnational capital any more than Lula could in Brazil.

And what have been the effects of neoliberal globalization on Mexico? While it has benefited some (most of the banks are foreign owned and Wal-Mart is the #1 retailer in the country), it has had a devastating effect on the popular classes, especially campesinos. Wages have declined and millions have been forced off the land and had to emigrate to the US in search of jobs. Foreign direct investment (FDI) has ended up pitting smaller Mexican businesses against transnational corporations. As was to be expected, the smaller ones have either failed in the competition or sold out to foreign capital that wanted a "national" cover in Mexico (e.g. Banamex—a bank name that sounds Mexican—is actually owned by CitiBank).

NAFTA's export oriented development model (EOD) envisioned the *maquiladoras* as a leading sector whose dynamism would stimulate widespread industrial development. In fact, they have had the opposite effect. As off-shore production platforms for transnational corporations, *maquiladoras* assemble products from components brought into the country duty free and then exported mainly to the US, again duty free. There are no linkages to the Mexican economy either backward or forward and thus the *maquiladoras* do not promote a network of domestic suppliers. The only factor of production that is Mexican is the cheap labor that carries out the unskilled assembly labor. Eighty percent of Mexico's exports are from the *maquiladoras*, although by rights they are really intra-firm transfers rather than true exports. For all intents and purposes *the maquiladoras are not part of the Mexican economy. They are part of the global economy that happens to be located on Mexican territory because of certain competitive advantages.* They are points in the global assembly lines of transnational capital.[19]

Far from promoting the development of the nation, globalization has strengthened its dependency on transnational corporate capital. And it is the globalized state of Mexico that has facilitated this neo-colonial situation.

Empire

Similarly the core state, the United States, has also become a globalized state. Indeed, the US is *the hegemonic* globalized state. Since the end of World War II it has used its dominance to construct a globalized capitalist system. And initially it was able to do this while also maintaining liberal welfare policies. That was possible because at that time capital was still national, and amidst the devastation of the other core industrial countries, US capital had no competitors. However, by the 1970s, that was to change.

The two world wars were a consequence of inter-imperialist rivalries among European and Japanese capital acting through their respective nation-states. By 1945 the victorious states resolved to avoid another such war by creating *international* institutions to keep peace between states (the United Nations system) and build an *international* economic order conducive to capitalism (the Bretton Woods institutions of the IMF and World Bank and the General Agreement on Trade and Tariffs or GATT—later to become the World Trade Organization). The lead in these efforts was undertaken by the only state with an industrial base still intact, the United States. The US put itself forward as the leader of a peaceful globalization of capitalism to the common benefit of North and South alike. The liberal foreign policy establishment was united behind this project and supported whatever efforts were necessary to ensure countries of the global South would not escape from the capitalist orbit. To woo them, capitalism had to show a humane face.

The US undertook this challenge, however, not solely on its own behalf, but also on behalf of the European colonial powers now weakened by war. It was understood that to avoid a return to fratricidal inter-imperialist rivalries, this leadership must represent the interests of capitalist countries as a whole—a general rather than a particular interest. It was this that made recognition of US leadership possible. It was this that made US hegemony possible. I use the term 'hegemony' in the Gramscian sense of 'consensual domination.' Other core capitalist states accepted US dominance in the post-war alliance in a kind of 'collective imperialism' over the South—Europe's soon-to-be former colonies.[20] The US became the 'indispensable nation,' the first among equals, in the words of Clinton's Secretary of State, Madeleine Albright.

What has been constructed step by step over the ensuing historical era was a global system at once economic, political, cultural and military, designed to give capital unrestricted mobility as it seeks ever greater accumulation. Institutions have been built to regulate trade and remove barriers to capital penetration, overt and covert interventions have sought to secure dominance of local elites favorable to capital, and capital itself has been consolidated and concentrated into ever larger transnational corporations. While the US led these efforts, the system that evolved was no longer rooted in any national territory; it was global. It corresponded to the description of what Hardt and Negri called an Empire, as distinct from imperialism.

> Imperialism was really an extension of the sovereignty of the European nation-states beyond their own boundaries... Empire... is a *decentered* and *deterritorializing* apparatus of rule that progressively incorporates the entire global realm within its open, expanding frontiers... [S]overeignty has taken a new form, composed of a series of national and supernational organisms united under a single logic of rule. This new global form of sovereignty is what we call Empire.[21]

This evolving global structure of economic and political rule made possible the gradual detachment of capital from its historical roots in nation-states. As we have seen above, capital has expanded beyond the confines of the national economies that had once nurtured and protected it, taking the organizational form of the transnational corporation. And as capital has become globalized, so too has its chief state sponsor. The United States has become the hegemonic globalized state.

Just as in its nation-state stage of adolescence, capital had needed the protection of the state, so too the transnational corporations require protection that comes from the new transnational institutions of governance. The World Bank, the International Monetary Fund, the World Trade Organization have been crucial in opening new markets, destroying older competing economic structures, establishing rule-based trade, adjudicating disputes, etc.—all necessary functions for the orderly global expansion of capital. Perhaps in the future these might even become elements in a transnational state serving global capital, as Steve Martinot suggests in Chapter 6. But for now transnational capital requires the service of the globalized states that have morphed from nation-states. As we can clearly see in the WTO, the rules are being written by transnational corporations, advocated by core states, adjudicated by transnational technocrats and then legitimized enforcement is carried out by globalized states against each other and their own national populations.

It was only after the collapse of the alternative socialist camp that the humane mask could be removed. With that the Kantian vision of perpetual peace of the liberal establishment could be replaced by the neoconservatives' Hobbesean world. Multilateralism under US hegemony gave way to unilateral pre-emptive wars to extend the empire. This was even pre-visioned by the liberal establishment before 911 made it politically possible.

As *New York Times* reporter Thomas Friedman has so candidly observed as early as 1999: "[T]he hidden hand of the market will not work without a hidden fist... The hidden fist that keeps the world safe for Silicon Valley's technologies is called the United States Army, Air Force, Navy and Marine Corps."[22] When all else fails, there is still the US military ready to do the job.

Two and a half years later, George W. Bush would answer the neocons' call. It is not only neocons who have supported an increasingly interventionist imperialism in the post Cold War period, it is also the liberal establishment. Their criticism of Bush was just that he did a poor job of it. President Obama has been more effective in his interventionism. In spite of protestations to the contrary, it is the logical extension of their bi-partisan foreign policy that has guided the US for over 60 years.(23) By extending this to its extreme outcome, the neocons have thereby laid bare the entire imperial project of our ruling elite.

As the global hegemon, the United States claims a kind of *imperial sovereignty*, enforcing the requirements of transnational capital on disobedient states, a.k.a. rogue states, whose sovereignty is to be limited. This is a marked departure from traditional concepts of sovereignty. Since the Treaty of Westphalia in 1648 proclaimed the inviolability of national borders, states were not to intervene in each other's internal affairs. While this principle was often violated in fact, it was accepted as the norm for inter state affairs. But that concept of sovereignty has now been significantly altered. The US is now proclaiming a new norm: imperial sovereignty for itself and limited sovereignty for all others. Regime change is asserted to be a legitimate right of imperial sovereignty.

Imperial sovereignty means that a state can act unilaterally (not having to justify itself to others; being able to keep secret its reasons for action; being able to coerce others to accept those actions) and with impunity (being a superpower means never having to say "I'm sorry"; being unaccountable to international law, exempt from the World Court and International Court of Criminal Justice; US troops never to be under foreign command). Fundamentally modifying the Westphalian state system, there is an asymmetric relation between a state with imperial sovereignty and those with limited sovereignty. In the Bush doctrine of preemptive war, an imperial state asserts the right to initiate war to prevent any other state from becoming a possible future challenger to its dominance. As Henry Kissinger has pointed out, preemption "cannot be a universal principle available to every nation [*sic*]."[24] It is reserved for the state with imperial sovereignty, not subordinate states.

Since the early post WWII period, the US has come to increasingly function as an imperial state. Often its "leadership of the community of nations," a.k.a. "the free world" was exercised with the consent of other states, or at least core states (since they are the ones that really count). In recent years, this consent was often manipulated or even coerced. With the Bush administration, the consent required for genuine hegemony was all but dispensed with. This led many to assume that the US was turning away from a half century of building transnational governance institutions and toward a nationalistic projection of power in its own interests. The Bush administration was certainly very successful in stirring up nationalistic forces within the American nation and harnessing them in support of such policies.[25] However, the interests it sought to serve are no longer just national in scope since the US state has itself become a globalized state. The political elite has long served the interests of capital and continues to do so now—only now capital has become increasingly transnationalized and come to see itself as the unique agent capable of promoting the ongoing globalization of capital. In the absence of a single global federation of states to promote and maintain capitalism, the political elite of the US has volunteered for that role, using its state as the instrument— an imperial state claiming to represent the whole. While many in the foreign policy establishment have been critical of the unilateralist and militaristic methods of the Bush administration's neocons and worry that the other transnational institutions of governance are being weakened, they have long shared the same imperial aim. The debate is only a difference as to the most effective methods: global order through military dominance or under hegemonic consent.[26]

Even prior to the Bush administration, in the 1990s, sovereignty underwent serious erosion. So-called "humanitarian interventions" went far in gaining recognition that a government was accountable to other states for the way it treated its own people; the exercise of sovereignty was trumpeted as being limited by certain universal principles of human rights.[27] This served as the driving wedge for acceptance of limitations on sovereignty. The US was quick to assert this for others, but never for itself. It claimed the "responsibility" to lead "the community of nations" in holding so-called rogue states to the new standards— rogue states being those still outside the orbit of or resisting the dominance of global capitalism. It was thus that it claimed an imperial sovereignty for itself. But, we should remind ourselves, that was the way the 19th century European imperialist powers had always acted towards non-Westphalian peoples elsewhere in the world. In fact, the 'new imperialism' may be nothing but the wine of the old imperialism in the new bottle of globalization.

But that new bottle has arguably changed the wine. Far from it spelling the end of states, Ellen Meiksins Wood has argued that the globalization of capitalism requires a system of multiple states under the hegemony of an imperial state that maintains "a delicate and contradictory balance between competition and maintaining conditions in competing economies that generate markets and profit." [28] Such a system of multiple states requires a global policeman with sufficient military force to prevent the emergence of competing forces globally or regionally that could lead to inter-imperialist rivalries. In the words of the Bush administration's National Security Strategy of 2002, it requires "full spectrum dominance." The implication of this view of the so-called neoconservatives then is that military dominance by the US is not just an expression of unilateralist nationalism, it is also functional for the system of globalized states that global capital requires. Thus is the logic of capital confounded with the logic of state power (at least for the hegemonic imperial state). [29]

Whatever the ultimate outcome of the globalization of capital, so far it has not been able to dispense with states. Indeed the existence of multiple states has been functional in many ways. [30] So far Wood is right to assert that "the more universal [i.e. global] capitalism has become, the more it has needed an equally universal system of reliable local states" [31] just as it has needed a dominant imperial state. But that does not mean, as she claims, that "the 'globalized' world is more than ever a world of nation states." [32] Rather, it means it is a world of *globalized* states, i.e. states serving the interests of global capital rather than their nations.

State Against the People

> *"The governments of the US and Mexico have declared war on the Mexican people, and I don't know why.... The politicians are all paddling in the same boat together."*
> *—words from a Mexican popular song, August 2005*

As we have seen, there has long been a link between class interests within civil society that enabled the state to represent the nation while actually serving the interests of its dominant class. However, with the globalization of capital, it has become detached from the nation. Transnational capital now roams the planet in search of accumulation. Yet, the state still functions to serve the interests of the transnational corporations, even when that is against the nation in which it is based. Thus *the globalized state finds itself against the nation*. With neoliberalism, the state (in both core and peripheral countries) has abandoned the people in serving the interests of transnational capital.

We are seeing globalized states emerging in both the core and the periphery—states that can no longer represent the collective interests of their peoples because of a commitment to neoliberal trade and investment policies. With respect to their nations, they have become disarmed, whether by complicity or threat. The political elite turns a deaf ear to the people, claiming that international competitiveness prevents them from responding to their pleas for social justice. But with respect to capital, especially the transnational corporations, they remain powerful and active. *Thus the state becomes ever more transparently the instrument of capital than ever before.* And with that the liberal alliance between the popular classes and the national elite that had once made welfare and developmentalist national projects possible unravels.

While the state in capitalist society has always served the interest of capital, what made this politically acceptable during the era of national capitalism was that it could be plausibly claimed that the interests of the other classes were linked to that of capital. But now with capital transnationalized, that link is weakening, if not vanishing. As a result, national popular classes have little reason to accept the political elite that has betrayed their trust— or even to accept the system of capitalism that it serves.

This presents a legitimization problem. As neoliberal globalization has transnationalized capital and globalized states, it pits those states against their nations. More and more as the state is globalized, it is no longer able to promote the common welfare or to be seen to do so. It acts to *prevent* it. and can be seen as doing so. It can be seen as keeping wages low in the name of competitiveness; keeping workers disorganized (capital has long dreamed of a union-free workplace); loosening health, safety and environmental regulations ("get government off our backs," intoned Ronald Reagan); lifting the tax burden from capital as an incentive to investors (thereby starving social programs); encouraging corporations to move "off shore", taking jobs with them, and on and on. When the people cry out in protest, the state responds, "The market made me do it"—feigning impotence in the face of the very market that it helped to create.

How does the political elite try to get away with this con game? How do they seek to maintain the compliance of the subject population, cooling them out so they will accept their loss? In the case of the United States, the culture of individualism and the seductions of consumerism have played vital roles. Both have fostered a privatization and atomization of life that has depoliticized society. That used to leave the state and the political elite relatively free from demands of the popular classes. But as Frederick Douglass observed long ago, "power concedes nothing without a demand, it never has and never will." The new Occupy movement that came into being in 2011 is but the beginning of popular challenges to the legitimacy of the status quo.

Mass consumerism has been especially effective in placating the people of the US. Even in the face of declining incomes over the last quarter century, the flood of cheap goods from the sweatshops of the global South has fed the insatiable, media stimulated appetites of consumers. This has been sustained by growing personal and national debt which is not sustainable in the long run, although so far it has been an effective prophylactic against popular challenges to the neoliberal corporate globalization. WalMart made a significant contribution to the political quiescence of the American people. But can this be maintained for long?

If we look to the South we can see a different process contributing to the political stability of globalized states. Mexico again is a particularly instructive case. The US-Mexico border is the only place where a First World country and a Third World country border each other. The dialectical relation between these two is revealing. We noted above how the Mexican political elite was able to impose neoliberal globalist policies on a reluctant population, privatizing key sectors of the economy and downsizing social supports. It has also sought to dismantle the traditional small scale farming that had succeeded in feeding the growing population, replacing it with large scale commercial agriculture for export.[33] This has freed up more labor power from agriculture so as to supply industry with low wage workers. As a result, Mexican agriculture now supplies the US market with vast quantities of fresh vegetables while Mexico imports more and more of the food needed to feed its population. Displaced campesinos work in prison-like conditions in *maquila* industries or flock across the border to seek work. At the same time, that industry is part of a global assembly line supplied with components from abroad and consequently does not generate local suppliers. In order to be competitive in the global "free market" the system depends on low wage labor and as a result the standard of living of most of the population remains low or has even declined.

Meanwhile, north of the border, the US consumer economy depends on low wage migrant labor from Mexico and Central America as well as cheap, labor intensive goods imported from those low wage areas. What keeps the wages of immigrants low is not only the large supply of workers desperate for work, but also the fact that many of them are illegal and thus highly vulnerable and unable to make demands on their employers. This brings into focus one of the important functions of a territorial border such as that between the US and Mexico: by limiting the mobility of labor at the same time that capital enjoys high mobility, wage levels are kept low on both sides of the divide that the two states enforce. The territories controlled by states might thus be thought of as "population containment zones", to use an apt phrase of sociologist Philip McMichael. Robinson comments, "the nation-state system boxes in and controls populations within fixed physical (territorial) boundaries so that their labor can be more efficiently exploited and their resistance contained."[34] Here again we can see how a system of multiple territorial states can serve to maintain the inequalities between nations that is essential to the continued combined and unequal development of global capitalism.

The migration from Mexico to the US, both legal and illegal, is massive. For example, in the central Mexican state of Guanajuato (a traditional "sending state") there are whole villages where no able-bodied men can be seen, only women, children and the elderly. And many of the young women have also left for work in the *maquiladoras*. The families left behind are sustained by remittances sent home from El Norte. For the whole of Mexico remittances totaled $20 billion in 2005, up from an estimated $16.6 billion in the previous year[35], and even after a decline in the midst of the economic crisis, remittances remain the second largest source of foreign exchange for the country.

One might well wonder what would happen if the safety valve of migration were not available to the Mexican campesinos? Early in the 20th century similar dire conditions in the campo gave rise to a major peasant revolution. Now migration and the dollars that come home from it have given campesinos another option, another way to survive. Without it, the countryside could explode once again. Migration has been a major factor in political stability, insulating the Mexican elite from the consequences of their service to transnational capital. And how about other, more distant regions of the global South where the migration option is not so readily available? As those societies are more closely drawn into the global net of capital, their national economies are undermined, and their states globalized, might their elites be confronted by new revolutionary forces? Those nativists in the US who want to end migration should be careful—they might get what they wish ... and along with it some unexpected consequences.

What we can see in all of this is globalized states in both core and peripheral countries acting in the service of transnational capital even at the expense of their own national populations. The state's historical function of preserving the social order is increasingly accomplished with no more than a passing glance at the form of justice that had once ensured governability.[36] The governance exercised by globalized states amounts to providing macroeconomic and political stability while enforcing on its population norms established at the transnational level.

This last point is well illustrated by Chapter 11 of NAFTA, negotiated by technocrats for the three major states of the North American continent. It gives corporations the right to sue governments to recover lost future profits resulting from state action, even if that action was undertaken to promote the common good of its nation, e.g. protect health, the environment, working conditions, income levels, etc. Further, such suits are adjudicated not in national courts, but by a transnational body of experts operating in secret. States are expected to enforce its decisions on their own nation's taxpayers. This privileging of investor rights (i.e. the interests of transnational capital) over the democratic rights of a nation, agreed to by its own state, shows the extent to which that state is no longer a nation-state but a globalized state.

Consider some concrete examples. Several years ago oil companies started adding the chemical MTBE to gasoline to make it burn cleaner so as to cut down on air pollution. But it turned out that MTBE began to show up in ground water and it was discovered that it causes cancer. Now the water supply of many California cities is contaminated, as is also Lake Tahoe, once one of the purest bodies of water In the world. So the State of California decided to ban MTBE. But as it happened, this chemical is manufactured by a Canadian company called Methanex. Methanex proceeded to sue California for $970 million for the loss of anticipated profits. Under the free trade rules of NAFTA, Methanex claimed the state had interfered in its market and thus it was entitled to be compensated for its loss. Here we see government being discouraged from protecting the public health and well being unless it is willing to pay a private corporation for not harming it. Such an outcome would likely have enraged public opinion In the US So after much delay, the NAFTA court ruled that since the Canadian company made only a component in MTBE, it thus did not have a substantial enough interest for its claim. The court took the politically safer route by dodging the substantive issue.

Here's another example. In 1996 the State of Massachusetts passed a law preventing state agencies from buying goods or services from companies that do business with Myanmar, a.k.a. Burma. This was because of the repressive military junta that rules that country after annulling the election of Nobel Prize winner Aung San Suu Kyi as president. However, this selective purchasing law was challenged as in violation of WTO rules that require governments to not intervene into economic markets. As a spokesman for the EU said, "we don't believe this kind of action is fair to the trade and investment community."[37] Under the banner of "free trade" the citizens of Massachusetts are forbidden from making democratic decisions about how to spend their collective money. Morality is required to leave the market alone. Under this principle, the sanctions against apartheid South

Africa would have been forbidden and Nelson Mandela might still be in prison today.

The effort in 1998 by core states to globalize the principle of investor rights in a Multilateral Agreement on Investment (MAI) shows the direction transnational capital seeks to take the global economy. Although this effort, undertaken by the Organization for Economic Cooperation and Development or OECD (a club of the richest countries) was aborted due to worldwide popular opposition, it remains on the agenda of the transnational capitalist class. The successful (for the time being) resistance to capital points to the fundamental contradiction of corporate-led globalization: the contradiction between transnational capital and the globalized states that serve it and, on the other hand, the nations with which popular classes identify. And it points to the centrality of the struggle for democracy in resistance to corporate globalization.

States, even globalized states, require some measure of legitimacy in order to be able to govern. That means that political elites have to respond to concerted popular pressures, even those that oppose the agenda of transnational capital. The opposition to MAI was moved by the popular classes' realization that its adoption would deny them the opportunity to protect their own interests against foreign capital. It was born of a nationalistic concern to preserve sovereignty in hopes that democratic pressure would be able to make the state an instrument of the popular will. They were unwilling to surrender to transnational capital the last, best means for protecting the national interest— the nation-state.[38]

In these concrete democratic struggles we can see popular classes contesting the new world order transnational capital is creating. In effect the nation is pitted against the transnational governance structure being constructed by an emerging transnational capitalist class. Consisting of the owners, managers and technocrats of the transnational corporations, members of this class are the true citizens of the globalized world. National populations have no citizenship rights there. Policy coordination within this global ruling class occurs in the annual gatherings of the World Economic Forum, a kind of central committee of international capital. The WEF consists of the CEOs of the one thousand top transnational corporations who are its Foundation Members. Other members are by invitation or appointment only. There are one hundred World Media Leaders, key policy makers from national governments and international organizations (called World Economic Leaders), and select academics and experts from various fields (called Forum Fellows).[39] Their purpose is to figure out how best to rule the world in the interest of transnational capital.

Former US Treasury Secretary Larry Summers, writing in *The Financial Times*, April 27, 2008 observed that "the global economy encourages the development of stateless elites whose allegiance is to global economic success and their own prosperity rather than the interests of the nation where they are headquartered." While they are becoming stateless, they nevertheless need states, globalized states, to protect and promote their interests. As William I. Robinson has argued, "Globalization is not a national project but a class project... with a strategy that seeks to utilize the existing political infrastructure of the nation-state system and simultaneously to craft TNS [transnational state] structures."[40]

Within globalized states the ideal political structure is that of a polyarchy. Formally democratic because it is based on contested elections, a polyarchy is actually a form of elite rule. As defined by political scientist Robert Dahl, polyarchy is simply the selection in multiparty elections of leaders from among competing elites. Under this concept of democracy, the term simply means, in the words of Schumpeter, "that the people have the opportunity of accepting or refusing the men who are to rule them."[41] But between elections, the governing elite rules, largely insulated from the popular will.

Nevertheless, globalized states are more than simple administrative units of transnational capital. This is because in order to serve the interests of capital they must be able to maintain effective rule over their national territory and its population. In a word, they must maintain governability. Unless they are to rule by sheer coercion (a means of domination that is not very cost effective), a measure of legitimacy is necessary. And legitimacy is achieved by adopting the form of justice. As we saw earlier, this is the political elite's response to popular struggles and is reflective of the correlation of class forces in a society. Politics is still possible even in a highly globalized state. Thus, as Nicos Polantzas has argued, the class struggle is inscribed on the state.

It is against the transnational capitalist class and the ruling elites within nations that the global justice movement is pitted. As a loose oppositional network, the movement has adopted a multipronged strategy in opposition to transnational capital.[42] To date, the anti-corporate global justice movement has focused primarily on resistance at every turn to the efforts of transnational capital to legally institutionalize and consolidate its global rule. But it must also continue the popular struggle for the democratic retrieval of the state by the nation. It should not forgo the powerful appeal of an enlightened nationalism to the popular classes to "take back the state" from the globalizing elite who have betrayed the nation. The nation-state remains an important terrain of political struggle even in a globalizing world. We must bring the struggle for global justice home.

As we have seen, a state may serve either the interests of a dominant class or popular classes. Which it does, depends on the political activity of the various classes and the leadership they put forward. Globalized states are led by political elites beholden to transnational capital. They have put forth a neoliberal project that identifies the interest of the nation with that of capital, and especially transnational capital. But this identification has worn increasingly thin as economic inequalities have widened within nations and between them as well. In response, radical social movements have emerged. Some, such as the *piquetero* movement in Argentina and the popular and indigenous movement in Bolivia, have even been able to topple neoliberal governments. The social movements of Latin America are putting forth alternative projects for nations and even redefining what the nation is. Some have been anti-state while others have recognized that to the extent the state can be captured by popular forces, it can be a powerful instrument against transnational capital. Witness Chavismo in Venezuela, which has given rise to participatory leadership and power in poor communities in a kind of "nationwide social movement-cum-political party."[43] This kind of extension of a revolutionary state into civil society and extension of civil society into the state is similar to the early development of Committees for the Defense of the Revolution or CDRs in revolutionary Cuba. In other cases social movements remain outside the state, thereby avoiding cooptation by entrenched political elites and preserving the ability to act independently through civil society to affect state policy, as for example Movimento los Trabalhadores Rurais Sem Terra or MST in Brazil.

In sections of the global South, particularly in Latin America, social movements have reclaimed the nation-state. There, the negative effects of neoliberal corporate globalization have been felt for many years. Popular forces have gained control of the state in Venezuela, Bolivia, Ecuador, and much earlier in Cuba. As a result the state has sought to promote the national interest while protecting the society from the forces of globalization. There we have nation-states responsive to the emancipatory interests of popular classes. Beginning with adopting new constitutions, there has been a re-forming of the state and its relation to society from the neo-colonial state of an earlier era.

The Bolivarian state in Venezuela is an interesting case. Blessed with an abundance of the world's most valuable commodity—oil—the Venezuelan government has been able to fund worker cooperatives, thereby forming the beginnings of a domestic alternative economy to the still dominant capitalist economy. At the same time, resources to local communities have been channeled through community councils, thereby empowering popular classes. Following Cuba's example of Third World solidarity, Venezuela has joined in partnership with it to forge a regional network of solidarity relations based on mutual benefit called the Bolivarian Alternative in Latin America (ALBA). Bolivia, Ecuador, Nicaragua, and other states have joined in this alternative to corporate dominated globalization. Nation-states are not necessarily chauvinistic. When guided by the interests of popular classes, they can be very progressive, even socialist, and exemplify the highest values of international solidarity.

Often social movements are better able to represent the general interest of a nation than political elites, tied as the latter are to the particular interests of dominant classes. This is because in order to grow to the scale of a mass social movement, its leaders must universalize their agenda in order to attract broad support and build alliances. It is even possible for a social movement to build a kind of parallel power to the state and the dominant class. This can be done by creating alternative economic institutions (e.g. cooperatives as in Mexico's Yucatan or occupied factories in Argentina) and autonomous participatory structures of governance (e.g. the Zapatista's *Juntas de Buen Gobierno* and their *Caracoles*), that strengthen civil society as an alternative to a globalized state. In this way, popular forces can literally reshape the nation out from under the control of the state. Which of these various relations between social movements and the state is optimal depends on conjunctural factors such as the country's political leadership, the correlation of class forces within civil society, pressures from outside by transnational capital, etc. Pragmatics, not ideology, must shape strategy.

It is important to recognize that such popular struggles are not solely motivated by material self-interest. As we said earlier, a nation is an imagined community. As such, the *image* of what that community is, is crucial. How do the members of a nation understand themselves? What are the core values they share? What kind of life do they aspire to for all members of the nation? The answers to these questions define what a particular nation is. People will be motivated to struggle in defense of that image as much as, or sometimes even more than, their self interest. That is because the nation they belong to is a part of their own identity. "I am an American" or "I am a Mexican" or "I am a Cuban" defines more than one's place of origin, it also to some extent defines one's being. Thus a threat to what the nation represents in one's imagination is a threat to one's very self, to one's identity. In defending it, one is standing up for what one *is*; one is defending one's dignity.[44]

This national self-image can play a vital role in the struggle for the democratic retrieval of the state. For example, Americans see themselves as a kind, generous, well meaning nation. The aggressiveness of the Bush administration's foreign policy violated this national self-image. Thus many Americans found it profoundly unsettling. Invading other countries or bullying small nations is not what America is about in their mind. The political elite had to justify it in terms of "national security" or "defending freedom" or "promoting democracy." But if these rationales can be exposed and people are able to learn that their political leadership has been carrying out such actions for many years, they feel violated, betrayed. When the skeletons are brought out of the closet, discovering reality can be a radicalizing experience.

As globalized states lose legitimacy with their own national populations, there arises the possibility of a politics of national unity. If led by the popular classes, this unity can include the petty bourgeoisie and, in the periphery at least, even those sectors of national capital threatened by transnational corporations. This is similar to the politics of national unity advocated by Jose Marti in order to win independence from Spain for the Cuban nation. And it is the same politics of national unity being followed today by the leadership of the Cuban Revolution. The Cuban Revolution was unique among the many revolutions in the 20th century: it was the one that occurred in the most highly neo-colonized society. For the first half of the century Cuba was a dependent satellite of the US. While nominally independent, the Cuban state represented US interests more than those of the nation. The resulting loss of legitimacy contributed to its demise

Today in the era of globalization, globalized states are in a similar position, only now they are beholden not so much to a foreign country, as to transnational capital (albeit enforced by the global hegemon). Nations find their interests betrayed, their established social relations disrupted, their livelihood threatened, their people impoverished—and their own political elite is complicit in this. Such are the conditions that may give rise to the national revolutions of the 21st century The contradictions of globalization are giving rise to its supercession. History may yet record that the Cuban Revolution was not so much an exception as a precursor of what was to come. It was just ahead of its time—It was the first revolution of the 21st century.

Endnotes

1   Benedict Anderson, *Imagined Communities: Reflections on the Origin and Spread of Nationalism* (Verso, 1991).

2   This point is succinctly made by the title of Chris Hedges' book *War is a Force That Gives Us Meaning*, Public Affairs, 2002. Indeed, it is what makes us, *us*.

3   Cf. William I. Robinson, *Promoting Polyarchy: Globalization, US Intervention and Hegemony* (Cambridge University Press, 1996).

4   Cf. Peter Bachrach, *The Theory of Democratic Elitism: A Critique* (Little Brown, 1967).

5   I thank Milton Fisk for the theory of justice and the distinction between the form and function of the state used here. Cf. *The State and Justice: An Essay in Political Theory* (Cambridge University Press, 1989).

6   Cf. Cliff DuRand, "Cuban National Identity and Socialism" (1992) at

http://www.globaljusticecenter.org/wp-content/ctrip1.pdf

7   William I. Robinson, *A Theory of Global Capitalism: Production, Class and State in a Transnational World* (Johns Hopkins University Press, 2004), p. 11.

8   David Harvey, *The New Imperialism* (Oxford University Press, 2003).

9   As Noam Chomsky has aptly put it in the title to his book *Year 501: The Conquest Continues* (South End Press, 1993).

10   Robinson, *op. cit.*, p. 78.

11   Samir Amin has suggested the term 'market states' in "Capitalismo, Imperialismo, Mundializacion", *Marx Ahora*, Nro.4-5, 1997-1998. But this fails to focus on what is new in the present stage of globalization. The function of the state has always been to serve capital. Today's globalized state undertakes to serve *global* capital. Similarly, the term 'neoliberal state' and 'national state' (Robinson) fails to focus on the fact that states have become reoriented away from their nation and toward global transnational capital.

12   Cf. Cliff DuRand, "Neoliberalism and Globalization" Chapter 1 above.

13   World Bank, *World Development Report 1997: The State in a Changing World* (Oxford University Press, 1997), p. 152.

14   Mike Davis, *Planet of Slums (*Verso, 2007).

15   Elisa Servin "Another Turn of the Screw: Toward A New Political Order", *Cycles of Conflict, Centuries of Change: Crisis, Reform and Revolution in Mexico*, Elisa Servin, Leticia Reina & John Tutino, eds. (Duke University Press, 2007).

16   Quoted by Charles Bowden, "While You Were Sleeping: In Juarez, Mexico, Photographers Expose the Violent Realities of Free Trade," *Harper's*, December 1996, pp. 44-52.

17   Dan La Botz, "Carlos Salinas and the Technocratic Counter-Revolution" chapter 6 from *Democracy in Mexico: Peasant Rebellion and Political Reform* (South End Press, 1999).

18   William I. Robinson *Promoting Polyarchy: Globalization, US Intervention and Hegemony.* Cf. also Cliff DuRand, "Democracy and Struggles for Social Justice" at http://www.globaljusticecenter.org/2011/11/04/democracy-and-struggles/

19   For a fuller account of the impact of NAFTA on Mexico, see my "The Exhaustion of Neoliberalism in Mexico" in *Confronting Global Neoliberalism: Third World Resistance and Development Strategies*, Richard Westra, ed. (Clarity Press, 2010).

20   The term 'collective imperialism' comes from Samir Amin, "The Alternative to the Neoliberal System of Globalization and Militarism Imperialism Today and the Hegemonic Offensive of the United States" February 25, 2003.

21   Michael Hardt and Antonio Negri, *Empire* (Harvard University Press, 2000), p. xii.

22   Thomas Friedman, "Manifesto for a Fast World," *New York Times Magazine*, March 1999.

23   Andrew J. Bacevich, *Washington Rules: America's Path to Permanent War* (Henry Holt, Metropolitan Books, 2010). Indeed, this is but an extension of the imperial project of the US elite since before 1776 as

neocon Robert Kagan shows in *Dangerous Nation* (Alfred A. Knopf, 2006). Cf. my 2009 review of Kagan's book at http://www.globaljusticecenter.org/2011/11/04/dangerous-nation/

24   Quoted by Noam Chomsky, *Z Magazine*, 18,2 (2005), p. 40.

25   Cf. Jerry Harris, "To Be or Not To Be: The Nation-Centric World Order Under Globalization," *Science and Society*, 69,3 (July 2005).

26   Cf. my review of Robert Kagan's *Dangerous Nation: America's Place in the World from Its Earliest Days to the Dawn of the Twentieth Century* (Alfred A. Knopf, 2006) at http://www.globaljusticecenter.org/2011/11/04/dangerous-nation.html

27   Edward D. Marks, "From Post-Cold War to Post-Westphalia," *American Diplomacy* http://www.unc.edu/depts/diplomat/AD-Issues/marks-westph.html

28   Ellen Meiksins Wood, *Empire of Capital* (Verso, 2003), p. 157.

29   Cf. David Harvey, *op. cit.* and Giovanni Arrighi, *The Long Twentieth Century: Money, Power, and the Origins of our Times* (Verso, 1994).

30   Even William I. Robinson, who is otherwise a critic of state-centric theories in this era of globalization, admits that "National boundaries ... are mechanisms functional for the supply of labor on a global scale and for the reproduction of the system. Here we see how the continued existence of the nation-state serves numerous interests of a transnational capitalist class." *Transnational Conflicts: Central America, Social Change, and Globalization* (Verso, 2003), p. 274.

31   Ellen Meiksins Wood, *op. cit.* p. 152.

32   *Ibid.* p. 154.

33   David Barkin, "The End of Food Self-sufficiency", *Distorted Development: Mexico in the World Economy* (Westview Press, 1990), pp.11-40.

34   Quoted by Robinson, *A Theory of Global Capitalism, op. cit.*, p. 106.

35   Fred Rosen, "From Mexico to New York Labor Joins the Struggle", *NACLA Report on the Americas* (May/June 2005), pp. 8-11. Cliff DuRand, "Mexican Immigration and Globalization," http://www.globaljusticecenter.org/2011/11/07/mexican-immigration/

36   A Gallup International poll of 50,000 people in 68 countries found that 65% do not think their country is governed by the will of the people, even though 47% thought their elections were free and fair, according to a BBC World Edition report, http://news.bbc.co.uk, accessed September 14, 2005.

37   Quoted in *Corporate Predators: The Hunt for Mega-Profits and the Attack on Democracy* by Russell Mokhiber and Robert Weissman (Common Courage Press, 1999), p. 56.

38   Another example is worth mention—this one from the eastern Caribbean. Here the small banana growers of these former colonies are supported by the European Union, which has agreed to buy their bananas at a preferential price—a kind of reparation, if you will, for years of colonial domination and slavery. However, such a preference violates the free trade rules of the WTO. The United States, acting on behalf of Central American banana producers, filed a complaint before the WTO and won the right to impose $520 million in sanc-

tions against the EU unless it abandons its banana policy. Under WTO rules it is irrelevant that eastern Caribbean bananas are produced in a relatively more socially just way—on small farms headed mostly by women— as opposed to the Central American plantations where workers are underpaid and exposed to pesticides, and unionization efforts are routinely smashed. But why did the US take such an interest in the case? After all, the US doesn't grow bananas. Well, the Central American banana plantations are owned by Chiquita, whose CEO, Carl Lindner, is a major campaign contributor to both Democratic and Republican parties. So, the US Trade Representative declared that the "US economic stake in this case is clear"—even though no US jobs are at stake. What is at stake is the livelihood of small, impoverished farmers who now may be pushed into the illegal drug trade instead.

39   Kees van der Pijl, *Transnational Classes and International Relations* (Routledge, 1998).

40   *Op. cit., A Theory of Global Capitalism*, p. 137.

41   Joseph A. Schumpeter, *Capitalism, Socialism and Democracy* (Harper and Row, 1975), p. 285. Cf. also William I. Robinson *Promoting Polyarchy, op. cit._*

42   Components of a multi-pronged strategy include:
a. exposing and disrupting the emerging transnational governance structure
b. democratic retrieval of the state by the nation
c. building a global civil society as a future global nation with popular democracy (cross-border solidarity leading toward the transnational power of popular classes no longer mediated by nation-states)
d. alterglobalization from below: a global Lilliputian strategy of cooperative localism
While these strategies may point in quite different directions, together they can go far in arresting corporate neoliberal globalization.

43   Jonah Gindin, "Chavistas in the Halls of Power, Chavistas on the Street", *NACLA Report on the Americas*, Vol. 38, No. 5 (March-April 2005), pp. 27-29.

44   The same BBC poll, *op. cit.,* found that a third of those surveyed used nationality to define themselves. Latin Americans had the strongest identification (54%) with their nation.

Chapter 4

THE SUSTAINABILITY OF THE NATION-STATE MODEL IN A GLOBALIZING WORLD*

Armando Cristóbal Pérez

In recent years, it has become fairly common for political scientists to profess the belief that the nation-state is undergoing a process of disappearance, or at least of reduction in its functional size and scope. The expectation is that at some time in the near future, the state will have become essentially extinct in its present form. For many now dubbed "failed states", this is a destiny that is already being approached in earnest. For this fate, two fundamental reasons are generally given.

The first is the economic expansion of the neoliberal project called "globalization." Though globalization can be understood as simply a variation on the classical capitalist process of its international extension in its quest for profit, there are significant aspects of this present form that go beyond that. In particular, this international expansion serves as both a theoretical and a material basis for establishing a non-national form of global political organization. Rising above mere economic

---

*Translation by Ida Maria Ayele Rodríguez and Steve Martinot

considerations, such a political organization is projected to eventually substitute itself on a global level for the current network of supposedly sovereign nation-states.

We saw this expectation of the disappearance of the state expressed in prophetic form over twenty years ago by Robert Reich, as Secretary of Labor for the Clinton administration.

> There will be no national products or technologies, no national corporations, no national industries. There will no longer be national economies, at least as we have come to understand that concept. All that will remain rooted within national borders are the people who comprise a nation. Each nation's primary assets will be its citizens' skills and insights. Each nation's primary political task will be to cope with the centrifugal forces of the global economy which tear at the ties binding citizens together—bestowing ever greater wealth on the most skilled and insightful while consigning the less skilled to a declining standard of living.[1]

The second reason, on the cultural plane, is the rise of new identities and new nationalisms whose tendency is to fracture the nation-state from within. These identities may have a racial, ethnic, linguistic or regional foundation. Whatever their source, they tend to produce a regrouping of people. Some actually lay claim, whether real or invented, to supposed "historic" territory. But whatever their claim, their emergence as new political communities produces demands on political power, demands which get expressed by a wide variety of means (including extreme violence).

It is to this process that Samir Amin has referred in a more recent statement.

> The present epoch is surely characterized by an awakening, or reawakening, marked by collective social identifications which are starkly different from those defined by membership of a nation-state or a social class. Regionalism, linguistic

and cultural assertion, tribal or ethnic loyalties, devotion to a religious group, attachment to a local community, are some of the multiple forms this reawakening has taken...They constitute an important aspect of the crisis of the state, and more particular of the nation-state, however notional the nation in question may in reality be.[2]

Here I will focus on the first of these two reasons. And as a prologue to that discussion, let me first specify the sense in which the terms 'State' and 'Nation' are to be understood here.

With respect to the "state," there is a wide variety of notions and definitions, expressed in a variety of ways by classical and contemporary philosophers, as well as in international law. I myself tend to adopt a Marxist conception as a philosophical starting point. Nevertheless we may briefly synthesize them, and express the common core of their diversity as lying in an historical process in which a territory is given boundaries and a specific community within those boundaries constitutes a political organization for itself, the function of which is to exercise coercive and hegemonic power over the population as a whole in service to the particular economic interests of a part of that community.

The variety of philosophical theories and descriptions that have been brought to bear upon this foundation, of which the Marxist is one, is not the topic that needs to be pursued here. Our focus is a critique of the projection of obsolescence and disappearance onto the state. In general, it is enough to recognize that each different characterization of the state arises from the particular philosophical perspective taken by each political theorist. We do not have to develop a typology of states nor of their forms of government. The subject of the question to be pursued here can be simply grasped as what can be called the *modern state,* that is, the form of state that originated in Western Europe during the high Middle Ages, and spread to the rest of the world.

The modern state can be characterized as exhibiting certain operational or structural aspects as follows. It is that institution in which various structures of power are subordinated to a single central authority. That authority establishes and maintains boundaries for its territory, the limits and contours of which are constituted through alliances and contestations with surrounding external powers and forces. Within its defined territory, the modern state centralizes itself in a capital city, to which it transfers all or most local responsibilities, and over which it constructs a hierarchy of subordinate powers, to which it demands consensual adherence. It creates a professional army (including mercenaries) to which it gives the responsibility for territorial defense. It builds an ever-growing bureaucratic apparatus of paid public functionaries, whose job is to guarantee the management of state functions (including the judiciary and the police). On the other hand, as a bureaucracy, these functionaries become detached from actual concern in real social or political affairs. One of their functions is to oversee and redefine the difference between public power and the private domain. Another is to break all political connections between the state's own political power and existing church hierarchies, or at least to subordinate the latter to itself. The state facilitates the free movement of the people within its borders, including fostering the growing urbanization of its territory in the interests of its socio-economic system, thereby producing new relations between the city and the countryside.

The "nation," as a concept, on the other hand, can be summarized as follows.

> The nation is a stable human group with a common history, a common territory, arising from complex processes involving ethnic, socio-cultural and class related aspects, which are conditioned and overdetermined by its unique economic system. Its emergence is manifest in a coherent and cohesive cultural and knowledge-based framework which materializes itself in a common literature and a common structure of language. An essential aspect of a nation is the recognition among its members of a common origin (whether real or mythic), along with a shared history and a common awareness of membership in a self-defined group or ethnicity. It presents itself as an historical entity to which all or most of its members express a strong sense of allegiance and a self-conscious sense of belonging. As a community, it integrates itself

through the construction of a socio-territorial organization, which can then be understood as the state.[3]

Today, sociologists and ethnologists tend to agree that the basic organization of every human group or community is of an ethno-social nature, regardless of specific form of political structure it had generated for itself. Though the actual sense of communality in a nation may not necessarily involve the totality of the nation's members (which depends on many factors), nor even express its internal diversity (as the state may be inhabited by many internal nations or peoples), it is through such communality that a nation's members attain a sense of themselves and their particular development. In other words, for each national community, there is a conjunction of socio-historical commonalities for which a sense of identity constitutes the cornerstone.

Most political scientists, on the other hand, when they consider the nation, tend to focus on the more concrete phases of its historical emergence as a political entity, rather than on the ethno-social foundation which sociology addresses. This is probably because that is how the political structure of the community most strongly manifests itself. Nevertheless, many political scientists engaged in analyzing the role of the "nation-state" today in its global or macropolitical context tend to co-opt terms from other disciplines, such as sociology, and to deploy them out of their original contexts, without attempting any critical bridge to translate those terms from their normal disciplinary domain to the categories of political science. In that way, they often end up constructing arbitrary definitions and descriptions to the principal advantage of substantiating their own particular political theories—though those theories may or may not be useful in other regards.

But there is a reductionism in this approach, owing to which what is essentially a consensus has evolved among political scientists that all human communities on the planet today which exhibit a form of political order and organization of their own, and which we have lumped together as the "modern state," can actually be considered or called "nation-states." That is, the tendency is to equate the two concepts. But as a renowned investigator dedicated to researching this matter has said: "according to rough estimates ... during the early 1970s, only about 10% of all states could claim to truly be "nation-states" ..., that is, those in which the borders of the state coincide with the nation, and in which the whole population shares a single cultural formation."[4]

How then did the contradictory nature of this term, the "nation-state," originate and become so common or habitual in the contemporary social sciences? What was its historical origin? After all, it integrates two different and incommensurable phenomena in a single conceptual notion, which thus already introduces a significant ambiguity and non-objectivity into any "scientific" attempt to comprehend the issue. In fact, at no time has the term "nation-state" been scientifically well-formulated, either as a concept or social category, despite the many empirical descriptions given to various specific and ungeneralizable aspects of it as a political phenomenon.

If what typifies the nation-state is the existence of a unique ethno-social body, for which it is its political organization, then it is evident that the majority of contemporary states cannot be considered nation-states—especially outside Europe and the United States. This is well understood by scholars of international minority rights, the international law that relates thereto, and indeed the international organizations and supporting scholarship that promotes these rights, e.g. organizations such as FUEN in Europe, or international instruments such as the UN's Declaration on the Rights of National, Ethnic, Linguistic and Religious Minorities, the Declaration on the Rights of Indigenous Peoples, etc.

During the period when the modern state was evolving, there was a search for a sense of collective identity that could be substituted for the social gel that religion and the feudal estates had provided prior to that time. In that context, many contemporary political theoreticians, both republican and monarchist, intuited that, in some generalizable sense, in each and every human community, the existence of an ethno-social identity offered the possibility of manipulating social behavior.

At first, of course, that possibility could only be constructed, whether theoretically or practically, in terms of the conditions existing in Western European societies of the time (which the modern state would later reflect). For instance, it was the basic structure of the medieval city-states that was subsequently extended and adapted to larger territories, such as the monarchies of England, France, and Spain. Indeed, the modern state, emerging from the specific circumstances of those regions, soon demonstrated the possibility, through the use of its centralized power in particular, of achieving high levels of social homogenization.

The dominant sectors of the economy and their ideological representatives discovered that new forms of hegemony could be constructed, and that a new social uniformity was made possible, through strengthening of a sense of national self-awareness. At the same time, they discovered that the use of force itself, deployed to incorporate surrounding ethno-social communities from outlying territories, actually assisted in generating and consolidating that internal social uniformity.

It was as a logical extension of this phenomenon that, in the wake of the seizure of power by the bourgeoisie, capitalism would produce wave upon wave of expansion into other areas, in a process of colonization that not only imposed the modern state on regions residing in totally different circumstances from those of the colonizing society, but also consolidated the hold of that modern state over the society that was being engaged in its colonization. For the European powers, the modern state became an instrument of dual domination, a machine for creating a colonial periphery and a homogenous core. The effect, on the scale of the entire system, was the formation of a vertical hierarchy between states reflecting that which had characterized the European monarchies of the 15th century.

What this incorporation and homogenization process implied, whether intentionally or not, was national amalgamation on the one hand and the dismemberment of autonomous human communities on the other. It was a violent process that resulted in the commission of genocide and ethnocide, the destruction of many ethno-social communities at various levels of development. Whole tribes, tribal federations, nationalities and nations, entire languages and extensive ethnic domains were annihilated.

Of courses, as this process unfolded, it produced concomitant political effects within the three European states from which it first originated. In France, for instance, the language of Oc (whose name is the etymological root for the term "occident," and is now the name of a zone called Occitania), which was spoken in the region extending from Catalunia through the Midi of southern France to Italy, was destroyed. In Great Britain, the conjunction of the dominant anglo-saxons with the island's original inhabitants constituted the subsequent English identity from which the on-going antagonism toward the Irish derives. In Spain, in contradistinction, the formation of the kingdom of Aragon never succeeded in totally eliminating either the Galician people or the Basque national minority. And on the overall map of Europe, accompanying these internal transformations, both the Slavic peoples of the East and on the Balkan Peninsula, and various Nordic communities, were reduced to serving as a marginalized periphery for the central three.

With all the force of the capitalist social-economic system, manifested through the political power generated by these states as they became world powers, the model of the "nation-state," in both its monarchical and republican form, was imposed on the peoples of the Americas, Africa, Asia and Oceania. A wide variety of means were used to impose that European model, from conquest and military occupation to massive settlements, seizing and building residence on the lands of indigenous peoples, all through the use of force. The result was a system of colonies or protectorates. When, in the 20th century, a worldwide anti-colonialist movement forced the European powers to "dismantle" their colonial system, the modern state "model" was again applied, under the guise of decolonization, as a way of maintaining the arbitrary territorial divisions created by the fire and blood of earlier imperial conquest. These state territories only corresponded to what had been established by conquest, rather than by conforming to the territories inhabited by specific peoples as nations. Yet the state structures imposed on those supposed political communities by this decolonization process were nevertheless dubbed "nation-states."

Perhaps it can be said that, in the time that has transpired since the system of states constructed by the Treaty of Westphalia (1648), and in light of the earthshaking events that have transpired since WWII, a sense of the obsolescence of the nation-state has been generated. But we have to recognize that alongside the tendency of the modern capitalist state to produce a homogeneity among the peoples within its borders, there remain those ethno-social communities that had been marginalized and not amalgamated into "political nationhood," who are now reclaiming their rights to political autonomy and self-determination. Ethno-social communities that have found themselves politically divided between or trapped within different multinational states are now demanding their self-determination via reunification or secession as a human right. This notion of the "nation-state" (that each nation should have its own state) is one of the causes of a new nationalism that has emerged with force on the world scene, to the surprise of many.

To this demand, neoliberal globalization has responded through a variety of means, while striving to preserve the ability of world market forces to meet its own needs. One has been to establish guidelines of a new unification, requiring all states to collaborate in one way or another through transnational organizations. Another has been the dispersal of production facilities transnationally, coordinated through new technologies, where only product components are produced in each state. But both these developments, in overlaying a uniformity of political control and of economic production on the globe, presuppose, as an underlying purpose, *the prevention* of the disappearance of states as political entities. It is from this complex process involving the arbitrariness of state borders, the formation of a global political organization, and the need to preserve existing states as political entities, as the terrain of economic and political control, that the dilemma outlined at the beginning of this essay arises.

The notion that the nation-state is disappearing can then be seen as only a reflection of a theoretical reduction of the situation, based on specific biased and non-scientific analyses. Clearly, in light of what has been said, the issue is not the disappearance of what is called the nation-state, nor the national identity that is intended to serve as the unifying paradigm for its population. It is rather a question of the replacement of old forms with a new overlying structure of power, one through which global capitalism as a world system can satisfy its new needs for expansion and unequal development. What we are witnessing is a realistic transformation of the prior capitalist state into a new form, rather than its disappearance.

Instead, what the notion of the state's disappearance proposes is some kind of elimination of national functions for each state, accompanied by a cultural homogenization of their distinct populations. In other words, it seeks to divest the peoples of any political power of their own, which would be wholly in the interests of the centers of power of northern industrial capital, and a derailing of any natural processes of ethno-social and political development of the peoples of the peripheral states (understood as either geographic, the south and east, or as an economic and social periphery constituted by minority groups in all areas, and indeed even including the US, whose elites are the leading force in this entire process).

If, in some manner, the existence of Cuba has analytic significance concerning the role of the nation-state in the 21st century, with respect to the neoliberal globalization of capitalism, it would be through its alternative trajectory, its oppositional response to the aforementioned historical developments and conditions.

The process initiated in 1959 by our revolution actually mirrored something of ongoing occurrence in Cuban history. Cuba has a long tradition of resistance to external forces when those forces act counter to whatever organic transformations are gestating indigenously in the womb of the nation. The current transformation of the character of Cuba, its decision to construct a socialist society, is a response to just such internal developments and changes, and thus constitutes a logical extension of former processes. Yet at the same time, of course, it breaks with them. The sense of continuity arises from the nation's aspiration to be free of all external domination and to govern itself autonomously as a sovereign country. This has long been the character of Cuba's cultural and patriotic traditions, as well as of its arts and literature. It has expressed itself in forms of populism, and in the strong popular embrace of its ethnic diversity. In a word, it reveals a developed political culture carrying on a heritage that is two centuries long.

But a break with the past has nevertheless occurred, grounded in the economic sphere. Cuba's transformations in that domain are well-known. But they have been accompanied by transformations in the political realm as well; in particular, in the construction of a new State. And what has been most characteristic of it has been the construction of new democratic structures, structures of participation that are neither merely formal nor restricted to the electoral. Without minimizing representation as an organizational paradigm, the most important element of Cuban democracy is the increasingly direct participation of people in decision making.

Now, to introduce into the arena of neoliberal globalization a nation-state such as Cuba's, insofar as it represents a socialist society, engenders a number of practical issues, not only for Cuba but for neoliberal globalization as a whole. While those issues raise a number of truly complex theoretical problems, beyond the scope of this essay, a few general aspects can be mentioned in the context of this critique.

We know that one purpose of announcing the alleged disappearance of the nation-state as a consequence of neoliberal globalization has been to create a general conceptual horizon that must be confronted by each individual state, at least theoretically. What that horizon portends is the inevitable development of a global market economy, for which a central concern would be the adequacy of an overall political organization that could circumvent or prevent conflicts between states within the operations of this system—that is, the governance of market stability in the face of built-in inequalities and asymmetries.

However, if one's point of view actually focused on a horizon of inclusiveness rather than conflict prevention as purported, it would materialize in projects to which the market economy would stand opposed. A socialist society need not seek to produce a homogenous society, but can embrace its diverse expressions, in both the long and short run. For the neoliberal project of a global political structure, the mere presence of a socialist society would alter its complexion and give it a different meaning. At the very least, what the existence of Cuba signals, against the global project of cultural homogenization, is the fact that socialist societies, as alternative societies, have not totally disappeared. It demonstrates that alternate forms of democratic organization of the modern state have given birth to themselves. It means that other societies with different objectives and methods, even under conditions such as those of neoliberal globalization and the market economy, have the possibility of both developing as sovereign entities, and uniting for solidarity and justice. And finally, and most important, Cuba has demonstrated that its very ability to participate actively in the given (neoliberal) conditions stems precisely from its independence, and that it is its autonomy as a state that permits it to do so.

In conclusion, insofar as it is an historical entity, the State has an origin, a process of development, and therefore also an ending. Nothing is eternal. Its end will come when the conditions that gave it birth and continue to make it necessary have disappeared. Though some of the conditions that have been at the foundation of the "modern" or "national" State may disappear, that in itself would not be sufficient for the disappearance of the state-based system. While a market society may govern the process of globalization and seek to disempower the ability of states to act for domestic benefit, the conditions which require existing human communities to have local political structures to fulfil their needs, and function as the State persist (whatever the form or name it may have been given). And as long as communities require and can independently produce a State for themselves, it will be impossible for the process of neoliberal globalization to realize itself and its innermost desires universally. In the present circumstances, it is precisely the existence or the inevitable human drive to construct alternative better states, national or not, that renders the neoliberal project for the generalized disappearance of the State impossible.

REFERENCES

Amin, Samir, *Capitalism in the Age of Globalization*, Edit. Paidos (Estado y Sociedad), 2001, Barcelona / Buenos Aires.

Cristóbal, Armando, *Dimensión política en el origen del estado-nación en territorio occidental de Europa en el siglo XV*, Tesis doctoral inédita, Fondos bibliográficos de la Fac. Historia y Filosofía, 2001, Universidad de La Habana.

Fung, Thalía, *Reflexiones y metareflexiones políticas*, Edit. Félix Varela, 1998, La Habana, pág. 68

Gramsci, Antonio, *Gramsci y la filosofía de la praxis*, Edit. Ciencias Sociales (Col. Filosofía), 1997, La Habana, pág. 68.

Reich, Robert B., *The Work of Nations. Towards the Capitalism of the 20th Century*, Javier Vergara Editor S.A., Argentina.

Smith, Anthony, *National Identity*, Editorial Trama, 1997, Madrid.

Endnotes

1   Reich, Robert B., *The Work of Nations. Towards the Capitalism of the 20th Century* (Argentina: Javier Vergara Editor S.A.).

2   Amin, Samir, *Capitalism in the Age of Globalization* (Barcelona/Buenos Aires: Edit. Paidos Estado y Sociedad), 2001).

3   Cristóbal, Armando, *Dimensión política en el origen del estado-nación en territorio occidental de Europa en el siglo XV*, Tesis doctoral inédita, Fondos bibliográficos de la Fac. Historia y Filosofía, 2001, Universidad de La Habana.

4   Smith, Anthony, *National Identity* (Madrid: Editorial Trama, 1997).

Chapter 5

ON THE AUTONOMY, SOVEREIGNTY AND INTEGRATION OF PEOPLES AND NATIONS*

Orlando Cruz Capote

This paper is a contribution to the extensive work now in progress on the issues of the nation-state, national identity and autonomous self-governing localities. The central questions inextricably linking these issues today are those of sovereignty on the one hand, and the diversity of ethnic, racial, communal, gender and sexual identities that cross borders, both naturally and transgressively, on the other hand. The problem is how to integrate the two.

For the most part, debates concerning the sovereignty of nations and national identities have focused on the cultural domain. The cultural element must be included in our considerations because of the importance it holds, in particular for those who are not members of the dominant majority and wish to preserve that identity. But it must not be made exclusive. And we must take care to recognize that in our discussions of cultural phenomena such as race, gender, etc. we are dealing with social constructions. This paper will argue, with respect to

*Translated by Steve Martinot

110

the existence and durability of both sovereignty and diversity that, within the vast spectrum of political issues they address, and in their processes of emerging, stabilizing, and diminishing, they maintain their own legitimacy in their confrontation with globalizing processes. In particular, it is their ability to actively oppose the dehumanizations of neoliberal transnational capitalism and its ideology (as articulated by its conservative intellectual circles and think tanks) that marks the nature of and substantiates their legitimacy.

Ultimately, this paper will address certain aspects of contemporary social and political discourses that signify possible alternatives to the many adverse effects of the globalization process. Our perspective is that only the construction of a new society at the global and local level, on both a regional and national basis, founded on a humanist and socialist solidarity, can provide an adequate response to the processes of globalization that challenge us, both those inherited from the past and those produced in the present.

The Present Reality of Globalization

The present processes of globalization have expanded in both the spread of hegemonic neoliberal capitalist theory and in its politico-ideological practice. As a complex process, its increasingly profound adverse affects and consequences have not been uniform among nation-states, national identities, and self-governing autonomous communities. Different countries and different peoples have suffered degradation and atomization in unequal ways and at different rates.[1] But clearly, the most negative impact has been on third world peoples, including marginalized immigrant communities and national minority cultures within the industrialized countries. One result has been the vast movement of peoples across borders, fostering an increased multiculturalism, with its complex heterogeneity of identities, such as is found almost everywhere today. Though some of this mixing of peoples and cultures has been inherited from the past, what now confronts us most directly is that which has come to reflect the reality of contemporary globalization. Though overlaid upon a natural heterogeneity of nations and peoples, this contemporary globalized multiculturalism, which has invaded the daily lives of peoples around the globe, has found itself subjected to forces seeking to produce uniformity and a greater homogeneity.

This push toward uniformity characterizes what can be called the "fast world," with its speed of transportation, its flood of information, the growing flow of tourism, and the invasion of the transnational corporate media. It is particularly evident in the unbalanced, unequal, and asymmetrical international trade between that "fast world" at the center and the peripheral third world. Yet it is precisely because of the impoverishment wrought by this imbalance that there have been massive and uncontrollable migrations of people from rural areas to the cities, and from poorer countries to richer ones. The emergence of many civil wars and foreign military interventions further adds to emigration.

The cultures that people bring with them suffer from this homogenizing process. The corporate media, with its endless flood of information from the capitalist world to the peripheral areas, has produced a degraded and inferiorized vision of cultural identity, whether reflected in the nationalism of states or in the cultural identities of internal groups. This gnaws away at the patriotic convictions and sense of belonging and collective solidarity that characterize these identities. The genuine originary historico-cultural traditions that people carry with them, including their present day beliefs, rituals and myths, are often reduced to a form of folklore.

All this has produced a phenomenon that could be called "identity nomadism." While it has promised a hybridity, a fertile mode of cultural exchange between peoples engendered by their mobility and diversity, it has also shown itself to contain a self-defeating aspect. Against its very promise, it has exacerbated backlash ideologies for the possession or even the reconquest of social space, which has traditionally been the foundation for racism, discrimination, xenophobia and other exclusionisms.

It is in this context that many neoconservatives, right-wing postmodernists, reformists, and a variety of superficial thinkers have advanced the various discourses about the end of history.[2] These are grounded on the idea that the nation-state, and autonomous self-governing communities and regions, have simply exhausted their possibilities and potentialities as agents of socio-economic development. Instead, it is the export market that is given the central position as the historical axis for development, whose implicit focus is the legitimization of neo-liberal transnational domination. There is another principle that accompanies this, of course: the idea of western bourgeois democracy. But while this latter idea pretends to prioritize public space, the focus on the market transgresses the barrier between the public and the private and subjects public space to advanced processes of erosion and diffusion.

Confronted with the fact that neoliberal political strategies have become instruments of the state, of its agencies and institutions, one begins to suspect that humanity in its entirety, insofar as it is beset by the steamroller of globalization, has only one choice ahead of it, to either search its horizons for new forms of democratic action, participation, and debate or submit once and for all to the hypnotic circularity of market operations, forever under the seductions of the fantasy world of merchandising.[3]

It is within this unfolding process that many people have tended to politically prioritize cultural identities, both regionally and locally. In some cases, they have actually succeeded in reanimating a slow integrationist process or program designed to bring diverse identities and movements into coalition. But the tendency to focus on the cultural also can be symptomatic of the collapse of the self-proclaimed project for "real socialism," a loss of legitimacy of the nation-state, and a disintegration of regional multinational configurations into smaller and weaker national entities (sometimes even at the hands of the exponents and designers of the so-called Global Village idea). [Some examples would be the division of Czechoslovakia, or the disunity of the different republics of the Caucasus.] On the other hand, the emergence and mutual recognition of heterogeneous identities, that has given rise to the new social movements—often composed of quite dissimilar groups and social forces (the World Social Forum is an example)—is a collateral effect of the relative decay of revolutionary nationalist movements (and here we are not speaking of the fundamentalist or cadre versions).[4]

The other side of the process of nation-state erosion is that governments, to the extent that they represented the interests of local elites, have tended to be reduced more or less to police functions to control their own people. In particular, they have sought to control the unemployed, the marginalized, the discriminated and the excluded by this means, rather than addressing their needs. While this tendency has generally been on the rise, it is especially true for the governments of what is called the third world, that is, for those countries that are trying to crawl out from under underdevelopment and dependency. But it also characterizes what has been happening in East Europe (the former Soviet bloc) and at the margins of the industrialized north. Politically, this increased policing has created the necessity for states to suppress their ability to plan or regulate their own economies, in effect eliminating their right and ability to determine which industries and services will be built within their own borders (including banks, the media, and cultural institutions) and where they will be located. Thus, they open themselves more to the impositions of the transnational system. These governments have fallen under the control of the forces of privatization (some domestic but largely external), which determine for them what transnational capital investments will go where, what new technologies will be used, what target markets will be served, as well as which sectors of the local oligarchy will be privileged, and which ecological standards or environmental protections will be repudiated. They end up violating or invalidating their own national or local laws and indeed, their national self-interest.

We have to remember that the Washington Consensus of the 1990s[5] actually stated its purpose to be to "drastically reduce the state, to *erode the concept of a nation*, in order to open it to the greatest extent to the import of goods and services and the entrance of risk capital." The means of accomplishing this centered on a "restructuring of the state," involving attention to "fiscal discipline, public expenditures, tax reform, financial liberalization, direct foreign investment, privatization, economic deregulation, and intellectual property." Ironically, the conference arriving at the Washington Consensus took place in a famous seminary in the US capital. It involved the participation of Institute for International Economy, the International Monetary Fund (IMF), the World Bank (WB), the Inter-American Development Bank (IADB), the General Agreement on Tariffs and Trade (GATT, which later became the World Trade Organization). It even included some Latin American economists. Its foremost principle was the "absolute sovereignty of the market."[6]

By means of this restructuring, the transference of productive and service enterprises from industrial areas to regions of cheaper labor was facilitated. It amounted to a process of denationalization and deindustrialization of the traditional industrial nations, and the imposition of greater overt levels of cruel, undisguised domination on the target areas, those regions that were too weak socially or politically to protect themselves against it.

The Problem of Integrating Diversities

In opposition to this neoliberal globalization process and its new forms of hegemony, many new movements have arisen.[7] Some of these new political and social movements have underestimated their essential need for a fundamental integration of many diverse social formations, from autonomous and self-governing communities to the national and even the international, in order to launch such an opposition. Or perhaps they have forgotten the potential (and lost) utility of the state. But only on the basis of the diversity of an area, integrated across its differences, will a powerful resistance be possible.

Insofar as regional diversity will reflect a "conflict of cultures,"[8] any solution to the problem of its diversity can only institute a relative subordination of the constituents to an integrated whole. But insofar as an integrated movement does attempt to unite autonomous communities and movements, sovereign and self-governing entities, it must do so without subverting their autonomy. What actually provides the foundation for the existent diversity of identities is their sovereignty; in turn, the sovereign state can facilitate institutional and rule-making means for the protection and expression of their authenticity and autochthonous character.

But let us look at one level of the diversity that we face. We can see that the process of capitalist globalization, which passes from its former configuration of many discontinuous (although contiguous) forms of domination to a single multileveled globalized system, is not an inevitability. It occurs under a complex of intentional processes and decisions. And because of that, its forms of hegemony share with the growing resistance that it itself induces a similar capacity to organize diverse political and social forces on the local, national, regional and world level. This parallelism has to be part of our thinking, both theoretically and practically, that is, part of our principal critique of neoliberal hegemonic globalization. Many leaders and intellectuals of the left, including democrats and progressives, and a broad ideological spectrum of organizations, who are attempting in some sense to construct power from below, have themselves advocated a general globalization of solidarity and humanity. That is, they proclaim a better world to be necessary, possible, and imperative. But they foster an integrationist approach which they legitimize simply on the theme of popular democracy. And in the process, they bar themselves from reflecting politically, socially, and historically on the extant configurations of what they confront.

That configuration even includes autonomous communities that constitute what could be called "black holes" in the social fabric of the world. These are areas into which transnational phenomena have not yet penetrated, or only barely. Either the process of globalization was weak, or they encountered enormous resistance at the hands of local traditions (religious, ethnic, tribal, local and nationalist). Such entities would be left out of the global democratic alternative to capitalist globalization.

On the other hand, this historical epoch of neoliberal capitalist globalization has naturally been a period of an intense unification of the human world. This has been given a number of names, such as "Americanization", "Europeanization" or transnationalization. While they all signify globalization, they also include different kinds of "indigenization," whose purpose is to feed off regional or national characteristics, to project a smoothing out of differences and heterogeneities, as a milieu in which to promise expanded productivity, earnings, and underneath that, the extraction of greater surplus value. As Leslie Clark has said, "to a certain extent, economic globalization has made possible the incorporation of local societies into the transnational networks of the multinational corporations, which has permitted it to take advantage of the local people and resources, advantages which it then shares in part with local elites."[9] In many cases, there have been theoretical and "scientific" discourses put forth in both political and civil society (by governmental and non-governmental organizations) that pretend to take the "bigger picture" into account as their point of departure with respect to these local or indigenous areas. But they often understate or omit relevant components of the system, the many inequalities, asymmetries, and inequities involved.[10] And in particular, they leave out the existence of alternative movements and their critiques of that system. New power in integrationist processes and individuals have been emerging that act against that system on the local and regional levels, in both traditional and modern modes. Some are even attempting to build a New International Order. This diversity remains an important consideration for activists and their popular democratic activities, within nation-states, autonomous communities, or local self-managing cooperatives (large or small). Multilateralism is indispensable in such a political environment, if the necessity for a just and democratic resolution of globalization is to be constructed.

In this sense, the question of independence, sovereignty, and autonomy, along with the urgency with which the rights of others are to be respected, stands out as an essential problem. It is the problem of how to construct and integrate collective societies, and how to place them on the basis of the most direct democracy possible. That is, a vision is needed of how to construct a juridical and judicial framework that would need no mediators. And that would be a vision of a true and just democracy, of equality, freedom and social justice, where individuals and collective groups may regulate their social lives based on norms that are both ethical and legal. For the mobilization of civil society whose diversity is an important driving force for this kind of democratic collective endeavour, integrationist processes are essential because they have roots in both the local and the national.

Part of the necessity for turning to this diversity lies in the fact that the majority of discourses concerned with taking power, which are based on a solidarist homogenizing unity (usually reflecting the dominant group) rather than a multilateral integrationism of autonomous entities (reflecting their equal status), have remained nothing but deferred promises, now open to serious question to the extent they have not fallen into frustrating unbelievability. It is only through an integration of the diversity of social and political movements that act in opposition to capitalism's multidimensional system of domination that it will be possible to recover and catalyze a broadly based alternative political culture. But such a culture is already implicit in the multiple forms of autonomy and autonomous communities that have been emerging, with their implicit, attempted or actual restructuring of the nation state and national identity.

The richness and complexity of this politico-cultural reality also reveals many paradoxes. Some can be deployed as strengths in our challenge to the system, while others reveal weaknesses that would affect us from within. For instance, in focusing on the democratic interests of the "local", the "national," and the regional, we confront the danger that these same interests can be fruitfully used by nationalist politicians and populists, and by the so-called national bourgeoisie (and even more so by nationalists of the worst kind, by various fascist tendencies). That is, similar "democratic interests" can be used by those whose objective is to subvert or counteract working class activism and the many movements in opposition to globalized capitalism's new configurations and structures. Beyond our diagnoses of this diversity, a lot depends on our calls to action, and on our way of seizing the historical initiative.

The Problem of Bourgeois Nationalism

The problem with traditional nationalist movements is that, whatever initiative they take on a national level, even though they dissociate themselves from the interests and power structures of transnational capital (and most essentially, from that of North American imperialism), they produce a false dichotomy between the foreign and the national, between the national and the local. The outcome of this dichotomy is too often a confusion of national capital with the nation as such, which then abjures the role of class struggle at the level of the nation. When progressive intellectuals and social movements, parties and organizations of the left in a transnational anti-globalization struggle negate the role of class struggle or a class focus for their political programs, they cripple their own movement, their own resistance, and their own ability to develop cadres-activists working for an alternative to neoliberal hegemony. It becomes a clear sign of ideological weakness. It is what Gerard Greenfield has called the deployment of "an anti-imperialist rhetoric without challenging capitalism." [11]

Thus, the question of nationalism has to be clearly understood in the context of the nation-state itself. Under the force of globalization, some countries have undergone a restructuring of the nation-state toward a managerial model. For such a model, the nation-state reorganizes itself as an agent or middle management for transnational capital. As a new means of maintaining public order (as in Thailand, for instance[12]), this managerial model of governance often masks the construction of a new nationalism which then appears to transcend the traditional authoritarian mode by which the state had historically defended the interests of a bourgeois oligarchy. This new model gets converted into a strategy for inserting local capital into the overarching internationalization of capitalism. Local capital remains national, while seeking to immerse itself in both the regional and transnational (as with Nike in Asia). Thus, it becomes different from a "national bourgeoisie." And one of its political purposes is to derail anti-globalization movements, which it facilitates by ignoring class confrontation between labor and capital or subordinating those conflicts to its own capitalist nationalism.

Paradoxically, many of the demands of the world's very diverse left wing opposition against transnational capitalist hegemony have been made to coincide with the nationalist interests of local or national capital by various social agents. It is easy to forget Nicos Poulantzas' suggestion that "there can be no doubt that bourgeois politics, when confronting the nation face to face, is threatened by its own specific interests; in fact, the history of the bourgeoisie is characterized by a continuous oscillation between identification with—and betrayal of—the nation."[13] By supposing the existence of a national bourgeoisie, that left-wing opposition tries to hide the contradiction that the bourgeoisie has necessarily become both national and international because the world is ever more transnational.

On the other hand, Bob Jessop reminds us that there is a sense in which a local transnationalized capitalism also gives rise to a domestic bourgeoisie that is not totally dependent on foreign capital. It thus differs from a "comprador" bourgeoisie which is created within the nation by the interests of foreign capital. The "comprador" remains economically, politically and ideologically subordinate to foreign capital because it lacks a foundation for its own accumulation. The domestic interior bourgeoisie of which Jessop speaks has a certain degree of independence, with its own economic bases for local accumulation. It is able to maintain its own political and ideological orientation, as well as a certain national opposition to North American and other capital.[14] However, it has an ambiguous position with respect to real independence or autonomy because it is not sufficiently stable to play a leadership role in any genuine anti-imperialist struggle, as had the pre-globalization national bourgeoisie, which had its own national status as a class.

As an operational concept, this interior domestic bourgeoisie opens two important avenues of analysis: its role in a gradual national integration into the circuits of foreign capital, and the economic foundations for its own processes of capital accumulation. With respect to the first, as an important consideration for antiglobalization movements, the defense of local interests can be appropriated by transnational capitalism for its own self-legitimization. For this reason, from the perspective of strategy and tactics for movements working toward alternatives to globalization, a narrow dogmatic or formulistic view of confrontational struggle on the one hand, or the nationalist positions that appeal to a traditional sovereignty or even national self-sufficiency on the other, can end up promoting programs that, by reinforcing the internal logic of local capital, reinforce that of transnationalized capitalism as well. They even run the risk of compromising political alliances through their pretensions about defending the nation against foreign intervention. In lacking a sufficiently complex and conscientiously critical view, leftist politics can lose its way and be converted into a boomerang dangerous to its own thought and action.

Once one loses one's focus on a class conjunction of national, regional and international affairs, for instance, by substituting ambiguous terms such as "destitute" or "ordinary" or "marginal" or "poor" for the exploited and the oppressed, one can easily identify such concepts with the nation as such, and lose sight of the need to include class struggle in the equation. Class struggles are always part of the conception of alternatives, in their given heterogeneity and multiculturality. That has to be part of the point of departure with respect to the problematic of neoliberal globalizing processes.

On an Oppositional Multiculturality

Multiculturality today goes beyond its historically given sense. The relations between uniformity and plurality, universalism and particularism, have changed. This is one of the things implied in the radicalism of indigenous resistance movements, or in the movements for the recognition of a national mestizo culture (even including its power elites, which continue to exist). In fact, as many have come to realize, cultural, ethnic, and national diversity are not obstacles to the positive modernization of social institutions. These movements can and do assume parallel and alternative forms that coexist in both harmony and disharmony with contradictions we have been examining.

Multiculturality and hybridity, as forms of daily life, are constantly interpenetrating each other and intercepting each other in both natural and artificial modes. Socio-cultural heterogeneity on the one hand, and the challenges that tradition poses on the other, are social factors that respond to influences external to themselves with their own linguistic counter-influences. In each region, nation, or locality, there are varieties of coexisting semantic codes, as well as complex and irregular networks, which express themselves through the signs of civil practices whose diversity or universality can lend themselves to oppositional purposes. Indeed, within and among these new heterogeneous social systems and networks, neither modernity nor postmodernity are substitutes for pre-existing traditions. Instead, there are exchanges among these networks, adaptations of knowledges, symbologies, myths, beliefs, religions and cultures.

Though many peoples are moving toward more technically advanced socio-economic forms, there are also increasing interchanges of information and knowledge among indigenous cultures—for instance, concerning natural medicine, curatives for loss of energy, etc.—especially among the peoples of the Third World, Latin America and the Caribbean, but even with respect to the industrialized countries. They comprise a diverse multitude of ethical beliefs concerning more adequate ways for humans to comport themselves ecologically in their natural environment. Even for the more advanced scientific discoveries of the technologically advanced cultures and civilizations (those of the industrialized western world), they provide valuable wisdom and useful elements of cultural education. All these modes of knowing, both the traditional and the modern, insofar as they serve as alternative and complementary knowledges, can assist in curing the many ills that beset humanity, such as biological disasters, psychological disruptions, and ecological catastrophes. However, a hybrid product of multicultural traditions is never completely attained or articulated. In particular, it does not eliminate the inequality of access to social wealth by different classes, ethnic groups, sectors, segments and social strata, nor their exploitation or alienation, oppression or marginalization. It does not demand a reformulation of the Manichean conceptions that separate the foreign from the national, the popular from the elitist, the traditional from the modern.

The construction of history, then, must stop being a reflection simply of western self-consciousness, which begins and ends self-referentially. The rich north likes to build national, cultural, and historical meta-narratives about itself and impose them on others. But the others, those of Asia, Africa, Oceania, Native American indigenous peoples, the Latin American and the Caribbean, have their own histories. Though they are often locked into their traditional conceptual systems, due in large part to the exclusions and exploitations to which they have been subjected, they must no longer be seen as men and women without a history. What is most essential is that these other histories, those of the exploited, the marginalized, and the excluded, however one wishes to narrate or dramatize their story, must be included and incorporated in the historical world as relevant expressions of transcendent temporalities and spaces of humanity.

Conclusions

Between the complex and contradictory processes of capitalist globalization, on the one hand, and the methodologies, theories and conceptualizations that people use to interpret and intervene in those processes for the purpose of lessening and transforming their impact on the movements of social classes on the other, little room for doubt is left concerning the present delegitimization and disintegration of the nation state. The disarticulations and atomizations to which it has been subjected bear a direct relation to the centers of transnational capitalist power. These centers have not hesitated to strengthen the principal states, to multiply their machinery of domination and control, and to enlarge them in order to form a kind of transnational state (the European Union, for instance). The purpose of this transnational state is to augment the capitalist prerogatives over nations, regions, and international bodies, and to seek to determine the internal politics and social relations of nations and regions through the instruments of internal and external commerce and exploitation.

The Hungarian Marxist István Mészarós reaffirms this when he says that, in spite of the "[n]eoliberal fantasies relative to the 'retreat of national borders,' the capitalist system would not survive a week without the strong support of the state."[15] The fact that public expenditures in developed countries greatly overshadow those in the developing countries testifies to this. The capitalist or imperialist powers developed instruments of control and domination over their own working classes as well as the oppressed peoples of the Third World in their anxiety to perfect their system of exploitation. For the US government, for instance, the growth of bureaucracy as well as of monetary expenditures for the departments of Defense (the Pentagon), Treasury, Security and Commerce mark a decided restructuring and strengthening of the state. Though the transnational corporations, whose home offices may be in the US, are owners of a major percentage of the world's assets and investments, for that very reason they need new and more powerful means of coercion against the world they exploit as well as an ability to defend themselves at home.

But what these corporations today face in the world is a panoply of sovereign entities, of popular nation states, national and cultural identities, autonomous communities and self-governing movements and organizations. In time and space, in the present and the future, in immediate and mediated forms, it is the active coexistence of these many sovereign structures, as a form of eco-cultural system, that is the transcendent destiny of humanity. And that destiny includes the transcendent necessity for forms of justice and democracy that complement its heterogeneity with forms of integration at the regional, national, and local levels.

For Marxism and other allied theories of critical social thought, it is more than ever necessary to grasp the interrelation between heterogeneity and integration in the context of capital's interior logic. Many diverse proposals and calls to action, with diverse forms of mobilization, decision and direction, can find a space for themselves on this road; and above all, those that extend the framework of popular democracy. For this reason, it is more than ever necessary to analyze and critique the present form of capitalist state structures.

Ultimately, of course, these structures must be destroyed and replaced by a new form of nation-state, one that is communist in essence and which will gradually move toward its own extinction. But Karl Marx's predictions about the final demise of the state are not really on the horizon today, and thus can only be a vision for the future. In other words, no one should feel that they have a hold on any absolute truth. Unity in diversity, on the basis of equality, social justice, and mutual respect should be the important aspects of our alternative possibilities.

The capitalist system has not globalized itself in the same way for all nations or regions. Its inherent nature is to act and realize itself asymmetrically. All discourse in a polycentric capitalist world that pretends to some universal principle of equality among states belongs to the realm of fantasy. 'Pluralism' in the world of capital means nothing but the plurality of capitals, which does not admit any thoughts of equality."[16] It is in that sense that the goal of the "modernization of the Third World" only accentuates the fundamental problem of its own capital development. Insofar as it "has shown itself unable to finish imitating the form of global capitalism in its own system, it is because it succumbs to the crushing economic rules that govern its own extraction of surplus value from exploited labor."[17] But this implies that there is a critical difference between the globalizing tendency of transnational capital economically and its "ongoing political domination of nation-states as its structure of total control of the social order."[18] This then is the name of the system's most important contradiction and limitation. István argues that,

> We are arriving at a new historical stage in the transnational development of capital, one in which it is already impossible to avoid confronting the fundamental contradiction and structural limitation of the system. In other words, it is in its failure to construct a state of the capitalist system as such, as the complement to capital's transnational aspirations, wherein it fails to supersede the explosive antagonisms between

nation-states that have characterized the system over the last two centuries.[19]

In these terms, the phrase "think globally, act locally" that pretends to reflect the era of neoliberal globalization, is actually a cynical semiotic and ideological play on words. It is theoretically and practically an empty discourse insofar as, in a neoliberal vein, it implies the "inevitability" of multinational globalization and the weakness of national governments as well as "intolerable nationalisms" and even generalized ethnic conflict. It essentially asks Third World people to leave strategic matters (global, regional and national) to the decision making power of the imperial center, with the US, as the world's unequivocally most tyrannical military power, policing those decisions at the global level. Instead, it is necessary to focus on the relations between national communities within their integrationist regional networks, with the ultimate objective of resolving the problem of constructing a new international order, that is, *acting globally*. The goal must be to put an end to war and to offer a harmonious and complementary framework in which the inalienable rights of national states, of ethnic groups at all levels, and of the many diverse autonomous socio-cultural formations, can resolve themselves. That is, it must frame a just and functional multilateralism based upon a respect for peace, for social justice, and for equality.

The actual experiences of many alternative social and political movements against imperialism, neoliberalism, and their globalization, have demonstrated how a realistic response can be constructed, both theoretically and practically. With much patience, they could gradually be brought into relation and conjunction, each with others and with all, to set us on the road toward the construction of a more just and equitable society.

In Latin America, the achievements of the peoples, the rise of dissimilar leftist national popular processes in Argentina and Brazil, the force of the revolutionary spirit in Bolivia, Venezuela, and Cuba, and the will of their leaderships, the programs for social change advanced in many of the indigenous areas, especially in Chiapas, Ecuador, Peru, and Guatemala, are the authentic demonstration of the strength of alternative ideas against the global neoliberal capitalist order. Gradually a system of mutual relationships has been developed among the nations of Latin America in the economic, commercial, and social spheres, in health and education as well as in the cultural. The integration of these countries has been facilitated by various international organizations and agreements, such as ALBA (Alternativa Bolivariana para las Américas), Petrosur, Mercosur, Caricom, etc., formed in opposition to the so-called free trade agreements proposed by the US and Canada. But above all, the ongoing struggle of the exploited and oppressed social classes has accelerated the reform and transformation of governance in general.

We all should learn from this, and share with humility our ideas and projects, our learning and our teachings, with an eye toward adding to these struggles, and toward confronting together the many challenges of the contemporary world.

There are so many alienating contradictions and antagonisms generated by the capitalist system and its mode of production, alienations generated by social class, alienations of an ethnic, national, or racial character, divisions originating in sexualities, generational differences, and levels of social organization, among others. Only the socialist road, of a truly democratic, integrative, and coherent nature,[20] "within the framework of global planning directed actively by all the world's people,"[21] can be a competent response that would prevent the end of humanity and construct a better, more just and equitable world for all—a world of truly human freedom.

Endnotes

1   Serbín, Andrés "Tendencias y contratendencias del sistema interna-cional: una mirada desde América Latina y el Caribe", President of the Coordinadora Regional de Investigaciones Económicas y Sociales (CRIES) (Regional Group of Economic and Social Research), Master conference presented in the opening of the Seminario Académico Internacional "Diplomacia y Relaciones Internacionales en el Gran Caribe" (Academic International Seminar "Diplomacy and International Relations in the Great Caribbean), (Havana: Instituto Superior de Relaciones Internacionales Raúl Roa García, December 5, 2005).
2   Theories of the end of history, the end of ideologies, the clash of civilizations, etc.
3   Jorge Velásquez Acosta *Democracia y Mercado ¿Nuevos modelos de legitimidad?* in *op. cit.*, p. 204.

4   Some of these movements are indigenous, ethnic, racial, ecologist, alter-globalization, antiwar, unionist, communitarian, against the external debt, feminist, gay, peasant (the Sin Tierra Movement in Brazil), anti-NAFTA, religious (the theology of liberation), the Madres y Abuels de la plaza de mayo (Plaza de Mayo Mothers, Grandmothers), pro-human rights, among others.

5   The first meeting of the so-called Washington Consensus was held on 6-7 November, 1989 in Washington.

6   Report of the Ambassador to Brazil, Paulo Nogueira Batista, "The Washington Consensus, a Neoliberal Vision of Issues", in Jorge Wilson Pereira de Jesús *A Reforma do Aparéelo de Estado*, 1998; in Thalia Fung, *La dinámica de la sociedad civil y el Estado a principios del siglo XXI, op. cit.*, p. 91.

7   Colectivo de Autores (GALFISA) *Las trampas de la Globalización* (Instituto de Filosofía (Havana: Editorial José Martí, 1999).

8   Martin Hopenhayn "¿Integrarse o subordinarse? Nuevos cruces entre política y cultura", in *Cultura, política y sociedad. Perspectivas latinoamericanas*, (Daniel Mato, Compilador) (Buenos Aires: CLACSO, 2005), p. 21.

9   Leslie Clark, *The Transnational Capitalist Class* (Oxford: Blackwell, 2003), p. 256.

10   Gilberto Valdés Gutiérrez, *El Sistema de Dominación Múltiple del Capital*, Tesis de Doctor en Ciencias Filosóficas, Instituto de Filosofía, CITMA, 2000.

11   Gerard Greenfield, "Bandung *de vuelta:* Imperialismo y nacionalismo antiglobalización en el sudeste asiático", en *El Imperio Recargado*, Editores Leo Panitch y Colin Leys, *Socialist Register* (2005) (Buenos Aires: CLACSO, 2005), p. 196.

12   Nidhi Aeosrivonge "Thai Nationalism Under the Trend of Globalization", 1229, 5-11 de marzo, *Metichon Weekly*, ISSUE, 2004, p. 33.

13   Nicos Poulantzas *State, Power, Socialism* (London-New York: Versoa, 2000) p. 117.

14   Bob Jessop *Nicos Poulantzas: Marxist Theory and Political Strategy* (London: Macmillan, 1985), p. 172.

15   István Mézáros *Socialismo o barbarie. La alternativa al orden social del capital* (Havana: Editorial de Ciencias Sociales, 2005,) p. 13.

16   István Mézáros, *op. cit.*, p. 25.

17   *Idem. Prefacio a la Edición Latinoamericana*, p. XVII.

18   *Idem.*, p. 15.

19   *Idem.*, p. 20.

20   The popular masses participating genuinely represented, calling, in permanent state of mobilization, controlling and taking crucial, strategic and tactical decisions.

21   Idem., *Prefacio a la Edición Latinoamericana*, p. XVI.

Chapter 6

SOVEREIGNTY AND THE FAILURE OF GLOBAL CORPORATE GOVERNANCE

Steve Martinot

The Emergence of a Transnational State

The concept of "corporate governance" may have a slightly fantastic tinge to it, like something out of a science fiction movie. But we have lived with its unfolding since the early 1980s. Corporate governance does not refer to a form of nation-state government, though it is born from that womb.[1] Nor does it refer to a variation on the Italian fascist experiment called the "corporate state." It refers, instead, to a global or "transnational political structure" that is operated by and for the corporations and corporate investment profitability.

It is important at the outset to be clear about our subject. As will be described more fully below, the corporations themselves, for which this transnational political structure would be a governing organization, emerged from what were known as multinational corporations—corporations that had subsidiary operations in many nations. To the extent that these multinational corporations have developed operations that transcend the boundaries, laws and resources of local economies, they form an international community of corporate entities that simply use national economies as ground and resource. In that sense, they are more properly understood as "transnational," that is, as massive enterprises that cohere with each other in a transnational economy. It is primarily to this transnational economy and its form of organization that the term "corporate globalization" refers, and which will be the subject of this present discussion.

To compose a portrait of transnational corporate governance, the images of three structures and their histories will have to be coordinated: 1) that of the modern corporation itself, 2) the historical relation of the corporate structure to the state, and 3) the way the cultural and ethical norms of a society dominated by corporations, as for instance in the US, reflect both the corporation's inner structure and its relation to social organization.

To tell the story of how transnational governance evolved, as well as how a community of corporations is conceivable which can "think" for itself, and form a political constituency for the state, we must begin with a brief description of the socio-political landscape it inhabits.

In the US, the predominant political fact of the 1970s was the unwinnability of the war in Vietnam . The Vietnamese desire for autonomy and independence was unconquerable. For 35 years, they had fought for it, first against the Japanese at the onset of World War II, then against the French who attempted to reclaim their former colony at the end of the war, and finally against the US, which stepped in financially after the Korean War, and militarily in 1960. An anti-war movement formed in the US that also believed in the principle of national sovereignty and the right of peoples to self-determination. It sufficiently imparted this principle to the GIs in Vietnam to render significant numbers of them non-combatant. The US military command sought to compensate for this deficit by shifting to endless air attacks with electronically guided bombing and artillery. While they succeeded in killing humans and animals indiscriminately, the raw criminality of those tactics constituted another factor in the US defeat.

The outcome on the US of the Vietnam adventure was crisis on many fronts. Though Vietnam was only one of many national liberation revolutions, the US had chosen that one to demonstrate to all others what the cost of their struggles for independence and sovereignty would be. Yet this brought with it eventually the concomitant recognition that the political and financial costs of militarily defending its empire were beyond US means or capability. In particular, its massive spending on war and military operations, including all its foreign bases built under the auspices of the Cold War, produced an outflow of gold reserves that threatened the domestic solvency of the dollar.[2] In 1971, the dollar was taken off the gold standard, and in 1973 it was allowed to float on currency exchange markets. This threw the multinational corporations into crisis. They had grown swollen and fat, as vast networks of subsidiaries, on the military largesse of the war, as well as the huge system of Cold War military bases the US had built. Because this network of subsidiaries stretched across national boundaries, it needed a stable currency to calculate the value of the goods that it passed from one subsidiary to another, as well as to maintain accounts that would be denominated in multiple currencies. The dollar played that role. As the international currency of record, it constituted the very bloodstream of the multinational corporations.[3] When the dollar went into crisis, so did they. And in the long run, their response to that crisis was to overcome their detachment from each other, and transform themselves into a transnational community that could organize itself politically.

In 1973, the Trilateral Commission, a think tank of corporate directors, economists, and politicians from Europe, Japan, and the US was organized to stem the crisis. In 1975, the US backed out of Vietnam, and watched the Vietnamese take back their country without bothering to admit to the massive criminality of its war policy. The Trilateral Commission rapidly developed a program to defend the empire by means other than traditional military counter-insurgency.[4] The first task was to restabilize the dollar, and to sustain its role as international reserve currency. The second task was to establish the means of controlling local politics in any nation or region of the world through global control of economic factors. For the trilateralists, this could be accomplished through centralized computerization and coordination of imports and exports, currency exchange rates, and interest rates, among other things.[5] The third was to build a transnational political structure to enable the corporations, as they cohered transnationally, to oversee, control, and govern themselves as a community. The central purposes of this governance structure were to prevent undue competition among themselves, and to regulate the relation of individual corporations to the overall process of (globalized) control. It was a project of coloniality significantly beyond the structures of traditional colonization.

The first two tasks were essentially mechanical problems. Euro-American economic leaders originally sought a replacement currency for the dollar. They found none, and decided to use US Treasury bonds as a stop gap substitute for gold. But real restabilization of the dollar was ultimately attained only by providing an alternate material backing. The natural substitute for gold was oil, since it was a substance in constant demand. In 1979, Kuwait lent itself to this project by agreeing to the "financialization" of its oil reserves. It established a state bank and investment office that accumulated international dollars and invested them in industrial enterprises around the world, backing those dollars with its oil. Before the dollar crisis, dollars that had accumulated in foreign state banks could be repatriated to the US in exchange for gold from the US gold reserves in Fort Knox. What the Kuwaiti Investment Office did was substitute its oil for the US gold that was no longer available. The dollars that then accumulated in foreign state banks could be exchanged for oil through the Kuwaiti bank. Kuwait became the new Fort Knox.[6] This explains why, during the Iran-Iraq war of the 1980s, US President Reagan warned Iran that if it attacked any Kuwaiti oil tankers, the US would reflag them, making such attacks acts of war against the US itself. Reagan's focus wasn't the safety of a tiny emirate; his concern was the stability of the international currency.

The second Trilateral project was facilitated through shifts in the lending strategies of the World Bank and the IMF. Insofar as most major investment banks in Europe, Japan and the US had become multinational, they had simply to centralize or coordinate some of their operations through the World Bank. By manipulating the availability of import and export financing, the availability and the price of loans (interest rates) for economic development, the IMF and World Bank could reshape and redirect the further development of local economies, thereby partially determining their internal political affairs and issues. In addition, the IMF and World Bank adopted the strategy of attaching Structural Adjustment Programs (SAPs) to their loans to developing countries. These programs required the loan recipients to privatize their social assets so they could be bought and sold by foreign corporate investors. Privatization became the condition for access to funding for international trade. Loan recipients were also directed to cut back on social welfare programs, reduce subsidies to local economic enterprises, and repeal any legal obstructions to corporate investment.[7] The use of economic sanctions, embargoes, loan restrictions, divestment, pricing discrimination, and the financial starvation of specific nations have become common levers to enforce within this general economic program. The purpose of an embargo is not to punish recalcitrant leaders, but to create misery and starvation through derangement of the local economy to the point where economic desperation would pry open that area to corporate investment and resource exploitation, free of any political restraint. It was this kind of economic aggression that derailed the socialist experiment in Mozambique, for instance. On the whole, the principle of economic sovereignty was subjected to economic assault through the demand for the privatization of social assets. And this is what is meant by "free trade." The term "trade" does not just refer to access to markets in order to sell consumer goods. Human consumers are ancillary. It refers to the ability to invest (and to trade corporate stock and securities) free from unwarranted disruption on the part of local political institutions, laws or events.[8]

The ideological name for this mode of economic domination is "neoliberalism." It marks the process by which corporate capital sought to reverse the sovereignty that previously colonized countries had sought to win for themselves (under the label of "independence") during the decades following World War II. The process of privatization sought to turn that independence against itself.

The Trilateral Commission's third project, a Transnational Political Structure (TPS), was more complex, and depended on the first two having been achieved. By the early 1980s, when sufficient monetary and financial stability had been accomplished, the outlines of the process of TPS construction begin to appear. They become discernible in the sequence of military assaults committed by the US (sometimes under the umbrella of NATO) against various sovereign nations. Though each event in the "sequence" appears as a separate affair, a number of commonalities of a conceptual nature are to be found. Among these are the emergence of a new form of impunity on the part of the US, the use of that impunity to destroy the sovereignty of the target nation, the deranging and forceful transformation of the conceptualization of international law, and the massive demonization of those political figures or state structures that prominently insisted on national sovereignty.

Though each event takes on an aura of unintelligibility when viewed through traditional political thinking, certain conceptual commonalities within them, in their peculiarity (and horror), reveal the outline of an underlying unifying project.

The Post-Vietnam "Attack Sequence"

The "attack sequence" began with the assault on Grenada in 1982, a tiny island nation no bigger than Boulder, Colorado. It then unfolded with the arming of a paramilitary force against the Sandinistas in Nicaragua (namely the Contras), the rearming and reorganizing (under US control) of the army of El Salvador to repress a multitude of popular movements and organizations in that country, the arming and supplying of UNITA in Angola (an African "contra" army), the emplacement of Marines in Lebanon, the assault on Panama (1989), the bombing of Iraq and the US takeover and occupation of Kuwait (1991), the invasion of Somalia (1992), the invasion of Haiti (1995), the bombing of Serbia (1999), the invasion of Afghanistan (2001), and the invasion of Iraq (2003). These last two continue as the people of these countries fight wars of liberation—like the Vietnamese—for their sovereignty and independence against US occupation forces. Though the US has ostensibly withdrawn from Iraq, it remains to be seen to what extent it has loosened its grasp on Iraqi politics. We shall see this in the form and intensity of resistance movements to the "new" Iraqi government. And this withdrawal had already been balanced by increased military force applied by the US on Afghanistan. It is a strange war, because the only evident resource Afghanistan has to offer the Euro-American economies is heroin and opium. Yet the US war effort there is forceful enough that it is overflowing into Pakistan.

The bombing of Iraq of 1991 was economically unintelligible. During the 1980s, under Reagan, the US had transformed itself from the largest creditor nation to the largest debtor nation in the world.[9] Yet to build an alliance to militarily evict Iraq from

Kuwait, it was willing to spend five times as much money as it would have taken to buy Hussein out (judging by prior deals with him). Furthermore, Hussein showed himself willing to negotiate Iraq's exit from Kuwait.[10] For some reason, it was of greater benefit to the US to demonize Hussein in order to organize an international mob against him, and militarily evict Iraq from Kuwait rather than negotiate its withdrawal. The effect was the destruction of Iraq's social infrastructure through bombing (with international complicity). "During six weeks of assault, Iraq was pounded with the conventional equivalent of six Hiroshima-size bombs. Power plants, desalinization plants, sewage treatment plants, water systems, etc. were all destroyed.[11] Bombing does not liberate people; it weakens them and destroys their social cohesion. In other words, it strengthened Hussein with respect to the Iraqi people. Thus world attention was misdirected at Iraq while the US military took over Kuwait (its real target).[12]

The invasion of Somalia in 1992 was socially unintelligible. It occurred without preliminary events, prior disputes or conflicts, without reason or rationale. Claiming Somalia was in chaos and needed relief, the US invasion succeeded only in obstructing existing relief organizations and adding to the political chaos. Promulgated by a lame-duck president (Bush), it seemed merely to be a parting shot to embarrass the one newly elected (Clinton). Only later was the discovery of oil reserves in east Africa revealed.

The bombing of Serbia in 1999 was unintelligible in terms of its wantonness and impunity. What brought the Yugoslav Federation to western governmental attention was its insistence on its sovereignty and the cohesiveness of its federated structure. Yugoslavia had rejected Structural Adjustment Programs proposed by the IMF in 1988. And perversely, it simply refused to fall apart when the Soviet Union did. In 1997, a "Kosovo Liberation Army" (KLA) was fabricated by NATO and sent into Kosovo, a small Muslim area of Serbia that no one had ever cared about before, to attack Serbs there. At the time, negotiations between Serbia and a Kosovar independence movement had begun to arrive at some common political agreement and a peaceful resolution to their differences. The violent presence of the KLA was therefore not to advance the independence interests of the Kosovars, but simply to trouble the waters. When Serbia counter-attacked the KLA, it was charged (in the person of its president, Milosevich) with crimes against humanity. The US then presented an ultimatum to

Serbia (at Rambouillet) that would have negated its sovereignty. As foreseen, Yugoslavia refused the ultimatum, and the US (under cover of NATO) bombed Serbia's social infrastructure for 72 days, rendering various areas uninhabitable through the use of depleted uranium, and the destruction of various chemical plants. While its stated purpose was to free Kosovo, in practice the attack established a NATO occupation of Kosovo to oversee the construction of an oil pipeline from the Black Sea through Bulgaria.

The invasion of Panama in 1989 was juridically unintelligible. It was ostensibly undertaken to arrest Panamanian ex-President Manuel Noriega for having violated US law. No Panamanians had been party to writing that law, whose jurisdiction constitutionally stopped at the US border. And Panamanians had their own law. Under the rule of sovereignty and democracy, that was the only law to which they could be held responsible, other than treaty law freely entered into. But the US indicted Noriega for drug trafficking, in violation of US law. US actions implied that the US had taken it upon itself to extend the laws governing the US to individuals in other nations. To subject the citizens of Panama to two separate judicial systems effectively dissolves the foundation of the judicial (viz. jurisdiction), and undermines the concept of nationhood itself.[13]

Two threads weave themselves through these events. The first is a judicial thread, an appeal to law, whether US domestic law or international law, under cover of which impunity for violence and aggression is practiced, thereby rendering that appeal specious. Impunity signifies not simply a refusal of legal restraint, but a dismissal of law per se by acting as a law unto oneself. That is, abrogating to oneself impunity for criminal acts undertaken in the purported defense of the law reveals a criminal intention hidden within the rubric of law. Thus, in practice, the combination of this military and political impunity with the juridical discourses in which it was couched produced an internationalization of US law coupled with a nationalization of international law, as if internationally law as such was a US possession. Hence the inherent oxymoronics contained in the often-used concept of "humanitarian" military intervention. The second thread is the establishment of a military presence with respect to major planetary oil reserves. This serves a dual purpose with respect to military operations. On the one hand, military operations are mainly dependent on oil, so they attempt to monopolize control of it to keep it out of the other side's hands. On the other, the global corporate structure, for the development of which US military operations are a central dimension, seeks domination if not monopolization of the world's oil as a means of controlling governments and local economies.

In contradistinction to the US appeal to law, and its effort to internationalize its own law, the world has witnessed the astounding hypocrisy of the US refusal to recognize the World Court in the Hague or to ratify the Rome Statute of the International Criminal Court. When, during its efforts to unseat the Sandinistas in Nicaragua, the US mined Nicaraguan harbors in violation of international law, Nicaragua sought to charge the US with war crimes in the World Court. The US replied that it was not bound to the court, not having been a signatory to the treaty that established it. Instead, it fostered ad hoc International Tribunals, set up through the Security Council. Thus, the tribunal established with respect to Yugoslavia was essentially a continuation of US policy already expressed militarily.

The Transnational Political Structure (TPS) and its Globalized Judiciality

Any judicial activity, even of a criminal sort, points to an executive or administrative structure that deploys it and to which it adheres. Through its appropriation of the right to exercise global police functions (holding wrongdoers to the "law"), the US held the citizens of many nations to a law they had not been a party to forming. The demonization or criminalization of a national leader was but the cover for the invention of a law that the person in question was then charged with violating—a law invented in order to charge that violation. When that leader's personhood (as criminalized) was grafted back onto that nation's body, the nation as a people could then be held responsible for what its nation-state, personified in its leader, could be charged with committing. It is necessary to criminalize the nation one wishes to invade in order to make one's aggression appear as an act of justice, since it is that entire people who suffer the aggression. What they think of the matter must cease to be a concern. And this holds true for the injustice of imposing an embargo, such as on Cuba or Zimbabwe, whose aim is simply to starve people. Though clothed in a pretense of protecting human rights, naked assault (whether economic or military) on a nation's sovereignty (in most cases won through anti-colonialist struggle of many kinds, from Serbia to Mozambique) requires a blanket dehumanization of that nation's people. It is the criminalization of that nation (through the demonization of a leader: Hussein, Milosevic, Castro, Qadhafi, etc.) that then decriminalizes the assault. And this testifies to the existence of an administrative power that requires that self-decriminalization.

Thus, the question that this "attack sequence" raises is what that executive or administrative structure is. In the context of a burgeoning transnational corporate community, what is implied, at the level of political structure, by the US actions insofar as they depart from the rationality of former colonialist endeavors? What is being signified by this confluence of a globalized corporate economy, an international militarist-oriented judiciality, and an unintelligibility when seen through past colonialist experience?

The impunity flagrantly exercised by the US in the attack sequence was not gratuitous, nor were the attacks undertaken simply for its own economic aggrandizement. The attack sequence testified to the existence of an executive project that conceived of itself as having *superseded nationhood and national sovereignty*, albeit expressing itself through US military and propagandistic power. Each element of the attack sequence marked the establishment of a new juridico-political principle in the world that only later could be grasped as steps toward a project beyond mere US interests. Though the political project that the Trilateral Commission had set for itself provides a certain foresight, it was nevertheless in silhouette. The actual organizational forms that would eventually institutionalize what that silhouette suggested have only slowly loomed into view. The IMF and the World Bank started changing their policies, and writing these horrendous Structural Adjustment Programs that simply sold out the ideals of the new anti-colonialist regimes that they were supposed to assist. The World Trade Organization came into existence, connected somehow with NAFTA. The European Union formed. But the underlying strategies remained hidden because that institutionalization occurred piecemeal. What the commonalities and paradoxes of the "attack sequence" provide was both a preview and a window.

If this underlying strategy is institutionalized as an administrative power, let us call it a Transnational Political Structure, which is essentially what was proposed by the Trilateral Commission in 1975, and examine its economic dimension first.

As mentioned earlier, after 1975 the World Bank and the IMF required structural changes to local economies in order for them to qualify for loans. At the same time, the World Bank established a fair degree of centralized control for itself over world banking and the possible corporate sources of such loans. It thus had the power to withhold international funding from recipient nations pending privatization of their social assets, such as social welfare programs, health care and education, water supplies, other utilities, and natural resources. All such assets were to become commodities for purchase and investment by corporate capital. This was the major hoop through which a state had to jump, along with its removal of any labor law or environmentalist obstructions to corporate profitability. A general anti-union labor atmosphere was demanded. In effect, state subsidies established by the recipient nation for the welfare of the citizenry were to be shifted toward alien investors.

It is necessary to understand the historical context for this focus on privatization. Massive anti-colonialist movements had swept the formerly colonial countries after WWII. Many of the newly independent states that emerged from those struggles socialized facilities and assets in order to neutralize the unconscionable inequalities that former colonial hierarchies had produced. These included utilities, land reform, and the engineering of infrastructure development. By coordinating employment and giving subsidies to local producers, these new states began the construction of economies that would at least provide sustenance for their people. The socialization of economic and social assets was a natural avenue toward sustainability for a nation impoverished by former colonialism. Against this, the neoliberal agenda proposed privatization as its primary counter-strategy.[14] Privatization would remove social assets (the assets of the people) from state protection and lay them prostrate before the profit-making venality of foreign capital. It was an essential element in bringing those formerly colonized areas back under capitalist domination and Euro-American financial control.

In effect, the debt necessary for an underdeveloped nation to begin the process of economic development was accompanied by conditions that made autonomous economic development impossible. The structural distortions that the SAPs imposed subordinated fiscal policies to debt service while subjecting the debtor nation's resources to foreign corporate control. In effect, for the World Bank and the IMF, "development" was a synonym for the development of corporate investment and profit-making.[15]

The World Bank's centralization of international funds for commerce and industrialization made it difficult if not impossible for small (post-colonial) nations to find alternative financing. They had either to accept the bank's terms or suffer destitution. If they refused, their destitution would then be blamed on their own bad leadership, on the state's exploitation of its own people, which in turn would be used as a rationale for sanctions or an embargo against the recalcitrant nation. For those that accepted the World Bank's terms, debt service, which in many third world countries has grown to the point of absorbing over 50% of their GDP, becomes a form of debt servitude, leaving no funds or resources to sustain the people's wellbeing, or for any social development outside the infrastructural needs of the exploiting corporations. The neoliberal program, through IMF loans and their SAPs, became a type of impoverishment machine.

A classic example of the devastation imposed by a SAP is Rwanda. The local economy in the 1980s was centered on truck farming, including livestock, with some economic surplus for international trade produced by fishing in Lake Kiva and Lake Tanganyika. The fisherman were small entrepreneurs, whose labor intensive activity supported much of Rwanda's employment profile. Gasoline was government subsidized to support the truck farms and markets. The nation was poor, but the economy was sustainable. The SAP ended state protection of the lakes, opened them to corporate fishing, removed subsidies for gasoline, and permitted imports that outcompeted and undermined the markets for food crops on which local farmers depended. Farmers could no longer afford to take their produce to market. Corporate fishing pushed local fisherman aside, fished out the lakes, and left. The result was mass starvation, a generalized unemployment situation, and the desperation that led to the catastrophes of the early 1990s.[16]

The neoliberal emphasis on international financing, endless debt, the prohibition of barriers to corporate investment, and the privatization of all resources and social assets, was designed to eliminate the social coherence of poorer nations, and substitute global administration and corporate investment for it. As Jonathan Cahn said in the *Harvard Human Rights Journal*, "The World Bank must be regarded as a governance institution, exercising power through its financial leverage to legislate entire legal regimens and even to alter the constitutional structure of borrowing nations."[17]

In general, the SAPs have created massive hardships and misery for the peoples of the target countries. The World Health Organization reported, during the late 1990s, that 33,000 children were dying every day from starvation or curable diseases because of the destruction of local sustainable economies. A second effect of these policies has been the enormous migration of people out of their devastated countries to the US and Europe, to nations that have grown fat on the wealth extracted through that devastation. Though these industrial nations complain about their immigration problem, they use it to generate a racism (often specific to each metropole country) against the alien immigrants that is useful for domestic control of their own people.

The creation of the World Trade Organization (WTO) in 1994 was the next step. It was an attempt to constitute an actual legislative body to provide the administrative machinery for governing the global impoverishment structure that the transnational corporations constituted. The WTO was the end product of the General Agreement on Tariffs and Trade (GATT) negotiations that had been in process since the end of WWII. GATT's original purpose was the regulation of economic relations between industrial nations, to prevent competition (seen as one of the causes of world wars) and coordinate their economic control over nonindustrial countries. In the late 1970s, GATT shifted its focus to the construction of a body with the power to oversee and govern the world that the SAPs and their neoliberal demands would bring into existence. It would be a body that would meet periodically, with the power to make rules and policies in real time concerning relations between transnational corporations and signatory governments. As a treaty organization, the decisions and regulations it would make would be binding on its signatory nations. That is, its decisions would have the status of law in those nations.[18] In other words, the WTO would function as a rule-making assembly (a legislative branch) for its global corporate constituency, with all of its signatory states bound by treaty to carry out its decisions.[19] As Akio Morito, the head of SONY, put it, the WTO would "begin creating the nucleus of a new world economic order that would include a harmonized world business system with agreed rules and procedures that transcend national boundaries."[20]

In effect, the WTO would be a global legislature, made up of delegates not elected by nor addressing the needs of the people of the states represented in it, but chosen by the transnational corporations that would constitute its real constituency. Thus, the member states would represent the local interests of the communities of corporations which constituted industries that were now functioning on a multinational level.[21] The WTO was to be a global governance body wholly beyond any structural connection to the peoples of the world, but whose operations and decisions would then be binding on those peoples through the conditions it would impose through their state governments. Its decisions, as a "treaty organizaton," would supersede local democratic enactments on such issues as labor conditions, environmental protections, and social welfare. Under its provisions, when local labor standards, pollution controls or living wage provisions hindered transnational corporate investment, the state in question would have to repeal those standards or face penalties. In other words, building the WTO was a wholly anti-democratic project.[22]

This is not strictly speaking new. Corporate enterprises in colonial or semi-colonial areas have always acted in concert. It is what Lenin referred to as the imperialist phase of capitalism, carving up the world for itself. According to Juan José Arévalo (former president of Guatemala), corporate investment has historically given US financial institutions control of Latin American trade and production, and through that, control of their political structure. Traditionally, before the 1970s, such investment (typically in agricultural products and mining, both labor intensive), enjoyed a profit rate of around 20%, owing to low wage scales and non-union labor conditions enforced by military rule. That is, capital outlays were recuperated in a mere 5 years. The entire structure functioned like a funnel into which the natural wealth of the colonized country was poured, draining it into the pockets of the rich. The resources of those nations or peoples were extracted and brought to the US, to be used to manufacture products. The profit from resource extraction (including labor) was also brought to the US. Some of those manufactured products were then sold in Latin America at a profit, which was then also brought to the US.[23] And the system worked because of concomitant control of hemispheric finances by US banks, which obstructed any autonomous local industrial development, condemning Latin America to the status of a captive market. In short, the peoples and states of Latin America weren't poor; they were actively impoverished by a relational process that enriched the US.

But in the present era, as the corporations extended this impoverishment system to the entire globe and become multinational, a requirement that transcended Lenin's analysis emerged. A governance body was needed to regulate issues of property, to adjudicate the "border disputes" between industries and the conflicting interests that property rights often incurred, to maintain the stability of the currency, and to coordinate trade to prevent "trade wars." Rather than engage in trade wars for markets, groups of corporations had come to see each other as important markets for each other, which implied a different level of trade coordination. In short, common political desires to affect policy around the world brought them together. And their size and preponderance formed a matrix for a kind of economic hermeticism in which they functioned as significant elements of each other's spheres of activity. It is no longer a question of dividing up the globe among colonialist powers or investors, but of uniting that globe as a single resource under the auspices of a single community of entities acting in concert. It is in this process that the multinational enterprises constructed a transnational economy for themselves, constituting themselves as transnational corporations (TNCs).

What the fluidity of capital investment permitted was a new level of atomization of the working classes. Manufacturing enterprises constructed transnational forms of factories, which then functioned as stages on "international assembly lines." Different processes in the manufacture of a finished product are performed in different host countries, by various subsidiaries of a parent corporation. Each subsidiary would import the materials it would work on (parts for assembly from a previous stage in a different country) duty free. It would use local labor and material resources, pay little tax, and export the factory's product duty free to another factory in another country for the next stage in production. The advanced technologies of transport, computerized accounting, and a low wage bill made this a highly profitable arrangement. These factories, known as *maquiladoras* in Latin America, are generally located in special areas called "Export Production Zones." These EPZs are an interface between the community of TNCs and the host state. The host government has simply to keep the work force under control, in a low-wage condition.[24] And since each factory relates only to the extended production process of the parent corporation, it remains essentially out of context with the host economy, except as an employer.[25] This lack of connection to the host economy is a form of insurance against nationalization, should the government change to one more adamant about its economic sovereignty.

This reduction of the economic relevance of corporate investment to the host country then induces a parallel reduction of the political relevance of the state government to the people of that country. In its agreements with the TNCs, the state begins to function as an intermediary, a form of middle management (labor control) for the TNCs. The marks of this reduction of a nation-state to middle management for TNCs are precisely its debt servitude to the World Bank, its acceptance of IMF structural adjustment, and its entry into membership, more as a cypher than a participant, in the World Trade Organization. In short, as the community of corporations takes over the role of "citizen" in the world, it reduces states and the nations and peoples, the real humans who constitute the constituency of those states, including the peoples of the nation-states of Europe and the US (nation-states constructed and imposed by the process of capitalist growth) to a form of irrelevancy (except insofar as they work).

In the developed countries, this process of rendering people irrelevant is actually deeper, because part of a longer tradition. In the US, for instance, political space has been severely reduced through consolidation of a monopoly over politics exercised by the two party system that goes back to the 1870s, and developed slowly. Party leaderships decide what will become a political issue for policy debate or concern, and what will not. There may be demonstrations of protest to various policies, or calls for an end to corruption, but these have no weight if the two major parties decide to ignore them. Anti-war movements, for instance, have appeared throughout the west in opposition to each moment of the attack sequence. But the call to reaffirm the sovereignty of the nations subjected to the injustice of assault has had no effect either on policy nor on what the two political parties have decided will be debated as policy in the halls of government. Wars proceed without debate or declaration.

Other examples are legion. The deregulation of banking remained undebated and uncontested (though not unprotested, e.g. the Occupy Wall Street movement), even after having caused the greatest economic crash since the Depression. Military bases, norms of torture, police brutality, the size of the prison industry (the largest in the world), remain reduced to questions of numbers and reputations, unexposed to ethical discussion or political referendum. And the privatization of education, prisons, utilities, and health care (which has been priced beyond the means of most people) has occurred in the US as well as in the third world. In other words, even in the US (or perhaps especially, since the US is the birthplace of that atrocious notion, the personhood of corporations), the corporations take on the role of citizens, while rendering real humans increasingly irrelevant to political and economic processes, again except insofar as they work.

This even holds for corporate management, directors, police, politicians, lobbyists, etc. who must fulfill the needs of the structure in which they function, and are required by that structure—corporations, political parties, government departments or officialdom—to direct their thinking, energy, and policy-making toward what that structure requires; they are not irrelevant to political processes as officials, but they are as humans. The obverse of this is that those most irrelevant to the system— laborers, service workers and other forms of impoverishment—

have the most unfettered possibility of forming alternate political structures and an alternate political culture. We will get to that below.

This indicates a second necessity for the form of the transnational state (TPS) from the perspective of its constituent corporations. The central problem that lurks in any system that sustains itself through the massive impoverishment of people is the possibility of their resistance. Despite the dogmatic proclamation of prosperity through investment, foreign corporate investment in underdeveloped areas remains the motor of the neoliberal *impoverishment* machine, and thus the enemy of the people's well-being. Past third world experience with Euro-American corporate investment, the enormous profitability it produces which leaves only destitution in its wake, has engendered peoples' recognition of foreign investment as an economic vacuum sucking up wealth in poor areas and depositing it in the pockets and accounts of the rich. that recognition now informs a refusal to accept corporate propaganda and drives popular resistance. It was to protect them from the possibilities and power of such resistance by the impoverished that the community of TNCs needed an international structure of governance.

Indeed, within this globalized context, new battle lines have been drawn. In Bolivia, when Bechtel Corp. "bought" the water rights to the country from a government privatizing that most essential of public assets, the people rose up and evicted Bechtel, starting a process of reclaiming their national resources from foreign corporations that has totally changed the political constitution of that country. The Argentine economy during the 1990s, for instance, had been brought to the point of owing more in interest to corporate banking each year than the entire economy produced as earnings, and which finally brought the economy to a standstill. In a massive movement of enterprise seizures, people took over factories, farms, and markets, establishing workers' cooperative control, and got the economy working again. They elected a government that had the fortitude to throw the IMF out and end its debt servitude. In Venezuela, Chavez renegotiated the oil leases that country had inherited from its past, from which it had received next to nothing for its oil. With the proceeds of its new royalty agreements, it has established a network of clinics, a livable minimum wage, education for all

Venezuelans, and a social safety net for a country in which 80% of the people had lived in poverty. It has initiated a movement of productive cooperatives to employ the unemployed, and it has begun the process of decentralizing political power to local community councils. In response, the US has recommissioned the 4th Fleet, based it on islands 50 miles off Venezuela's coast, and begun maneuvers in the Caribbean.

The Nation-state and the Structure of the Corporation

Ironically, it is the very nature of the nation-state itself, as a structure, which Europe and the US succeeded in imposing on most of the anti-colonial movements under the rubric of a proclaimed independence, that facilitated this debt-servitude form of neo-colonialism. Imposing a republican structure, its separation of powers, its representationism by which it shunts democratic political participation into banal formal procedures,[26] that has provided the fertile ground for processes of privatization and anti-democratic structure. Without the matrix of the republican nation-state, the corporations could not have grown to the point of inventing themselves as the world's primary citizenry.

Two anti-democratic aspects of the republican form of nation-state lie at the center of the corporate rise to structural prominence. The first is its fundamental guarantee of property rights (different from the personal right to own property), which strictly delimits the extent to which a legislature can represent the real interests of people to resist their exploitation by those property rights. It is the political guarantee of property rights that allows owners to use their property for personal aggrandizement, irrespective of social need or public benefit. That guarantee prohibits subordinating the prerogatives of capital to majority rule.[23] A legislature cannot contest the exploitation of people by economic power regardless of the economic injustices committed, or the social needs of those exploited. The effect of this is to embed in governance a categorical separation between the economic and the political.

Because of that "immunity," corporations easily developed the power to threaten the economic stability of any electoral district, and thus to contest the interests of majority rule. For instance, at the present time, the insurance companies own more than 45% of all the outstanding corporate stock in the US economy. This gives them the power to destabilize or bankrupt any corporation in the nation by dumping its stock. They can thus disrupt any electoral district, and indeed throw it into economic depression by artificially bankrupting the corporate enterprises in that district. They control Congress in this manner, district by district, and have consistently used that control to defeat anything that would cut into their business operations, such as free health care.

This is, of course, simply an extension of the fundamental relation between the corporation and the state. Chartered by the state, the corporation was originally invented (in 17th century Europe) to be an extension of the state, as state functions became too complicated for a sovereign or even a parliament to direct. In the US, at first, they were chartered primarily for infrastructure development: canals, roads, bridges, etc. Other functions, such as banking, manufacturing, and other profit-oriented ventures, took precedence gradually, mostly after the Civil War.

The second aspect of the republican form of governance that yields to corporate dominance is the system of representation because the republican form of political representation is based on single delegate districts with winner-take-all elections, representation becomes impossible. Each electoral district contains a multiplicity of classes, communities, identities and ideologies, all with disparate and often conflicting interests. Single elected delegates are unable to represent that multiplicity of interests. Two things happen. As a group, separated from their constituencies by their inability to represent them in any coherent fashion, the members of a legislative assembly develop a form of hermeticism, an insular culture in which they offer support for each other on specific projects. In effect, the assemblage of delegates as a legislature becomes the real constituency for each delegate. The projects they promulgate take on political meaning only insofar as it will foster reelection. What really develops in legislative structure is a system of horse-trading of such projects. In that sense, the republican form of legislature serves to divide the social from the political.

The second thing that happens is that each representative is left to act in a discretionary manner, open to predominant influences—that is to say, to the highest bidder. And that "highest bidder" would tend to be the largest economic interest in each district.

These distortions of representation emerge from the multiplicity of interests in each electoral district, all squeezed into the person of a single delegate. If this system worked at all during the first 20 years of US existence, it was because late 18th century constituencies were more uniform, composed of white male property-owners. The political attractiveness of a candidate attached not to what could be promised to whom, but to how able the person seemed to maintain the social and political unity of the district. Later, as constituencies and the franchise diversified, representatives became increasingly unable to represent, or even to mediate between different interests, to the point where real economic differences could result only in Civil War. This occurred throughout South America during the early decades of the 19th century, in which internecine conflict appeared unavoidable between parties representing different economic groups. And it happened in the US between the industrial system in the north and the agrarian slave system in the south, two different forms of property that had no means of reconciling themselves in a republican legislature.

For these reasons, republican "representationism" can be neither democratic nor responsive to the people. Instead, the government acts, and the people, presented with the political decisions that the government makes, are then required to live in accord with those acts and their effects, under the false presumption that they express the popular will. War, for instance, or military spending, are obvious examples of representationism; neither are ever put to a vote or debated among the public at large, yet they have driven health care and education into the ground. In other words, "representationism" uses the rhetoric of representation to cover its operation of forestalling or obstructing any real political representation. The US left, unfortunately, has never abandoned thinking that majority rule can be used against elite-defined national interests, which are property interests—to end a criminal war, for instance. In so thinking, it is refusing to take into account this reversal of the representationist arrow.[26]

In the developing nations, this republican system had the effect of hamstringing the popular basis for independence.

Insofar as the legislature, representing the independence process, may have sought to stop or control the influx and imposition of foreign investment, it found itself doubly obstructed. It had no administrative power of its own, while at the same time it was unable to give the executive the power to contest the prerogatives of property. And the executive, which represented the nation to those foreign interests, was also left to deal with the highest bidder. The citizenry, and the independence movements, had no means of truly representing themselves or their popular independence interests through the government they had brought to power. Executive, legislature, and citizenry were all impotent, unable to defend themselves collectively because of the separation of branches of government against the new incursions of foreign capital.

What the growth of the corporate provided, in the US, in the shadow of these relations of non-representation, was the possibility of a new political uniformity (such as had existed for a few decades right after the promulgation of the Constitution). It did this by presenting the community of corporations as a constituency for the political structure, a constituency of "highest bidders" for both state and federal legislatures, replacing the multiplicity of conflicting interests to be found among real people. Whether this was envisioned in granting personhood and citizenship to corporations is immaterial. These processes of granting personhood and producing constituent homogeneity simply went hand in hand. Corporate citizenship was written into law by Supreme Court decision in 1844, in the Letson case.[29] And after passage of the 14th Amendment, corporations were given full rights as persons in 1886, in *Santa Clara vs. Southern Pacific Railroad*.

What the corporate form does is separate property from ownership, preserving the primacy of property rights while eliminating the political conflicts attendant upon contradictory forms of ownership. Ownership gets displaced into securities markets, dispersed among the multiplicity of shareholders, which then constitutes a different level of economy from enterprise ownership or the productive economy. The productive capacity of the corporation goes on at a concrete economic level, but it is run by the managerial staff of the corporation, and not by ownership, which resides in a different form of economic activity altogether, that of trading on securities markets far from production management. Ownership occurs in terms of pieces of paper that have value only if there is a demand for them on the markets in which they are traded, regardless of the worthiness of the production processes they represent. To be an owner (investor) simply means to trade in stocks and bonds, while having little or nothing to do with the productive assets owned. In other words, ownership loses all intrinsic character. Though the securities markets condition and determine the actual asset value of productive corporate property, they do so as a result of trading, and not as the result of any ownership intentionality. Stockholding becomes a separate mode of economic activity, with no power over corporate policy or its social or political activities.

Yet the trading in stocks and bonds is what determines the value of productive assets. This inverts the former relation in which the value of productive assets determined the worth of the company. On the securities markets, the value of a factory can be maintained only if there are people interested in buying the securities that represent that corporation whose property that factory is. It has little to do with whether the goods produced by the corporation can be sold. When the value of a corporation's assets falls because no one will buy its securities, the corporation finds itself unable to pay its debts, and it goes bankrupt, regardless of the health of its production process or its sales. It marks an essential separation between two economies: the productive and the financial.

We saw an example of this recently with the Nummi auto plant in Fremont, CA. It was owned by Toyota and GM. Because GM went bankrupt in the crisis of 2009, unable to pay its debts owing to bad investments in invented securities, it pulled out of Nummi. The resulting sale of its stock caused its value to fall on the stock market, and the Nummi plant closed as well. Nummi had been the most efficient and productive auto plant in the US in 2009, and its cars and trucks sold well. But the factory closed in April of 2010, because of what was happening on the securities markets.

The corporate form thus creates an economic category that supersedes an owning class. It rises above interpersonal and interclass conflicts, while preserving and indeed embodying the priority of property rights. Corporate economic interests become the predominant political influences on legislatures, both as particular interests and through overall control of local economies. In other words, as the republican form of state developed, and the granting of personhood to corporations kept pace, it was logical that the corporations would then invert their original relation as an extension of the state and see the state as an extension of themselves. This mutual extension of the state and the corporation in each other is itself a structure of political operations in which the corporations and the state achieve a new constituent homogeneity. And today, the TPS, as a project of the TNCs, simply represents the logical extension of this essential relationship to the international arena.[30]

We have to recognize, however, that corporate person-hood was not the only possible solution to the problem of representationist ineptness. One other solution would have been a strong executive that would reduce legislative power and obviate its endless betrayals of the electorate. That way lies autocracy or dictatorship. Still another possibility would have been proportional representation organized along party, class, ideological, and interest lines—that is, eliminating the single delegate travesty of representionism. But even proportional represention, if it be true to its ability to represent, would have to occur in a context free from all prohibition on contesting property rights. Parties that represent those exploited by property would have to have the ability to contest and regulate, if not eliminate, the right and the power to exploit, that is, to circumscribe or eliminate property rights. But the elite of the US chose to move toward corporate hegemony rather than democracy in the face of the ineptness of representationism.

The Corporation as Cultural Template

Historically, the corporate structure has been the central form of political organization at all stages of US development. The Virginia and Massachesetts colonies were settled by a corporation. Cities, counties, political parties, universities, and administrative agencies (e.g. port or transit authorities) are established as corporations. Even labor unions incorporate, which has had a distinctly anti-democratic influence on them. In a labor union (and this is true for unions all the way back to 1800), there is an executive committee, for which business agents and shop stewards (or their equivalent) serve as different levels of middle management. The membership is called to meetings for open discussion, but policy is made by the executive committee. Under the current labor contract system, the executive committee has the responsibility to negotiate and enforce the contract, giving membership little more than ratification rights. In short, not only did the corporation rescue government by representationism from its own inherent weakness, but it provided a cultural model for the entire society.

The main purpose of a corporation is to limit the liability of its personnel, its officers, members and employees, for anything the corporation does. That is, an abrogation of responsibility to the world is the central ethical element institutionalized in the corporate structure. Whatever injury or harm may result from corporate activity, its human component escapes liability. One could say that there was an ontological disconnect between its structural and its societal operations. But in point of fact, owing to its size and economic power, the arrow of social responsibility actually gets reversed. Society finds itself holding itself responsible for the continued existence and stability of the corporation, in order to preserve its economic function, on the presumption that thereby the well being of society at large is preserved. In the recent economic crisis of 2009, when a bank claimed that it was too big to fail, it was saying that it had so great a hold on economic activities that society bore a responsibility to prevent it from failing. Where representationism reverses the arrow of political representation, the corporation, within a corporatized society, reverses the arrow of social responsibility. It forces society, by its economic might, to take responsibility for what society should hold it responsible. Thus, representationism and the community of corporations find themselves in easy accord on the field of politics.

What characterizes the internal structure of a corporation is its stratification of command, from the directors all the way down to unskilled production workers. Each level is responsible to the next higher level, and has only to insure that at the levels below it the work gets done. One is responsible *to* others but responsible *for* no one. In form, then, all levels have essentially the same quality, that of fulfilling higher level commands, and commanding those below. Employees are known not by their class or relation to the means of production, but by their level in the corporate structure. As André Gorz puts it, each person in this structure impersonates an impersonal power, and their task is to guarantee the continuance of that power without having any of their own.[31] While prestige and salaries increase the higher one goes in the hierarchy, each level is imprisoned in the same relation of stratification. The responsibility of the top levels is to insure the overall profitability (productively or financially) of the corporation, which comes down to the single requirement of maintaining the stock market value of its assets. It is this need to maintain stock market values that dictates the directions of production or any other operations.

But this distinctive aspect of limiting liability not only rubs off on the reasoning and social behavior of those the corporation employs, but it purfuses the rest of society. It creates a social ethos in which the predominant sense of social responsibility becomes impersonal. The maintenance of hierarchy, the distinction of social strata, whether within an industry or social function, takes precedence over other social considerations. This is an ethos that had even infected the labor movement. In early craft unions, for instance, skilled workers actually withheld solidarity from the unskilled, even as the factory system began to equalize them. Their relative hierarchical position was more important than class unity.

What the ethos of impersonal power and limited social responsibility does foster, however, is a sense of organizational allegiance, which substitutes itself for both solidarity (between humans) and the class consciousness to which class solidarity would attach. Allegiance is the primary relation between individual and institution, the idea that one's primary responsibility is to the organization in which one has membership. It requires that corporate employees at all levels bury their own sense of social responsibility under the corporation's existential need to accomplish its task. And it requires that citizens at large bury their sense of justice in the face of US military intervention on another sovereign nation. In either case, allegiance is primary over the harm committed to others, as one's first responsibility. On the labor field, many a strike has been lost because allied unions saw fit to prioritize jurisdictional authority, with its allegiance to organizational sanctity, above class solidarity. And in the context of this ethos of allegiance, the US is unique in the industrial world as the only nation that insists on pledges of allegiance in schools, as if nationality itself wasn't enough to insure responsibility to executive decisions.

With respect to the attack sequence, the general acceptance by the citizenry of an unintelligible interventionism testifies to the reduction of ethics or justice to secondary importance with respect to allegiance. To call it "nationalism" leaves it unexplained behind a mere change of name. It emerges from a much more profound aspect of social organization.

Allegiance is part and parcel of the US sense of impunity toward the world, as the unquestionable core of its violations of social responsibility. Not only a sense of impunity but an actual enjoyment of it has always characterized US foreign policy, from Manifest Destiny to Hiroshima, from the genocidal elimination of indigenous cultures and languages to the attack sequence. It reflects the corporate ethic insofar as it means that the US can suspend all need for ethical approbation from the world, as its international "limited liability" condition. If the invasion of Iraq has killed a million and a half Iraqis, allegiance to the institutionality that did this is valorized in advance as part of the culture of organizational non-responsibility, irrespective of what it may do in any specific instance.[32] And this dismissal of external approbation is of a piece with the government's refusal to provide universal health care for its citizens, despite the practice of other developed countries.

This corporate ethos has a further ramification with respect to the state. Insofar as securities markets are the arena in which corporate asset values are determined, securities trading becomes a primary economic activity, separated from the vicissitudes of actual human need and production. Production, as opposed to productivity, remains a secondary detail for the community of corporations at the level of securities markets. This implies that, because the community of corporations is an extension of the state, the securities markets themselves must be considered part of the state. Beyond the corporations being inherently active political agents, through the logic of their personhood and citizenship, the securities markets present themselves as a fourth branch of governance—a branch for which representation has never been an issue. In their capacity as a citizenry, the corporations simply extend their state functions to a determination of local politics through stock market operations as a normative activity. The economic threats they hold over elected representatives, which amount to a form of blackmail called "lobbying," is simply an aspect of standard operating procedure.

From a human point of view, the political ramifications of this are catastrophic. In competition with corporations on the political field, humans lose in advance to the power contained in corporate size, wealth, and control of real economic resources. This is the meaning of the *Citizens United* case. Corporations supersede political representation through their real economic power in each electoral district. That is, they supplant humans in citizenship, and thus in political participation. The increasing irrelevancy of real people to the political process cannot be over-emphasized in a situation wherein the rhetoric of political representation still holds sway. Humans in the US, left with a degraded form of citizenship, are rendered degraded entities, against the honor given the corporate institution as such. During the financial crisis of 2009 (which resulted from an over-fictionalization and over-extension of increasingly abstract derivative securities), the government faithfully concerned itself with the losses by banks and insurance companies, while providing no bailout money to alleviate the condition of the people, or to stop the flood of housing foreclosures that catalyzed the crisis in the first place.

It is this catastrophe that we have seen played out in the attempt to form a TPS.

The Class Nature of the World under the TPS

We have been discussing the foundations of a trans-national corporate citizenship, within a transnational political structure, constituted by the confluence of US military impunity and neo-liberal economic processes which stand in subversive opposition to national sovereignty. And we have shown how it is a logical extension of the ontology and ethics of corporate operations.

On the basis of having raised their citizenship to a trans-national level, the corporations have been able to transform their relationship to all states. In particular, the specific aspects of the nation-state as imposed on post-colonial societies—its republican form, its representationism, the absolute sanctity it gives property rights, and the separation of governmental powers, all of which made this corporate citizenship possible— has given the corporate community new access and a new form of control over post-colonial countries.

This has taken the form of "neo-liberal" removal of investment barriers, the formation of international assembly lines, and the reduction of local political structures to the status of administrative adjunct to corporate operations (a form of "outsourced" middle management). Through these means, a form of global homogeneity has been bestowed on international capitalist economics. This unifying process has generally left the internal class structure of each subordinate country intact. And in some cases vestiges of local capitalist classes still struggle against foreign corporate domination (e.g. Brazil). But each country has also become a productive unit in the globalized economy, rather than a participant.

More to the point, a structural relation to the community of transnational corporations accrues to each nation-state that is analogical to the condition of workers within the capitalist class system. States are held to the decisions and rules that the WTO makes, as employees are held to labor law and to the rules of the employing class. Entire nations are tied by debt to IMF directives the way workers are tied to jobs by the debt incurred through their credit cards and mortgages. The productive operations that subordinate countries host on their territories as part of international assembly lines have no real relevance or meaning for their own domestic economies, just as the tasks performed by industrial or bureaucratic workers for the sake of an income have little or no meaning for their lives other than as jobs. In sum, nation-states and the societies they govern take on the analogic aspect of globalized productive workers in the scheme of corporate globalization.

This sense of a nation-state as a "worker" in a transnational economic system is further revealed by the way war itself has been transformed. The TNCs are no more interested in international conflict than a factory owner is in fistfights among his workers. On the other hand, racialized or ethnicized civil wars internal to a nation or a state are of considerable benefit to the corporate community insofar as war destroys not only assets but the social coherence of nations. Such civil wars render whole areas a new market for goods and construction, with very few defenses left against renewed exploitation. The wars in Bosnia, in Rwanda, in East Timor, in Congo and in Sudan have been exacerbated or simply allowed to go on to unspecified destructive ends for these reasons. They mark the production of death on which corporate institutions live and profit, leaving nations prostrate, like workers reduced to starvation and begging for a job.

Under this globalized duality of class relations, traditional class approaches derived from European experience during its period of industrial development no longer provide insight. In the traditional understanding of class relations, capital depends on a working class, and thus depends on its subordination and obeisence. The use of civil war to destroy social infrastructures, accompanied by a generalized political murderousness, not to mention the wanton bombing of whole populations (as in Iraq and Serbia) present a landscape for which those traditional accounts are no longer explanatory. In addition, corporate globalization has radically changed the arena in which oppositional and anti-capitalist movements can operate. People of one country fighting their own state for political powe are left open to being blindsided by an economic power that comes from elsewhere. Similarly, the effort to organize a multinational struggle against the multinational character of an industry will be fragmented into atomized economic skirmishes because the local constriction of political space only provides for the contestation of local managerial power whose real political power lies elsewhere.

It is as if there were two levels of class relations overlaid upon each other. Each nation-state's class systems persists, but without an independent, domestic capitalist class because it is held under the global hegemony of the TNCs, that is, without the investment rights and privileges that the WTO bestows on the latter. And each nation-state, in its capacity as "worker," is enmeshed in a single global capitalist system whose ruling class is the TPS itself. At least, that is the portrait that the process of constructing a TPS has suggested. There is evidence, however, that the project for a TPS, as originally envisioned, has not succeeded, and is today in a process of erosion.

The Failure of Global Corporate Governance

Structurally, the TPS was both logical and consistent with corporate history. To sustain the exploitation of labor (to prevent cooperativism or economic democratization), and to politically unify society around the exploitation of resources were the two common goals of the nation-state and the corporations it chartered. Both ideas had but to be extended to a globalized politics, to produce a neo-colonialism that spoke the language of political independence, democracy, and human rights while burying the first under debt servitude, the second under corporate domination, and the third under super-power impunity. By 1998, it looked like this plan was working.

The last ten years, however, have shown that it may be failing. The most tangible sign of that failure might be the general economic crisis of 2009, brought about by the deregulation of banking and real estate speculation in the developed economies, both being elements of privatization deployed domestically. But a more substantial list of events presents itself. The principal thread that weaves through this list has been the rise and reconstitution of national, communal, and organizational sovereignty, and the construction of local autonomies which have eroded globalized control and subverted the corporate project.

At the top of the list, without a doubt, has been the ability of Cuba to remain uncompromising on its national sovereignty, and to survive the assaults and crimes committed against it since 1959 for that very reason. Cuba provides a beacon of anti-colonialism and opposition to neoliberalism that illuminates the second half of the 20th century.[33] Second on the list, then, is the ability of the Iraqi and Afghani people to resist US occupation—one of the most significant facts of the 21st century's first decade. The invasion of Iraq, like the invasion of Afghanistan, was a wholly criminal act, an unprovoked aggression against a sovereign nation. If it represented a geo-political project for ultimate corporate and TPS control of Middle Eastern, Caspian, and east African oil reserves, the resistance of the people over whom this project ran roughshod has provided a massive roadblock to the consummation of that project.[34] Just as a failed war (the US failure to defeat the Vietnamese liberation effort) created the necessity for a TPS in the first place, so it has been a failed war that has begun to derail the TPS project itself. What neoliberal thinkers have not been able to fathom is the ability of peoples to resist impunity and corporate domination. And nothing better exemplies that ability to resist than that of the Palestinian people against Israeli occupation; but space limitations prohibit a proper analysis of the relation of Israel to the story of the TPS that we are telling here.

In the context of this resistance, precisely because it absorbed the political and military resources of the US, and thus of the TPS project, a second wave focused on the retrieval of sovereignty has swept South America. That is, with the US bogged down in Iraq, political space opened for the peoples of South America to begin to take back control of their own resources. Venezuela's Bolivarian revolution began the process of resocializing its social assets, including its major factories, its education and health systems. It has done this by taking back greater revenues from the exploitation of its oil reserves, and returning it to the people through enhanced social safety nets and a politics of local community control. In Bolivia, beginning with massive upheavals against the privatization of water, and the exploitation of Bolivia's natural gas resources for which there had been no return for the Bolivian people, a movement of the indigenous has transformed the structure of political power, and reaffirmed sovereign control over Bolivian society and Bolivian resources, as the bedrock upon which a new democracy could be built. Argentina has definitively broken with the IMF, settling the debt that had formerly prostrated its economy in mass starvation and political chaos for ten cents on the dollar. What powered this process was a massive wave of factory takeovers by workers, throughout Argentina after 2003, asserting their local community sovereignty over the economic entities that should rightfully belong to those who built and worked them anyway. A similar retrieval of resources, with the building of new forms of internal political cooperation, also characterizes the situations in Ecuador and Nicaragua. And key to this process has been the rewriting of constitutions (in Venezuela, Bolivia, Ecuador), as an important step away from the neo-colonial trap into which the republican representationist form of nation-state had thrown the people. On a continental level, Latin America has begun to construct a unity based on sovereignty, no longer tied to or dominated by the

US. If Cuba pointed the direction, the Iraqi and Afghani people provided the space.[35]

A third form of opposition to the TPS has emerged in response to US military impunity. New economic and political alliances have begun to form whose purpose is to strengthen the sovereignty of the post-colonial nations. These include the Shanghai Cooperative Organization, the development of the BRIC alliance (Brazil, Russia, India, China) as a new center of trade financing, and ALBA (the Bolivarian Alternative for the Americas).[36] These cooperative organizations have formed for the purpose of fostering the development of the underdeveloped countries without the anti-development strings that the neoliberal programs had imposed on them. They represent directly countervailing forces to a transnational state at the nation-state level.

Finally, in the industrialized countries themselves, the blatant atrocity of a global government of TNCs, its clear negation of local democracy, the massive starvation and deprivation to which the IMF's structural adjustment programs condemned the world's peoples, and the murderousness of the "attack sequence" and its impunity, have produced a massive anti-corporate movement in both Europe and the US.[37] It was this movement that organized the historical demonstrations that rocked Seattle, Genoa, Miami, Cancun, Davos, Geneva, and other cities—wherever the TPS builders attempted to meet. It was that movement which brought knowledge of the MAI (Multilateral Agreement on Investment, whose horrendous autocratic conditions would make local democracy impossible) out of the secrecy in which the WTO sought to hide it. The focus of the anti-corporate movement has been the popular sovereignty that remains the indispensible basis for local democracy. Those demonstrations, and the movements they represented, provided a political context in which other nations inside the WTO could gather strength and organize themselves to resist Euro-American domination. By presenting demands inside the WTO (on issues of agriculture, labor, tariffs, state subsidies, etc.) to which Euro-American corporate capital was unwilling to accede, they derailed its neoliberal agenda.

And finally, as this is being written, a massive movement calling itself "Occupy" has broken upon the world, and is standing in opposition to the corporate community inside the US. Taking inspiration from the massive movements that took over capital cities in the Arab world, beginning in Tunisia in January, 2011, hundreds of people "occupied" Wall Street, encamping there. Their purpose was to call attention to the control of the corporations over US politics, the vast economic disparity between the corporate elite and the people, and the shift of class struggle to a global struggle between the masses of humans rendered politically irrelevant by corporate monopolization of citizenship and those corporations themselves. As a first step toward creating a new relevance for real people, the movement spread rapidly to 1500 other cities in the US, and from there to other capitals in other continents. The fear that it inspired in the political elite of the US has been evident in the violence as well as the coordinated manner by which these encampments have been attacked by the police and torn apart. The attack on "Occupy Oakland" on the night of October 24, 2011, sparked a minor war the next day in the downtown streets of that city between the people and the police, and led to solidarity demonstrations all over the world. Recently, at the behest of the indigenous of Oakland, a discussion and debate has been initiated on shifting the name of the "occupy" movement to "decolonization." "Occupy Oakland" would then become "Decolonize Oakland."

On Sovereignty and Democracy

The term "sovereignty" has come to differ from its historical meaning. It has passed through many mutations, from the sovereignty of a monarch to the popular sovereignty of a constitutional republic and the national sovereignty of the anti-colonialist struggle. It has come to include the concept of both "local sovereignty" and "cultural sovereignty," signifying autonomy at the level of community, of organization, and of popular movements to collectively address their condition and choose for themselves how to determine their destiny. When the Farmer's Alliances of the 1880s (in the US Midwest and South) sought to build their own purchasing and marketing cooperatives, their goal was a class sovereignty free from the debt servitude to which commercial and financial interests were increasingly condemning farmers through crop liens and usurious loans. When the National Organization of Women decided not to take grant money or corporate money, but rather to finance all their activities internally from their own membership, they were insuring a level of organizational sovereignty for themselves.

Against the coloniality of corporate power, the concept of the sovereignty of a people, of their organizations, of their movements, and of their nations, stands in direct opposition, and forms the predominant avenue for alternate political structures, for an alternate political culture to that of the nation-state and its anti-democratic representationism. For the nation-state, organizational or community autonomy is clearly a threat. After Carey was elected president of the Teamsters by a powerful rank and file movement, the US government intervened in the internal affairs of the union to remove him as president for some minor corruption charge, sidestepping the union's internal processes for dealing with such matters, in order to impose James Hoffa Jr. on the union as president. Thus, the US government, as a nation-state, abrogated the democracy for which that rank and file movement had fought; its autonomy was clearly a threat to the state. Even "The Garden," in South Central LA. was a threat. "The Garden" grew and flourished on two large fallow blocks of land in an industrial section of the city, farmed by people of the neighborhood, and providing food and flowers for some 350 families. It was destroyed by police bulldozers, pursuant to a reclamation order by the owner, who then did nothing with the land.

Sovereignty is really the critical foundation for any concept of democracy. If democracy means the ability of people to determine their own destiny, they have first to be sovereign in that destiny to determine it. Their capacity to develop has to be entirely in their own hands. Any external intervention in a nation, a movement or an organization, because it violates sovereignty, makes democracy impossible. To intervene militarily in another country in order to "bring democracy" is a blatant contradiction in terms.

In short, democracy means that the people who will be affected by a policy are the ones who participate in both formulating as well as deciding what that policy will be. That is, policy must be made, discussed and formulated by the people who will be affected by it.

In the corporate model of representationism, people elect representatives without having first decided on issues, leaving it to those "representatives" to discuss politics for them, which the people as a constituency then "represent." In the corporate model, the top of the pyramid makes policy, and the lower levels represent it through obedience to its rule. The structural question is how to invert the pyramid that characterizes the corporate model. In the pro-democracy model, policy is first discussed among the people, in their most local assemblies and meetings, from which they then elect representatives who will represent the discussions that have occurred.

The imperative to develop an alternate political culture based upon a pro-democracy model has been thrust upon us by the corporate community's attempt to develop a transnational political structure for itself. It is the imperative of resistance. The urgent political question for the peoples of the world has become how to form autonomous organizations and communities, how to create the political autonomy from which an alternate political culture can flourish, and from which the impunity and supremacy of property rights at the core of corporate coloniality can be contested.

Endnotes

1   I am using the term "nation-state" as a technical term for the form of government that emerged in Europe gradually out of its own feudal era. "State" refers to a governance structure in general, and "nation" refers to a more complicated socio-cultural phenomenon that can organize its own governance in many different ways. "Nation-state" refers to a specific form of state that emerged from Europe as its capitalist and colonialist structure developed. It refers to a state that invents (as in the case of the US) or coalesces (as in the case of European peoples) a nation for itself, under the capitalist framework that it guides and nourishes. Essentially, the nation-state is a state that creates a nation by bringing people together under its rubric. The paradigmatic example of the nation-state is the US, which created itself as a nation through its constitution of a state for itself in the wake of its expulsion of the British. Spawned by colonialism, it has been used against modern anti-colonialist movements, as I will describe in this essay, to maintain Euro-American control of peoples and nations seeking to liberate themselve

2   Under the Bretton Woods Agreement at the end of WWII, US gold reserves were to be used to establish the dollar as the international

currency of reserve. This meant that dollars accumulating in foreign banks could be exchanged for gold at a fixed rate, thus preserving their value for international commerce. But oil imports, the hundreds of military bases the US built around the world, and the Vietnam War brought the international accumulation of dollars to a critical point. Their repatriation threatened to deplete US gold reserves below the statutory level needed to back the domestic currency.

3   Thierry de Montbrial, Foreign Affairs, vol 54(1), Oct. 1975. Montbrial was a French economic theorist for the Trilateral Commission, one of its charter members. See also Nobuhiko Ushiba, with Graham Allison, and Thierry de Montbrial, *Sharing International Responsibilities Among Trilateral Countries* (New York: Trilateral Commission, 1983). Also C. Fred Bergsten, *The Future of International Economic Order* (Lexington: Lexington Books, 1973).

4   Two major descriptive works on the multinationals, and the Trilateral Commission, are: Holly Sklar (ed); *Trilateralism: The Trilateral Commission and Elite Planning for World Management*; South End Press, Boston, 1980; and Richard Barnet and Ronald Muller; *Global Reach: the Power of the Multinational Corporations*; Simon and Schuster, New York, 1974. See also, Helga Hernes, *Multinational Corporations* (Detroit: Gale Research, 1977); and Lewis D. Solomon, *Multinational Corporations and the Emerging World Order* (Port Washington: Kennikat Press, 1984).

5   Laura D'Andrea Tyson, *The Impact of External Economic Disturbances on Yugoslavia : Theoretical and Empirical Explorations,* with Egon Neuberger (Washington, D.C.: Kennan Institute for Advanced Russian Studies, 1978); and *The U.S. and the World Economy in Transition* (Berkeley Roundtable on the International Economy, University of California, 1986).

6   Peter Dale Scott, *SF Chronicle,* 1/2/91, p. C1. The effect of this arrangement was that Kuwait became a "spoiler" in OPEC, voting for lower oil prices against the oil exporting nations that wished to raise them, because industrial revenues generally vary inversely with the price of oil, meaning Kuwaiti industrial investments gained from lower oil prices where its oil export lost.

7   C. Fred Bergsten, *Conditions for Partnership*; with Etienne Davignon, and Isamu Miyazaki (New York: Trilateral Commission,1986). Neil Hood and Stephen Young; *The Economics of Multinational Enterprises* (London: Longman, 1979).

8   "Free Trade" refers to the ability of corporations to trade with each other, and to trade securities freely without interference from local governments. In an economy characterized by corporatized retailing, free trade does not exist for human consumers. In supermarkets and big box stores, prices are already set according to the financial necessity of the corporation. For subsistence goods, furniture, cars etc., the price and availability of goods is controlled by the needs of profitability. "Free trade" means that corporations are freed from political interference by states, labor unions, local trade associations, labor laws, environmental protection laws, etc. Domestically, in the US, this has

been accepted as "economic development." In the global South, it has meant the privatization of communal resources.

9   The Reagan administration decided to make the US a debtor nation (mainly through increased military spending), (Bergsten, 1986) in order to free it from the threat of concerted default by its own debtors (principally Latin America). Foreign default could be passing through to US creditors. Ultimately, the 1991 bombing of Iraq was not a war but a technological massacre launched from an antiseptic distance whose purpose was to destroy Iraqi's social infrastructure, yet leave Hussein in power. Thousands died. See "The Gulf War Reader"; Mikah Sifry and Chris Cerf, eds. (New York: Random House, 1991). Also, Ahmad Chalabi (a London banker); Wall Street Journal, April 8, 1991.

10   The most general estimate of the cost of the war is $100 billion, including funds used to build the alliance, such as $7 billion of Egyptian debt forgiven for their allegiance, and another $7 billion in foreign aid to Russia. (SF Chronicle, 4/26/91) A fraction of the money spent building the alliance against Iraq, either directly or through cancelling debts, added to the military expense of the assault, would have been more than enough to pay off Iraq's war debt from its war with Iran, and buy Iraqi compliance with western policy. Clearly, the destruction of Iraq was the primary planned purpose for which this money was spent.

11   The Jordanian Press Agency, and the Red Crescent (the Islamic counterpart to the Red Cross), both estimated in March, 1991, immediately after the bombing, that at least 125,000 civilians were killed, 60% of whom were children. The US has estimated 150,000 Iraqi troops were killed. All urban water purification and sewage disposal systems in Iraq were destroyed, as was 95% of Iraq's electric power; medical care became, and remained practically nonexistent. UNICEF, WHO, and the Red Cross all issued reports in April and May, 1991, warning that the lives of millions of Iraqis, mostly children, were in immediate jeopardy from famine, epidemic, and collapse of the social infrastructure. A report on child mortality in documentary film form was released in March, 1992 ("A Just War?", dir. and prod. by Maj Wechselmann and Stefan Hedqvist, 1992).

12   Kuwait differed from the case of Saudi Arabia in not being an oil exporting country any more, but a factor in the stability of the international economy. While deals can be made in a market, and thus stringent alliances with the Saudi family were possible, the Al-Sabah family in Kuwait had to be rendered wholly subordinate. The US did not wish to have as important a factor as Kuwait in the hands of an Arab family. What had prevented an earlier takeover was the existence of the Soviet Union. Any military adventure in that area of the world would have brought on a Soviet response. With the Soviet Union out of the way, the US was free to act with impunity. And this relates to the massive destruction wrought on Iraq. Iraq was the only nation that had an historical territorial claim on Kuwait. Under British protectorate, Kuwait had been a fifth province of Iraq. When the British lifted their control, they Balkanized Iraq, inventing Kuwait as a separate state. It

was to forestall any possible claims on Kuwait by Iraq that Iraq was subjected to the bombing it was in 1991. Cf. note 7.

13   Law professor Anthony D'Amato of Northwestern Univ. Law School argued that "sovereignty," in the case of Panama, was of no legal consequence in the face of the human right of "Panamanian citizens to be free from oppression by a gang of ruling thugs." The Panamanians being shot at by invading helicopters from a US carrier perhaps more clearly understood what the term "thugs" referred to than did D'Amato. He goes on to say that treaty arguments "are far less important to international law than the actual customary-law-generating behavior of states." "The U.S. interventions in Panama and, previously, in Grenada are milestones along the path to a new nonstatist conception of international law." To substitute the "behavior of states" for treaty agreements as law openly espouses the reduction of law to power, to military might pure and simple. Anthony D'Amato, "The Invasion of Panama was a Lawful Response to Tyranny" 84 *American Journal of International Law* 516 (1990). Against this, Congressman Steve Chabot, speaking at a Congressional hearing on the "Military Extraterritorial Jurisdiction Act" of 1999, Thursday, March 30, 2000, House of Representatives, Subcommittee on Crime, Committee on the Judiciary, stated that "American civilians who commit crimes abroad are also not subject to the criminal laws of the United States, because the jurisdiction for those laws ends at our national borders."

14   The two central themes of the neoliberal project were to make all lands salable, and to remove all obstructions to corporate investment. In Mexico, for instance, this meant changing the constitution, which provided that cooperatively held indigenous land could not be sold. In general, in the third world, it meant leaving corporate operations unhindered by tariffs, taxes, permits or licenses to terrains or resources, and suppressing unions. When applied to the US, these same principles deregulated securities markets, opening them to highly exotic invented securities (collateralized debt obligations, loan swaps, etc.) and mortgage scams (false low-interest appearances) that together became the engine of the crash.

15   The strategy of the multinational corporations, embodied in the Trilateral Commission, is suggested in many articles of the mid-70s. See, for instance, Peter Drucker; "The Multinational Corporations in World Politics;" *Foreign Affairs*, vol 53(1), Oct. 1974. C. Fred Bergsten; "The Threat from the Third World;" *Foreign Policy*, no. 11, Sum. 1973. Raymond Vernon; "Does Society Also Profit?" *Foreign Policy*, no. 13, Win. 1974. Vernon claims, in fact, that one benefit of the multinational corporations as a phenomenon is precisely the "undermining of the nation state system." Mysteriously, this does not contradict the notion of sovereignty for him.

16   Joseph Stiglitz, *Globalization and its Discontents,* New York: Norton, 2003.

17   David Korten, *When Corporations Rule the World,* p. 165.

18   C. Fred Bergsten; *Toward an New International Economic Order* (Lexington: Lexington Books, 1975); *Managing International Economic*

> *Interdependence* (Lexington: Lexington Books, 1977); Joan Edelman Spero, *The Politics of International Economic Relations* (New York: St. Martin's, 1990).

19   See GATT, Article XVI, section 4.

20   Korten,122.

21   The idea that a governance body might be possible for the corporations is what permits us to conceive of the TNCs as a "community of corporations." Corporations meet through the discussions of personnel who speak together as elements of a corporate structure, while their respective needs form the matrix for each in what they say. For example, when the Business Roundtable was first organized in 1972, it was "in the belief that business executives should take an increased role in the continuing debates about public policy." (Korten,144) Its 200 members included the heads of 42 of the largest (Fortune 500) corporations. In its meetings, the heads of GM, Ford, and Chrysler (for instance) would come together to talk business, as would the heads of DuPont, Dow, and Monsanto. They "put aside their competitive differences to reach a consensus on issues of social and economic policy." And indeed, as the community of corporations has grown, they have become important consumers for each other, irrespective of actual human-oriented markets.

22   Herein lies the true nature of the relation between the "free market" of neoliberal ideology and democracy in its local reality. They are antithetical. The neoliberal ideology proclaims that the free market is the essence of democracy, its necessary precondition. But the free market for them is the free stock market, and the markets of securities by which they can profit from and determine the value of capital assets anywhere in the world. But that determination comes from above, leaving real people impoverished, with no democratic connection to these operations, nor their results. (DK,66)

23   Juan José Arévalo, *The Shark and the Sardines*, trans. June Cobb and Raul Osegueda (New York: L. Stuart, 1961). See also, Carleton Beals, *Latin America: World in Revolution* (New York: Abelard-Schuman, 1963); and John Gerassi, *The Great Fear in Latin America* (New York: Collier Books, 1965).

24   Korten,125.

25   Hood,143

26   I use the term "representationism" to designate that system of electoral politics in which people elect officials who then talk politics and make political decisions on policy, as opposed to a truly democratic representational system in which people in local assemblies talk politics and decide on policy for themselves, and then elect delegates to higher bodies to represent their discussions and policy decisions.

27   Property and property rights were the ostensible stumbling block in abolishing slavery. The guarantee of property rights was considered to require compensation for the "owner" of the emancipated man or woman for his loss. Few people thought to reply that it would not have hindered proclaiming humans to not be property as such, and thus emancipation not a loss of anything but the injustice of forced

labor.

28   In the US, the majority of the people have supported the government's wars of intervention and aggression. Though the US is signatory to the Nuremberg principle that no citizen should obey or support a criminal action or command on the part of the government, few people attempt to live that principle, and those who have attempted to stop the US war machine have been barred from making a Nuremberg argument in court. When a movement succeeds in electing representatives to oppose a war effort as unjust or colonialist (as happened during the Vietnam war), those representatives are impotent because Congress has no power to stop a war. It cannot order the withdrawal of troops. It can cut appropriations to the Pentagon, but it cannot direct the military where to deploy those cuts in funds.

29   The case emerged from the problem that corporations needed standing in federal courts. Corporations were chartered in particular states, but engaged in commerce in all. Being involved in interstate trade, they were often required to answer civil suits across state lines. The jurisdiction for such cases was the federal court system. Thus, corporations had to have federal standing in order to appear in federal court. This implied a form of citizenship. Corporate personhood in the US is thus an artifact of the division of powers between the states and the federal government. The question was decided by Justice Story in 1805, and further by Justice Taney in 1844. Corporations were then given personhood, with all the rights and guarantees of the citizen under the 14th Amendment, in 1886 in the Santa Clara case, which enabled them to function fully as political entities.

30   Michael Taylor and Nigel Thrift, in *The Multinational Corporations and the Restructuring of the World Economy* (London: Croom Helm, 1986), point out that as the multinational corporations get larger, they cease to view the world as an environment of objects whose aggregate they can control, but rather as a population of organizations (nations, corporations, state-owned enterprises, unions, blocs, cultures, etc.) to effect. They call this a "structural contingency model", in which efficiency in production is replaced by effectiveness of organization, and profit maximization is no longer of primary concern.

31   André Gorz, *Farewell to the Working Class*, p. 57.

32   Like the identity one gains from employment in a corporation, national allegiance, however devoid of ethics that nation may be, is a question of identity. A social or national identity produces itself through a social process of identification, which is a consciousness, a way of imagining a connection to others (as Benedict Anderson described for nations as "imagined communities"). The imagined community coheres because it imagines others cohering to the identification, and watching to see if one is doing so as well. It is the institutedness of that structure of watching across the multitude of identifications that erases the difference between the imaginary and social identity. In some cases, this institutedness is provided by the state, and in others by a para-political process, such as racial segregation and the violence that enforces it.

33   Cuba's uncompromising insistence on its sovereignty is the real reason for US hatred and opposition to the Cuban revolution, not ideology nor its former Soviet alliance. The US has never stopped charging dictatorship, but could do so only by hiding the fact that the revolution armed the people, and has carefully evolved a political system that is the closest thing in this world, besides perhaps the Zapatista municipalities, to direct democracy. It was the people of Cuba, not the revolutionary leadership, that early on rejected the corruption of a two party system. Imbued with that corruption, on the other hand, the US has never had any difficulty supporting dictators.

34   While the Afghanistan invasion seemed only to be about a pipeline, it had an additional focus. If one regards how these two invasions together with the 2005 attempt by US agencies to install a government in the Ukraine (the so-called "orange revolution" financed by the NED) relate to each other geographically, one can see that they were an attempt to surround the Caspian oil fields. The Ukraine adventure drowned in chaos and corruption, however, leaving the Caspian region out of reach.

35   As testimony to the extent South American autonomy and sovereignty has disrupted the neoliberal agenda, the US has reorganized its military presence in that area. It has refurbished the 4th fleet, stationing it in Aruba, a few miles off the coast of Venezuela. It has reinvolved itself in military coups, in both Venezuela and Honduras. And it has created several large military bases in Colombia, while attempting to instigate border conflicts between Colombia and Venezuela.

36   Indeed, it was the execrable gratuitousness of the bombing of Serbia in 1999 that convinced many nations that the US had crossed all lines of civilized behavior and had to be stopped. This could not be done militarily, however. The US accounts for 56 % of the world's military spending, meaning that it spends more on the military than the rest of the world put together. The purpose of these cooperative organizations has been to form alternate centers of economic and political unity, from which the US is excluded.

37   Lori Wallach and Michelle Sforza, *Whose Trade Organization: Corporate Globalization and the Erosion of Democracy* (Public Citizen, 1999). See also, Richard Peet, *The Unholy Trinity: the IMF, World Bank, and WTO* (London: Zed Books, 2003).

Chapter 7

NATIONAL SELF-DETERMINATION IN AN AGE OF GLOBALIZATION*

José Bell Lara

What are the necessary conditions for undertaking a real project of development in today's neoliberal, globalized world? The existence of a revolutionary and popular power—in other words, socialist, able to access and wield economic, political and military capacity and summon the popular will needed to confront and neutralize the pressure and confrontations of the global economic system's power centers. This includes:

1. The capacity to place the process of accumulation in service to the national interest, which implies national control of accumulation.

2. The political will and capacity to develop organizational structures that will facilitate popular participation and engagement in the project of national well being, an important component of national hegemonic consensus to take the project forward.

3. The constant *materialization*, within the limits allowed by the accumulation level and the results of economic activity,

*From José Bell Lara, *Cuba: Socialism Within Globalization* (Editorial José Martí, 2008), pp. 69, 83-91, 97.

of a policy of facing and solving social problems generated by underdevelopment, so that the people can see that they are deriving fruits from their efforts. This includes the distribution and the redistribution of the income to the benefit of the people.

4. A capacity to absorb and create technologies in order to be able to compete internationally.

The effects of these profound revolutionary changes bring about a *social accumulation*, a concept that combines economic accumulation and processes directed toward the transformation of human beings: education, health, social security, the creation of positive social values and different forms of participation in daily political tasks.

Social accumulation is not the simple sum of material change and changes in the living conditions of the people. It is that and far more; it is a complex process in which those two factors are interrelated with a subjective moral/ideological accumulation and the beginning of a new form of living, a new way of life. Cuba's social accumulation is at the root of the reasons why Cuba did not replicate the Euro-Soviet cycle: the crisis and defeat of the real socialism model and a peaceful transition to capitalism.[1] It also explains why socialism continues to be a majority option in Cuba.

As a matter of fact, the Cuban people even defied a very profound economic crisis known as the Special Period that began in 1991 after the dissolution of the Soviet Union, and thereafter of Comecon. The socialist paradigm did not go into a crisis even when faced with economic duress. The policy applied from the 1990s was that of resistance and of maintaining the revolutionary power that was the bearer of the socialist project, even in those adverse circumstances. Implicit in this orientation was the need to confront the objective pressures arising from the systemic functioning of the capitalist world economy that was entering its full stage of globalization, as well as other pressures specifically targeted at Cuba by the system's hegemonic powers.

The Cuban state assumed the major cost of the crisis in order to preserve the Revolution's essential gains in the social terrain: health, education and social security. A policy to limit inequalities and protect vulnerable groups was undertaken.

These anti-crisis measures also covered the political level of Cuban society, and among them we note the following:

1. Changes in forms of ownership, with an extension of the private sector.
2. Moving from a state-owned agricultural sector to a largely cooperative one.
3. An expansion of market spaces.
4. Greater utilization of monetary-financial mechanisms in the directing and functioning of the economy.
5. Extension of democratic spaces with the reform of the Constitution, the generalization of People's Councils to the country as a whole, and promulgation of a new Electoral Law.

By these means, Cuba has found a space for its survival in the current world, However, the situation is complex because the necessary measures taken include some which by their nature constitute challenges to the revolutionary project, as well as because some components of social accumulation have been eroded. However, what is key is that the socialist paradigm is still in force in Cuba.

What are the challenges that lie ahead? To continue existing as a nation and a revolution in a globalized world under a neoliberal rule, while continuing to advance Cuba along its road to development. Cuba has the possibility to do this because it possesses the basic requirements needed, summarized as follows:

1. Cuba is in prime condition to undertake a development project within the current world circumstances due to the existence of a revolutionary and socialist power that, with wide popular participation, managed to undertake a socialist transition while still achieving an impressive advance in social accumulation....
2. Cuba has the capacity to place the accumulation process at the service of its national interests. The role of political power embodied in the structures, actions and rules established by the revolutionary state is decisive when it comes to submitting the process of accumulation to national interests. This means having national control over that accumulation; in other words, control over the reproduction of the labor force, the centralization of surplus, the market, natural resources and technologies.

In the Cuban case, the state has ownership of the principal means of production, which allows it to form associations with foreign capital without losing control of the domestic economy; on the basis of that control it can direct investment policies, prioritizing sectors that it considers important for the country's development, all of which means the state has the resources that it can use in a centralized way on behalf of national interests. The foregoing is supported by a redesigning of the national financial system, updating it to function in the new conditions.

The state has majority control over the labor force, because even hiring by foreign companies is done via Cuban state-run employment agencies, and the state fixes the wages to be paid in this sector of the economy. The sector of the labor force that can be considered private—*campesinos* and self-employed workers—is a minority within employment as a whole, although it has an important monetary accumulation. The majority of domestic trade circuits are controlled by the state by means of state-owned retail chains and enterprises. Control is likewise maintained over natural resources which are exploited according to a codified policy. *The state command of the economy gives the Revolution the equivalent of the directive power of a transnational conglomerate to negotiate with other actors in the globalized economy, thus maintaining a degree of autonomy but not activated by the private profit motive.*

1.   Despite the crisis and the difficulties, the Revolution has maintained the post-capitalist *social* accumulation, which is the principal component of the socialist project and continues to constitute the principal reserve of Cuban socialism.

This reserve is maintained by political-ideological work, a constant expression of one of the forms that the class struggle is acquiring today in Cuba. The institutional network of the Revolution articulated in the agencies of People's Power and a series of social and mass organizations designed to channel the organized participation of the people form part of this social accumulation.[2] They have not been exempt from certain vices of formalism, but the participative framework exists, and through it a hegemonic consensus is maintained in favor of the Revolution, expressed in diverse forms and ways in the functioning of the political system.

2.   In thirty years, from 1959 to 1989, Cuba achieved superior levels in the principal life standards and life quality indicators to those of Latin America and underdeveloped countries as a whole. The level of indicators that measure results in this terrain were similar to those of the most industrialized

countries of the capitalist system.[3] The crisis of the 1990s has not fundamentally reversed that situation thanks to the policy applied in the face of the crisis to try and preserve the achievements attained in the social sphere....

3. Cuba has a capacity for absorbing and creating technologies supported by a material base. From its beginnings, the Cuban Revolution mounted an extraordinary effort to raise people's cultural and educational levels. That educational effort has to be seen as part of the accumulation-investment process for development, given that it has not been just a process of instruction in general, but also one geared to master contemporary science and technology.[4]

As a result of this, the country has raised its average ninth grade educational level; there are 46 higher education centers in which 21,600 professors are working. Cuba has 1.8 scientists for every 1000 inhabitants. The country has 221 research centers and invests $25 per capita in research and development, the highest figure in Latin America.

The principal axis of the Cuban scientific-productive complex consists of centers in which prioritized investigations are developed. At first sight they are similar to industrial parks, but in Cuba they have their own particularities. Cuban scientific complexes are agencies that ensure cooperation between research and production centers that take advantage of their special distribution to create specific synergies among themselves.[5] Currently there are 15 scientific complexes: 12 territorial ones and 3 specialized ones that bring together 465 agencies, institutions and working groups belonging to 24 organizations. More than 23,000 people work in them, of whom 43% are university graduates.

A study of Cuban economy's development demonstrates that its principal developmental direction is what we can call "the productive-scientific constellation of health," formed by a strong accumulation of biotechnological, chemical-pharmaceutical knowledge, the design and manufacture of short-series medical equipment with a computational base, and the loan and export of health services in specialized installations at the highest international level. This constellation has had and continues to enjoy notable development on the basis of its productive scientific results.

The Cuban Paradigm for Development**

The globalization process is not uniform, nor is it exempt from contradiction. Indeed, the old contradictions have been maintained while new ones have emerged. The contradiction between the North and the South has been maintained and the gap between the two groups has actually grown. The contradictions and competition between the economic blocs within the system persist and they likewise thrive within the interior of each of them. The contradictions and competition between the principal protagonists of the globalized economy, the transnational enterprises, are increasingly acute in their need for expansion and their struggle for profits. This also leads to a corresponding struggle on the part of the transnational fractions of the bourgeoisie, in both North and South countries. For Cuba, the important thing is for the Revolutionary State to fully exploit the contradictions which are generated in the globalization process with the aim of gaining increased room to maneuver in economic and political relations. The Cuban Revolution is showing that this is possible.

The characteristics of the Cuban paradigm for development can be elaborated, bearing in mind that the point of departure for this model is a country which has now completed a phase of primitive socialist accumulation.

The main elements of the paradigm would be the following:

1. The possibility of achieving development from within via the articulation of a body of strategies that imply the construction of competitive advantages, supported by the development of knowledge-intensive branches of the economy.

2. A strategy of selective global connection-disconnection.

3. A policy of agreements (or alliances) with a certain fraction of the international bourgeoisie so as to gain greater access to capital, technology and markets while maintaining the political command of the socialist power over the economy. This can allow the promotion of a sustained and sustainable, autonomous development, capable of achieving a type of

** from José Bell Lara, *Globalization and the Cuban Revolution*, Richard A. Dello Buono, trans. (Editorial José Martí, 2002), pp. 118, 121, 124-125.

175

accumulation that breaks with the throes of dependency and which tends towards socialism.

The kind of development strategy being visualized here overcomes the dichotomous discussion of "inner-oriented"/"export-led" development. The goal is not to create a socialist version of the import substitution model nor is it aimed at creating an export platform model oriented towards the world market, although certain elements of both are present. Rather, the goal is to program the productive structure so that it is supported by the endogenous capacities of the country, reaching for combination and complementarities between production for the internal market and production for the world market; an intensive production in capital and/or knowledge-intensive production in balance with more traditional labor-intensive exports; and an ongoing search for exports which display a high added value.

In Cuba, socialism is the guarantee for the continued self-determined existence of the nation. In the geopolitical conditions in which Cuba is situated, and in the context of U.S aggression, a capitalist restoration would imply an associated/dependent/subordinated bourgeoisie as a local ruling class, which would arouse internal resentment, possibly leading to an attempt to forge a closer integration with imperialism.

Socialism is the continuity of the Revolution. This means Cuba enjoys class support to limit the scope of action within the national arena of those tendencies which are imposed by globalization. This is, again, due to its social development. With these in place, the prospects remain present over the long run for a sustainable, non-capitalist society.

More than a decade following the fall of the Berlin Wall, socialism in Cuba continues to display its validity as a political option insofar as it signifies the preservation of national independence and of a social project that responds to the interest of the majority. In the short term, socialism legitimates the current struggles for development. If this banner and objective were to disappear, an extraordinary mobilizing element would likewise be destroyed.

Knowing the route is one of the premises for not losing one's way, even though circumstances may sometimes impose partial delays, detours, and even reversals in some areas. But the real options are clear: The choice is between acquiescing to an underdeveloped, dependent capitalism in conditions of capitalist globalization, or undertaking the project of a viable socialism that offers the potential for a society rooted in social justice.

These are the conditions in which the Cuban Revolution must continue to unfold. Its constant challenge is to try to consciously maintain the project of a societal alternative to capitalism. In so doing, we may sometimes have to use capitalistic instruments and our intelligence; however, we will remain on the side of our heart: *on the left*.

Beyond doubt, the new global conditions will affect the profile of the Cuban society of tomorrow. If the policy of development we have described is successful, that society will not be the one which the revolutionaries of the 1960s had dreamed of. But it will still be an alternative to capitalism, a plausible socialism. Only within that framework will Cuba be able to maintain its independence and its national standing.

Endnotes

1   José Bell Lara, *Cambios mundiales y perspectives de la Revolución Cubana*, pp13-31.

2   The CRDs bring together 84% of the population aged fourteen and above; the FMC, 80% of adult women; and the CTC, 99% of paid workers. The local agencies of the People's Power have municipal delegates and thousands of citizens are involved in 1900 working commissions. More than 98% of the registered electorate regularly participates in elections to those bodies. On the other hand, approximately 16% of these belong to what can be considered the most active segment of the population, the Communist Party of Cuba and the Young Communist League.

3   Beatriz Díaz, "Cuba, modelo de desarrollo equitativo," LASA-CEA, *Sistemas políticos, poder y sociedad (Estudio de casos en América Latina)*.

4   One example of this in Cuba is that in the 1980s expenditure on education represented 6.1% of the GDP and 13.2% of the national budget.

5   The complexes are the superior organizational level of science in Cuba; interface units that group together multiple institutions with the objective of participating in the country's economic and social development. They represent an ideal environment for bringing together the undertakings of politicians, scientists, producers and marketing agents to convert a scientific idea into a productive reality.

Chapter 8

THE NATION-STATE AND CUBA'S ALTERNATIVE STATE

Steve Martinot

The history of the Cuban revolution and its survival against the unremitting attacks by the US has been written from essentially two perspectives, those of Cuba and its struggle to preserve its sovereignty and the socialist and democratic principles of its humanism, and those of the attacker, the US, which seeks to isolate Cuba, creating an ignorance about it in the world within which to demonize it as a totalitarian, anti-humanist society. Cuba's responses to this hostility, its struggle to develop its economy, its maneuvers to break the isolation the US has attempted to impose (and failed), and its attempts to protect itself internally and externally, have formed the major part of most accounts.

In the process, Cuba's mode of internal organization and the nature of its political structure have evolved. They have changed significantly over time in relation to a single unvarying and overarching principle, the principle of sovereignty. On that, Cuba has been consistently uncompromising. As a result, the nature of its state stands in sharp contrast to the form of "republican" government that characterizes the US and Europe, though the latter also rest on the concept of popular sovereignty.

To contrast the two will be the purpose of this article. In order to grasp the depth of the distinction, a brief description of the concept of the nation-state that arose in Europe and the US, as well as its particular historical sense of sovereignty, will be given.

But first, a vignette might be in order to set the stage for this contrast. Because of the US embargo, most of Cuba's international trade (around 85%) was with the Soviet Union and the socialist bloc. When the Soviet Union collapsed, Cuba's economy went into severe crisis, and Cuban society faced terrible hardships. Economic activity fell by 50%. The usual political response to such a crisis, during most of 20th century European history, has been one of militarizing and regimenting society. Governments strengthen policing activity, centralize economic power, and augment political controls over daily life in order to keep society from flying apart. But in response to the crisis of 1990, during which the US actually increased its assaults on the island, Cuba did just the opposite. It decentralized administration, giving greater control over economic processes and development to local neighborhood and municipal assemblies rather than to the central government. And it cut back on military spending by 80% in order to have the funds and resources to continue its health and educational programs for the people.[1] To mention one small detail, shortly after the revolution, the Cuban government resolved to provide a quart of milk a day to every child under the age of nine. Even during those days of crisis and dire shortage, it never missed a day.

To better understand the structure of the Cuban state as it has emerged, and how it reflects the ethos this represents, we need to first set out the parameters of the nation-state as it developed in the capitalist societies of Europe and the US. Using those parameters as a political language, we can then describe how Cuba's state differs, and indeed inverts the capitalist state.

The Emergence of the Nation-State as a Structure

In general, the term "nation-state" refers to the republican form of state that emerged out of the growth of Euro-American capitalist society. It is characterized by constitutional government composed of a representative legislature, an elected executive, and a separation of governmental powers (executive, legislative, and judicial). These then relate to each other through a system of checks and balances. Ideologically, the state proclaims itself dedicated to the preservation of civil rights and civil liberties, and thinks of itself as providing democratic participation by the people in government affairs.

In practice, however, this ideological focus is constrained by the state's dedication to maintaining the rights of private property. This latter aspect requires a strong centralized mode of governance, to prevent local democratic processes in the hands of those exploited or dominated by property, most often forming popular majorities, from infringing the rights and impunities of the property-owners. In the US, this centralization is provided by a court system that judges law according to its impact on property's rights, and an executive with both veto and discretionary enforcement powers. ("Executive discretion," a technical term in US jurisprudence, means that the executive can decide what laws to enforce and what not.) In Euro-American society, this form of state has provided the institutional-legal framework for the massive economic development of capitalism.

If this form of state is based on the concept of a "sovereign people," that notion did not just suddenly appear. It emerged in two stages, both of which ironically involved a form of colonialism (the negation of other people's sovereignty). The first stage was the development of monarchy and trans-oceanic governance empowered primarily by the conquest of the Americas. The Americas provided the initial mass of capital from which capitalist development germinated during the 16th and 17th centuries (through seizure of gold and silver, the taking of vast lands for plantations, the use of enslaved laborers to produce its colonial wealth, and the enormous profit made from the slave trade itself). The European monarchies of those centuries fostered that development through their legitimization of slavery and the establishment of trade and settlement monopolies.[2]

In the second stage, modern capitalism emerged by shifting the concept of sovereignty from the monarch to the people, establishing government under the authority of a civil constitution. Under this "republican" concept, a people defines itself as sovereign by bringing itself into existence as a nation through that constitutional process, which then establishes the state institutions by which it then governs itself. Sovereignty meant a people enacting itself as a people through its political acts at a national level. For the US, this took the form of an independence struggle (among the white settlers, not among the colonized, the enslaved people of African descent or the indigenous nations from whom the land was seized), while in Europe it took the form of a dominant language group establishing a republican form of government for itself (on territory which often encompassed other ethnic, religious or linguistic minorities). The result was a racialized state based on a white franchise in both Europe and its colonies, and a messianic white supremacy imposed on the rest of the world through colonization. In effect, on both levels, the "republican" form of government became intimately involved in a new form of colonialism.

It was in the context of struggle against this colonialism that the concept of sovereignty took on a third sense. After World War Two, the colonized nations sought independence from their Euro-American colonizers, and used the notion of national sovereignty as a conceptual basis not only for independence but for autonomy from outside influence or control, whether as a single nation or a multi-national state. And this third sense of political and cultural autonomy, arising from the anti-colonialist process, then spread back to the colonialist societies, and was adopted by many forms of organization to signify their right and/ or ability, as organizations or communities, to govern their own affairs according to their own internal rules and desires. Since the civil rights movements of the 1960s and 1970s, this local sense of sovereignty has even been extended to social justice movements, labor unions, and communities in their struggles for justice, equality, and self-determination as communities. Labor union movements in particular have traditionally insisted on their organizational sovereignty, and most labor legislation has been designed precisely to curtail it (for instance, the Taft-Hartley Act). One of the most egregious violations of union sovereignty by the US government in recent years was its removal of Carey as president of the International Brotherhood of Teamsters. Carey had been elected by a rank and file movement (Teamsters for a Democratic Union). When suspicion arose that he had violated some internal election rules, which the union executive chose to ignore, the US government stepped in, removed Carey, and put its own man in the union presidency.

One of the reasons massive social justice movements arose within the "republican system" with its sense of popular sovereignty is that, for the most part, it didn't work. In the "republican" system of representation, representatives are elected from specific districts, in order to represent those districts in legislative assemblies. It is then the representatives and not the people who discuss politics within the halls of government, and make policy. Though delegates pretend to represent the districts that elect them, those districts are too complex for single delegates to speak for. They are, in general, made up of contradictory class interests, communities and cultures with conflicting identities and ideologies. A single delegate remains unable to represent them all, and ends up representing none. Ultimately the delegate is left to fend for him/herself in the assembly to which s/he is elected, prey to the "highest bidder." Three things happen. A legislative assembly becomes hermetic, its members taking the assembly itself as their real constituency. Second, "democracy" gets reduced to the rhetoric of electoral campaigns and the act of voting, as political spectacle. And third, political policy and decision-making occurs without input or participation by the people. "Representation" gets transformed into a structural disconnect between the people and the government. It is because democratic participation is thrown to the winds that protest movements become necessary and inevitable. What are called "protest movements" are actually demands for the democratic participation that the "republican" system obviates. Thus, the nation-state's rhetorical proclamation of a democratic ethos was betrayed at birth by reducing democracy to formal representation.

If the republican system worked at all in the US, it was only briefly at the turn of the 19th century. At that time, the electorate was homogeneous, composed of white male property owners, whom elected legislators could represent to a degree. Extension of the franchise, economic development, immigration and urbanization disrupted that homogeneity, producing the political crises of the 1850s and the Civil War.

In the wake of that war and the Reconstruction period, the US had two other sources of constituent homogeneity to fall back upon. The first was the construction of a forceful system of white supremacy (through legislation in the South and cultural emulation of that legislation in the North), involving the exclusion of black and brown people from all arenas of social and political life, enforced by para-military means. The name for this system was "segregation," or Jim Crow, and it became ubiquitous throughout the US. It has conditioned the domination of politics by a two party system, precluding the establishment of other parties that might reflect the interests of the dominated groups.[3] Where, before the Civil War, there had been a black political presence in the abolitionist movement, black organization and resistance was thrust into clandestinity until the Marcus Garvey movement. Only the Knights of Labor recognized black political rights, and it is one of the factors that led to its rapid demise in the early 1880s.

The other structure that has provided a form of constituency homogeneity has been the corporation, and the community of corporations as such. Having been given personhood and citizenship in 1844 and 1886,[4] this community (as a group of "highest bidders") has become the primary constituency for state and national legislatures. Their ascent to the level of citizenship has had the effect of thrusting humans out of the arena of participation, and rendering them politically irrelevant.

Internal Contradictions in this Post-colonial Situation

Not ironically, when applied to those peoples who sought liberation and independence from colonialism after World War II, this "republican system," based as it was originally on popular sovereignty, took on a distinctly self-contradictory character, and came to stand in direct antithesis to the growing demand for independence and sovereignty in those former colonies. That is, when newly independent post-colonial nations sought to emulate the "republican" system (or had it imposed on them by the terms of independence engineered by colonialist powers, or by the UN), a number of contradictions would emerge.

A major contradiction emerged from the necessity of guaranteeing the sanctity of private property, and thus of capitalism. The former colonialist hold on land as property demanded that it be integrated into the new national paradigm. The effect was to corrupt or block real liberation from the colonialist hierarchy. Thus, the republican system that many post-colonial governments sought to emulate stood in the way of real restitution of the nation.

A second contradiction imposed on post-colonial societies by the republican system was a result of the nature of capitalism itself. Capitalism is endlessly expansionary, especially in its corporate form, and needs increasing areas of colonization for investments and markets to remain viable. Insofar as the "republican system" functions to guarantee capital's ability to operate, it must exclude excessive regulation of capitalism's expansion and imperial interests. It is this essential exclusion of capital from domestic legislative control that forms a primary aspect of the political disconnect between the people and the government, especially in the developed countries. But when newly independent post-colonial societies attempted to emulate the republican system, internal capital had few areas into which to expand. In the absence of colonialist possibilities, many post-colonial nations turned inward, and invented or enhanced the prior racialization of their own people. This sometimes led to an internal colonization of different ethnic groups that had been included in the pre-independence colonial framework.

Finally, another major source of internal conflict arose from that fact of prior racialization by colonialism. But insofar as the republican system required a certain level of homogeneity if it was to be "representative," that racialization was maintained, and in some cases exacerbated as a complex social hierarchy. This was also true for the economic classes and their cultural communities. Attempts at class expression, and class struggles, were suppressed in the interest of a stability of representation. Hamstrung by multi-dimensional class struggles and segregationist policies, post-colonial society suffered internal political stresses that allowed foreign capital to maintain economic control. In effect, the newly independent society labored under a political structure that exacerbated its prior racialization while suffering a continuation of prior domination by foreign capital.

It was in this sense that the demand for sovereignty continued to be a revolutionary demand, both for political restructuring of the country's governance, and for cultural liberation. Cuba was one country that recognized this at the very beginning of its revolutionary construction. It is a primary factor today in the restructuring that is occurring in South America, led by Venezuela and Bolivia.

In sum, the system of "republican" governance that emerged in Europe and the US is epitomized by the development of a colonialist, racialized, patriarchal, corporate state that pretends to a representationism, but depends on an ability to dominate other societies, cultures, and markets. And when applied or imposed upon the newly independent states, the republican system of governance actually prevented the independence movements in these countries from politically defending what they had won against that continued foreign domination and its continuing distortion and warping of the independence project.

First, it separated the executive branch of government from the legislative, under conditions where neither was able to be truly representative of the independence movements that had brought them to power. The executive branch was constitutionally required to maintain the rights of private property, opening the post-colonial economy to corporate investment, on top of the foreign economic interests remaining from the colonial period. And the legislature, unable to truly represent the people whose multiplicity of interests reassert themselves after independence, was barred from being the major expression of the independence movement. The result was a foregone conclusion. Representationism, by not representing, leaves the legislative function in the grasp of an external "highest bidder," Euro-American corporations and financial institutions, whose domination is thereby protected from any authentic independentist administrative leadership. Insofar as the people still sought to defend their society against renewed exploitation by foreign capital, they were obstructed structurally by the hermeticism of the legislature, and its separation from the executive.[5]

In effect, in the "republican system," resistance to continued colonization by Euro-American corporations becomes marginalized or suppressed. Euro-American capital establishes itself at the core of the post-colony's economic life, and thus its political life. In other words, it gains control of the economy through the former colony's very attempt at independence, using the representationism adopted by that attempt to render the independence project helpless against external control. The movement's leadership cannot contest foreign economic domination because the institutionalization of its "independence" as a nation-state required its prioritization of property rights. Independence remained formal rather than real.

In sum, the nation-state, in a post-colonial country, creates a structural complicity with the very coloniality it had sought to escape in principle. The alternative ideas and political cultures implicit in national liberation movements (such as ending property in land, or the democratization of production) remained stillborn.

The Cuban State

If Cuba has been able to defend itself against the coloniality inherent in the republican form of nation-state, it has been precisely through having evolved an alternative political structure.[6]

In Cuba, political institutions are divided into three domains of governance, but not as a separation of powers in the traditional sense. Its elements are in fact incommensurable with the nation-state's division into executive, legislative and judicial branches. In Cuba, the three domains are 1) a multi-level system of elected assemblies in which systems of meetings (consultas) or constituent assemblies have replaced the role of political parties, 2) the mass organizations, and 3) the ministries.

The ministries are organs of centralization for the purpose of coordinating the procurement and distribution of goods and productive factors (as well as handling security). They manage the governance of things for economic and infrastructural development (critical in times of shortage and difficult international trade). The mass organizations organize and represent groups with common interests (such as labor, women, students, small farmers, etc.). That is, they present and negotiate on the specific interests of their constituent groups with respect to the ministries and the assemblies, through proposals for changes in policy. They also have the responsibility of facilitating assembly discussions (*consultas*) on political or institutional issues at the local and national levels. They thus constitute the matrix for dialogue among people locally, between constituencies and elected delegates at all assembly levels, and for a sense of responsibility of each domain toward the others. The emphasis on broad popular dialogue among the people has become a deep-seated cultural norm of Cuban political life. It marks its most fundamental difference from the US system (and with the nation-state in general). It is the foundation on which the Cuban system has been approaching a form of direct democracy.

In Cuba, the consultative process has sometimes taken years, with thousands of meetings (as was the case with the revision of the legal code in the early 70s; it took seven years, involving 33,000 meetings and discussions among the people, before a new code was written and agreed upon). Consultation is essentially a dialogic process, both among people, and between the three elements of governance.

The assemblies are the main policy-making bodies. By secret ballot, people elect delegates to the assemblies from a variety of constituencies—neighborhood, factory, school, agricultural enterprise, etc.—not just territorial districts. There are no electoral parties. Delegates do not run campaigns in which to make promises about the future. Rather, they are elected on the basis of community and organizational participation—in the consultas, the mass organizations, and the general dialogic life of the constituencies.

The local assemblies have the responsibility for administration at the local level. They coordinate production in their districts, administer the court system (whose description would take us too far afield here), and adjudicate political disputes. In effect, executive, legislative, and judicial powers are lumped together into the assemblies. Instead of a separation of these powers, the assemblies represent their democratization. What accounts for Cuba's success in doing so is the fact that administration and legislation in Cuba can concern itself with the interests of the people, while in a capitalist society, these powers have to concern themselves primarily with property and property interests.

The participation of the mass organizations in the structure of governance is the main innovation in Cuba's political structure. The mass organizations include organizations of women, students, labor, small farmers, professionals, neighborhoods, etc. (The actual organizations are the Cuban Federation of Women, various university and high school student associations, the Cuban Labor Confederation, the National Association of Small Farmers, and the Committees for Defense of the Revolution; others are formed as social groups coalesce or develop with specific needs.) These organizations are independent of the government, and decide their own policies autonomously in terms of the interests of their constituencies, which they then represent and express in the assemblies.

The striking aspect of this domain of Cuban politics is that these organizations represent within Cuban society what would be the various movements of exploited or dispossessed people under capitalism (unions, women's movements, student movements, etc.). Each mass organization represents a traditional form of resistance to hierarchical control (patriarchy, elite academic training, class exploitation, latifundia, and colonialist segregation and social domination of the colonized). While, under capitalism, the movements of resistance that the oppressed have had to organize to express their needs and interests remain marginalized, this is inverted in Cuba. These movements are brought into the center of governance. In representing a consciousness of the past (of past exploitation and suppression), they stand as resistance to the resurgence of that past. They constitute a consciousness of the persistence of oppression in the world, in ways that the ministries (which concern themselves with present reality) and the delegate assemblies (which have a future oriented responsibility toward policy) do not (and should not).

The responsibility of the mass organizations is first of all to represent the interests of their membership in the different levels of assemblies, to which they send delegates. Thus, they embody the real economic, political, social, and cultural interests in Cuban society. In addition, they administer the machinery of delegate election. For each constituency, they constitute, in an extemporaneous form, an electoral committee. And they organize the meetings, *consultas*, and dialogues between delegates and constituencies, and between constituencies and delegate assemblies.

The struggle to maintain and build the mass organizations has been one of the central processes in the evolution of the Cuban state. During the period of excessive centralization (1960s and 1970s), they almost went out of existence. This was the period when various attempts were made to form a leadership revolutionary party. At first, it took too much administrative responsibility upon itself, resulting in the erosion of the mass organizations. This was one of the primary experiences that led the Cuban leadership to realize the need for decentralization. The on-going decentralizing process with respect to administration and decision-making (adding intermediary levels of assembly, for instance) marks a second important difference with the capitalist nation-state system in general, and that of the US in particular.

There is a cyclic structure discernible in the interrelations between the ministries, the assemblies, and the mass organizations. The ministries act in a top down fashion, a centralization that is present-oriented economically and future-oriented politically. The delegate assemblies act in a bottom up fashion, with juridical decision-making power that is future-oriented politically and present-oriented organizationally. And the mass organizations mediate between the two on the basis of sociocultural and political interests that are present-oriented politically and past-oriented (as mass politics) organizationally.

What appears as executive power in the capitalist nation-state is split between the ministries and the mass organizations in this form of alternate state; the nation-state's legislative functions are split between the delegate assemblies and the mass organizations; and the judicial power is split between the delegate assemblies and the ministries (the ministries administer the courts, the legal system, and education at the national level). In other words, what is constituted as an institutionality of power in the nation-state appears as a mediation between domains of governance in Cuba. And conversely, these domains of governance are defined along conceptual lines that are incommensurable with the categories of the nation-state. In the place of the hegemonic power and detachment that representationism produces among legislators and the executive, Cuba has substituted a structure of responsibility that combines a political responsiveness with a dialogical ethics.

In other words, the categories of structural power of the nation-state have been rendered mediatory, ephemeral, and disseminated socially in the Cuban state. And what is marginalized in the property protecting nation-state (mass movements, organization of social and human welfare, and popular direct participation in political affairs unmediated by party organization) has been placed at the center of Cuban state operations.

In sum, the Cuban state inverts the governmental categories of the nation-state. The mass organizations invert the marginalization of the social movements in capitalist society, taking their place at the center, an inversion of center and periphery. The assemblies invert the process of representation in the nation-state. In a representationist government, the election of representatives occurs first, often based on the choices of elite party leadership, and it is those representatives that then discuss policy and make political decisions. In Cuba, political debate and discussion on policy occurs first among the people at the level of constituent meetings, consultas, neighborhood and enterprise assemblies, and in the mass organizations. Delegates are then elected to higher assemblies to represent what had occurred in those meetings. And the policy decisions of the discussions represented are then conjoined and amalgamated. Contested issues in the assemblies are remanded to the constituencies for discussion, organized by people themselves or by the mass organizations.

In the US governmental system, for instance, political parties mediate between constituencies and legislatures. In the Cuban state, the inverse relation of the assemblies to the constituencies is mediated by the mass organizations. In the nation-state, political parties are necessary to give the illusion of choice and participation. But political discussion is always carried on in the future by representatives meeting elsewhere and not among the people, to whom they have simply made promises. It is through those illusions that political parties can absorb dissent, and keep people "within" the system. In Cuba, parties are not necessary because debate and discussion is already collective at the constituent level.

There is one single party in Cuba, the Cuban Communist Party, but it is not an electoral nor a governing party. It is barred by law from accounting for more than 10% of all delegates elected to all assemblies. Instead, it serves as a moral leadership for the society as a whole, participating in the consultative processes in constituent meetings, and acting as a source of organization and ideas. Though a party heavy-handedness is always possible in such consultations, its operations have been decentralized in practice, and are open to criticism by the assemblies, primarily the neighborhood or municipal assemblies in which the people participate most directly. Thus, it inverts the ethic of obeisance to expertise that accompanies the market commodification of all things human in the nation-state.

Finally, the ministries invert the fundamental structure of capitalism itself. Their job is to coordinate supply and demand, as well as economic development. They thus play the role of corporate management for the economy as a whole. But they do so in an open manner of direct concrete responsibility toward social welfare as well as the economy, as opposed to the hidden and ephemeral ways the administration of corporations and the executive branch of the government operate, and the fundamental irresponsibility toward society that is the main motif of the corporate structure. Instead, the ministries have the responsibility for equalizing employment opportunity and the distribution of material resources to the various productive facilities. Thus, they serve to alleviate the competition between workers for employment that capitalism relies upon, while coordinating and planning economic administration, as opposed to the anarchy of investment and production that characterizes capitalism. In addition, the workers in each enterprise act through democratic management assemblies that overcome their division of labor through that administrative unification, while the ministries divide the overall managerial tasks of the economy among themselves. Thus, as an inversion of capitalism, management undergoes a division of labor while the workers are unified through their collective administration.

It is through this multiple structure of inversion and mass participation that the Cuban state represents a clear alternative to the capitalist nation-state. It is thus that the Cuban revolution, and the Cuban experiment in revolutionary society, has been able to escape the pitfalls that beset other post-colonial societies and maintain their national sovereignty. Like other post-colonial countries, brought into existence by national liberation movements, the Cuban revolution has based itself on the national character of the Cuban people, and established a state for itself to represent the interests of the nation. But Cuban nationalism has maintained its revolutionary character precisely because it rejected the republican form of government characteristic of the nation-state, which has enabled Cuba to preserve its sovereignty.

A Note on Race and Racism

With respect to the racialization of the Cuban people and among the Cuban people that Cuba inherited from its pre-revolutionary colonization, the Cuban state has unfortunately acted in an ambiguous and sometimes contradictory fashion. During the early years of the revolution, discrimination on the basis of race was outlawed in principle and through the dedication of the revolutionary spirit to equality. It was fought conscientiously by the revolutionary leadership. Social clubs, social facilities, and educational or health institutions that discriminated racially were fairly rapidly closed or taken over by the government and run on a non-discriminatory basis. All employment, government participation, education, health care, and housing has been opened to all, without discrimination.

But politically, in the wake of these actions (which were by and large successful at the time), the Cuban government took the stand that if racial discrimination had been eliminated, then race ceased to be a factor, and was not something that needed to be spoken about or addressed politically any more. The political motivation for this stance was the need for unity in the face of US hostilities. No specific laws addressing racial discrimination were passed, and organizations based on race, such as a number of black "societies" that had grown up during the pre-revolutionary period, were discouraged or even closed down. What the absence of discussion on racism and white supremacy assumed was that if race were not spoken of, it would disappear. But that simply allowed the structures of racialization in pre-revolutionary Cuba, the cultural matrix of white supremacy inculcated by colonialism, to persist intact. And it has reappeared from time to time when conditions permitted.

The government's refusal to include racialization and white supremacy as political issues is the one exception to the emphasis of discussion, dialogue, and consultation that has emerged as the center of Cuban political life. It is a policy that has begun to change, and to be reversed since the early 1980s. But the fact that the revolutionary leadership could make this omission testifies to the depth in Euro-American culture and its colonies at which the structures of white supremacy lie. And when the Cuban economy had to shift to tourism for economic growth (in the 1990s), the racism inherent in the dormant structures of racialization re-emerged in new and old forms of white supremacy. The Cuban government is now struggling with this problem on a number of fronts, which would be too complicated to go into in this paper.

REFERENCES

Isaac Saney, *Cuba: a Revolution in Motion* (London: Zed Books, 2004)_

Peter Roman, *People's Power: Cuba's Experiment with Representative Government* (Boulder: Westview Press, 1999)_

Max Azicri, *Cuba: Politics, Economics and Society* (New York: Pinter Publ., 1988)

Alejandro de la Fuente, *A Nation For All: Race, Inequality, and Politics in 20th Century Cuba* (Chapel Hill: Univ. Of North Carolina Press, 2001)

Anibal Quijano, "The Nation-State, Citizenship, and Democracy," in *Nepantla: Views from the South,* vol. 2 (2001) (Durham: Duke Univ. Press) _

Larry Tise, *Pro-Slavery: a History of the Defense of Slavery in America, 1701-1840* (Athens, Ga.: Univ. of Georgia Press, 1987

Steve Martinot, *The Rule of Racialization* (Philadelphia: Temple Univ. Press, 2003)

Endnotes

1   Isaac Saney in particular gives interesting descriptions of the actions of the Cuban government during this period. Isaac Saney, *Cuba: a Revolution in Motion*

2   Monarchs granted commercial and settlement corporations monopoly control over their domains in order to eliminate any competition that would hinder economic development. And the enslavement of labor was necessary as a means of controlling labor (obtaining obedience) because society's economic production had not yet fully commodified social existence. Once full commodification of society is achieved, under which an individual would require an income to buy the means of living (survival), then the threat of dismissal from one's job (one's source of income) became a sufficient inducement for laborer obedience. In other words, competition and wage labor were luxuries that capitalism could afford itself only after the long process of extensive commodification of society. But capitalism is grounded most fundamentally on monopoly enterprise and the enslavement of labor.

3   During the early 19th century, many in the US answered European criticism of it being a slave state by avowing that to be free, one had to control others, and since white people controlled slaves most absolutely, they were the world's freest. [Tise] From 1870 to 1965, the legislative and electoral systems both depended on a variety of mechanisms for disenfranchising black and brown people. For a description

of how the process of disenfranchisement of black people produced a two party system, see Martinot 2003, chap. 2.

4   The Taney Supreme Court first granted citizenship to corporations in *Louisville, Cincinnati, and Charleston Railroad vs. Letson* in 1844. The Santa Clara case in 1886 then extended the 14th Amendment to corporate rights. Cf. Austen Allen, *The Origins of the Dred Scott Case*. The latest extension of corporate personhood rights is in *Humanitarian Law Project vs. Holder* of 2010.

5   This was the fate of the Mexican economy after its 1910 revolution, only partial modified by Lazaro Cardenas's nationalizations. [Hugh Thomas] It is the situation in Kenya that Ngugi wa-Thiongo describes in his many books. And it has happened in post-Apartheid South Africa. [Pilger] It is a process that various papers in this volume present.

6   In this description, I am indebted to Isaac Saney, both his book and personal conversation, and to the writings of Peter Roman. But also to my own personal experience in Cuba, having visited a number of times.

Chapter 9

THE POSSIBILITY OF DEMOCRATIC POLITICS IN A GLOBALIZED STATE

Cliff DuRand

Surely by now there can be few here who still believe
the purpose of government is to protect us from the destructive
activities of corporations. At last most of us must understand
that the opposite is true: that the primary purpose of
government is to protect those who run the economy
from the outrage of injured citizens.
—Derrick Jensen
Endgame: Volume 1: The Problem of Civilization

In the fall of 2011 Occupy Wall Street sparked a long awaited social movement against financial capital in the U.S. Widespread public indignation at a state-led bailout of failed banks that stuck the taxpayers with the bill while all but abandoning underwater homeowners, this gross injustice finally found its voice in the Occupy Wall Street protests. A wave of outrage swept the country that bailouts and tax breaks were doled out for billionaires while austerity was imposed on the rest of us. There were other issues that fed the indignation as well: the downward mobility being experienced by those who had once fancied themselves as "middle class,"* three decades of outsourcing of jobs to low wage countries, the declining access to higher education that left those who did go to college with futures mortgaged by heavy student loans, a dysfunctional political system unable to address pressing social problems, a prison system that is the largest in the world and urban police forces for whom brutality against people of color has become standard operating procedure. And that's just a short list of what outraged a sizable portion of the population.

But why didn't this popular outrage have a voice in the elected representatives in the state structure—national leaders who profess to speak for the nation? In a genuine democracy one would expect as much. It took a protest movement to give this public discontent a public voice. Most USians, even those who believe in the system, feel themselves unrepresented. Why is this?

In its spirit and style, if not its demands, OWS was inspired by the Arab Spring. But those popular protests were against totalitarian governments. Wasn't the US different? Or was it maybe that the US had become what Sheldon S. Wolin boldly called an "inverted totalitarianism" in which economic and state powers were conjoined, but with more subtle control measures than found in classical totalitarianism?[1]

Almost all of the US public used to believe that their country was a democracy. Most of the world's peoples saw it that way too. That is no longer the case. It has become increasingly obvious that the US political elite is unresponsive to the views and interests of the majority of the people they claim to represent. Instead they represent the interests of the wealthy and their corporations whom they claim are too big to fail. As the popular

---

*The term 'middle class' is an ideological concept more than an empirical category. It is not the name of a class, but at best refers to the location of a class somewhere in the middle. Early in US history it was called the middling class. It referred to those who were not poor, but not (yet) rich. It referred to those who had the hope to be able to move up in the social hierarchy. Basically then being middle class meant the possibility of upward mobility. For a society to have a sizable middle class in this sense was seen as conducive to political stability. Ideologically being middle class (as measured by certain patterns of consumption) meant you were above the working class. The increasing downward mobility now becoming common for such people exposes the myth of the middle class. It reveals the reality that they were actually working class all along. As the middle class collapses as a result of globalization the class dynamics of capitalist societies changes drastically.

classes find themselves unrepresented, the system encounters a crisis of legitimacy.

In fact, the normal political process of access to state decision making that one might expect in a democracy has never been open to ordinary citizens. The US has had a long history of the wealthy shaping political power. Even an objective conservative commentator like Kevin Phillips has addressed the fact that throughout our history the nation's rich and politically powerful have worked to create and perpetuate privilege at the expense of the national interest and at the expense of the classes beneath them.[2] And there is an equally long history of popular struggles against wealth and power, as documented by radical historian Howard Zinn.[3] Indeed, sociologist Robert Bellah has argued that "The most important unresolved problem in American history [is] the tension between self-reliant competitive enterprise and a sense of public solidarity."[4] It is this tension between capitalism and democracy that has erupted once again in an open class war since the late 1970s. As Warren Buffett told *The New York Times* in 2006, "There's class warfare, all right, but it's my class, the rich class, that's making war, and we're winning."[5] It is only now, after 30 years of escalating attacks on working people that we are beginning to see a growing popular fightback.

People are just now waking up to that reality. Finding their concerns excluded from the political process, they find their voice in a social movement that is outside that process. Just as in earlier struggles for popular justice, social movements are the voice of democracy.

At this moment in our national history, there is considerable hostility toward the US government from among the citizenry. This comes from both the far Right as well as the Left. I submit this is for much the same reason, viz. the realization that government is not representing the people. This realization is grounded in familiar social policies that are widely unpopular. The 2008-09 financial bailout of the banks while leaving ordinary people stranded demonstrated that government was on the side of the rich, not on our side. It was not *our* government, a government *for* the people. It was a government for the wealthy. Similarly, government promotion of neoliberal trade policies in NAFTA-like agreements has benefited transnational capital while depriving US workers of their hard won living standard, their benefits and often their jobs. This is not *our* government, a government *for* the people. It is a government for the corporations. Then we saw state governments stripping their workers of bargaining rights, destroying the collective power of unions while giving tax breaks to corporations. This is not *our* government, a government *for* the people. It is a government for the corporations. I could go on with multiple examples that are making it clearer and clearer that in the class war, our governing political elite is not on our side, it is serving the interests of the wealthy, especially the top fraction of the 1%.

A Government Designed to be Undemocratic

If we are to get to the roots of the problem and invent radical solutions, solutions that pull up those roots, we need to recognize that the reason we now find government so undemocratic is because from its beginning it was designed to be undemocratic. It was designed to protect the wealthy against the common man. James Madison, chief architect of the US Constitution, made this abundantly clear in *The Federalist Papers* #10. He wrote there:

> Democracies have ever been ... incompatible with ... rights of property .... The interest in a majority ... must be *prevented* ... [because it would threaten] the unequal distribution of property. Those who hold and those who are without property have ever formed distinct interests in society ... and divide them into different *classes*. [emphasis added]

Living in a society already divided into propertied classes and those with little or no property, Madison and his co-conspirators sought to fashion political institutions whereby 1) the interests of the ruling class could be protected and 2) the multitude would not be allowed to prevail where that might injure the rights of others, particularly the property rights of the wealthy. The Founding Fathers who gathered in Philadelphia in 1787 were moved by what one delegate called "the excess of democracy" represented in the demands of indebted and heavily taxed yeoman farmers and mechanics. Another complained that things had become "too democratic." And so this gathering of merchants, slave owners and manufacturers resolved "to create a more perfect union." Indeed, the Constitutional Convention amounted to a conspiracy of the propertied classes to create a system of federal government strong enough to protect them from those in the popular classes, and yet weak enough not to itself be a danger to their interests. What was devised was a division of powers that at times would create gridlock and a system of representation that would make difficult the formation of a united popular will.

As Sheldon Wolin has pointed out, Madison in *Federalist Paper #51* took comfort from the fact that

> the geographical expanse, ideological differences and socioeconomic complexity of the new system would splinter the demos—'the society... broken into so many parts, interests and classes of citizens'—and thereby prevent it *permanently* from gaining the unity of purpose necessary to concert its numerical power and dominate all branches of government.[6]

The Constitution framed not a democracy but the removal of a supposedly sovereign people from government. Madison congratulated himself and his co-conspirators for their success in removing the people from the councils of government, ensuring that it would remain in the hands of those whom he deemed better qualified.

The resulting system of governance proved to be remarkably enduring under a continuous constitutional rule lasting well over two centuries. There have been democratic moments in that history, but its chief virtue lies in establishing a political system of representationism by which legitimate power can be passed from one part of the elite to another in an orderly way. Its essence is found in contested elections and in the deliberations among the representatives chosen thereby. The role of the people is to choose from among a political elite those representatives who are to rule them; the role of elections is simply to produce a government. Once this is done, we have discharged our civic responsibility as citizens and we are expected to return to the affairs of our private lives. While claiming to be a theory of democracy, this polyarchy (as political scientists have dubbed it) is actually an elitist theory of democracy, a kind of low intensity democracy at best. As Joseph Schumpeter put it, democracy simply means that "the people have the opportunity of accepting or refusing the men who are to rule them."[7] Wolin has called it a managed democracy. By whatever name, it is a far cry from the classical concept of democracy expressed in the original meaning of the Greek word—the rule or power, *kratia*, of the people, *demos*. Democracy means people's power, not the legitimating of elite rule.

So, the function of the US political system is to protect wealth against people's power. In the late 18th century wealth was in the hands of landowners and merchants. A century later new wealth came to be concentrated in corporations. The war for independence had been a struggle not only against the king of England, but also against the corporate bodies England had chartered and which enjoyed vast power over the colonies. Recall, the Boston Tea Party was a protest against the East India Company. As a result, the newly independent country was deeply suspicious of the corporate form of property. Corporations were carefully limited. They were to be chartered by state legislatures for specific purposes deemed in the public good for a limited period of time and could be dissolved if they failed to fulfill that purpose.[8] But with the industrial revolution and the building of the railroads, corporations became increasingly powerful economically as well as politically. As early as 1864 President Abraham Lincoln saw what was coming. In a letter to Col. William F. Elkins, he wrote:

> I see in the near future a crisis approaching that unnerves me and causes me to tremble for the safety of my country ... corporations have been enthroned and an era of corruption in high places will follow, and the money power of the country will endeavor to prolong its reign by working upon the prejudices of the people until all wealth is aggregated in a few hands and the Republic is destroyed.[9]

Before century's end Lincoln's fears had been born out. Now, another century later, those corporations have grown enormously and transnationalized beyond the confines of mere nation-states. At the same time capitalism has financialized, with its center of economic power in the hands of gigantic banks. Another prophetic voice from our past, Thomas Jefferson, warned of this danger in an 1802 letter to Treasury Secretary Albert Gallatin:

> I believe that banking institutions are more dangerous to our liberties than standing armies. If the American people ever allow private banks to control the issue of their currency, [...] the banks and corporations that will grow up around them will deprive the people of all property until their children wake up homeless on the continent their Fathers conquered.[10]

The polyarchic political system enshrined in the US Constitution has served well for a transnationalized capital in need of state power to establish a global system in the interests of capital while not being unduly burdened by obligations to a national population. It has been conducive to the transformation of a nation-state into a globalized state.

Participatory Democracy: The Core of the Democratic Ideal

In 2008 we saw in the U.S. an invigorated electorate focused on replacing the imperial presidency of a globalized state with a new leader who promised change. And although he came into office in the midst of a structural crisis in the economy—a circumstance that offered a unique opportunity for far reaching changes—the new administration sought to operate within the existing institutional structures of power. By all appearances, President Obama came into office as a community organizer. But once inside the capital beltway, he proceeded to govern within the established parameters of the elite. As a result all he was able to do was rescue financial institutions from their self-inflicted crisis. By relying on an existing political process that excluded popular participation, he not only demonstrated the dysfunctionality of that process for representing the popular will, he also demonstrated the extent to which one's position in the structure, be it governmental, corporate, or security, conditions even to the point of determining what one thinks, does and even accepts as ethical. By embracing the imperial role of the dominant globalized state, Obama also perpetuated an imperial presidency. The fundamental lesson is clear: an undemocratic polyarchy will be able to continue to rule until popular protest transforms the political and economic institutions and brings popular classes into power.

Throughout our history there have been periodic democratic moments when the power of the people has found voice. The labor movement of the 1930s and the civil rights and anti-war movements of the 1960s come to mind as high points of democracy in our lifetime. Those decades of heightened political participation, social protest and citizen engagement in public affairs were among the democratic moments in our history. Social movements made demands on the ruling elites, demands for economic empowerment, for racial equality, for peace, for social justice, demands that the institutions of government address pressing social problems. The spirit of citizen engagement was articulated in the call for a more *participatory* democracy by the Students for a Democratic Society's Port Huron statement:

> As a social system we seek the establishment of a democracy of individual participation, governed by two central aims: that the individual share in those social decisions determining the quality and direction of his life; that society be organized to encourage independence in men and provide the media for their common participation.[11]

This is a fundamentally different concept of democracy, one that resonates from deeply held American values. Rather than seeing citizens as passive subjects to be ruled by elites, it advocates active participation in all those decisions that affect one's life. This extends not just to government, but also education, the workplace, the family, neighborhoods—all of those spheres, both public and private, in which we live our daily lives. It is a call for all the institutions of society to be made more democratically participatory.

It is this concept of participatory democracy that I want to set against the dominant polyarchic elitist theory as better expressing the core of the democratic ideal. To return to my initial point, the present disillusionment with government reflects the realization that we have a system of elite rule that cannot represent the people. This is what we see in the rise of the Tea Party. This ersatz social movement is largely a creation of the economically powerful and their political operatives in their class war against the popular classes. But by drawing on the deeply rooted culture of self reliant individualism, they have transformed anger against a government that in fact protects the rich rather than the people, into an anger against government itself. Rather than seeking to make government into an instrument of a popular will against the rich, they seek to neuter the powers of government. This would free the rich from any democratic restraints. It is a brilliant strategy that at the time generated a right wing populism in the absence of an alternative Progressive populism.

Occupy Wall Street is a long awaited genuine social movement that has redirected this popular anger against financial capital rather than government. Overall, its as yet uncrystalized program proclaims: it's the economic system, stupid! The problem in Washington is that it has too long been occupied by Wall Street. Now a Progressive populism has refocused on the root key indicator of the problem—the concentration of wealth. The root of the problem is capitalism

At the same time it has modeled the kind of participatory democracy that it offers as an alternative to the hierarchical process of a polyarchy. The decision making process developed by the protestors occupying Zuccotti Park is a reinvention of the direct democracy advocated in the 18th century by philosopher Jean-Jacques Rousseau.[12] Rousseau spoke of a community of equals coming together under the shade of a large oak tree to discuss and make the decisions that will govern their life together. The occupiers have created a community of struggle. Their invention of the people's microphone makes it possible to have an assembly larger than a single oak tree could shade. All can participate in the discussion themselves either in the direct assembly or the smaller groups. The discussion is consensus-seeking, made possible by the existence of a common-unity (i.e. community).

As Rousseau pointed out, the best decisions are those that are unanimous, or at least nearly so. That is because such decisions are self-enforcing since each has willed them in their own heart. The strength of this process is that the decision has high legitimacy, even for those who had not agreed (but not so strongly as to block consensus). Another thing that the process illustrates is that democracy is a full time affair, even with the technological advantage of amplification which makes discussion in a large group proceed more efficiently.

What we see in Occupy Wall Street is what we find in all social movements—a people coming out of their seriality as separate individual atoms and becoming part of a collective entity that can act autonomously for a common good. And that is what democracy is all about... and what makes it so dangerous for elites who fear the power of the people united.

So what then is democracy? Here's my working definition: Democracy is the possibility of joint decision making for collective action in the common good. Let me unpack that a bit. It is not just individuals deciding for themselves, it is individuals as members of a body engaging in a joint decision making process with others. That involves dialogue with others and voting on what they agree to do. And what they agree to do then becomes a collective action by the whole. The agreement seeks to promote a common good, not just that of a part of the body. Of course, that does not mean that some may not benefit more than others. But that is allowed only if it is believed to contribute to a larger common good. So democracy is the possibility of that taking place—*the possibility of joint decision making for collective action in the common good.*

Democracy thus means the people doing for themselves collectively what they cannot do for themselves individually. In Lincoln's words, it is government of the people, by the people and for the people. A democratic government is the *instrument* of the will of the people. It is the means by which they carry out their decisions. The spirit of a democracy is not hostile to government—as long as government is an expression of the popular will.

A Crisis of Democracy or a Crisis of Polyarchy?

The last great upsurge of democratic aspirations was in the social movements of the 1960s. It is instructive to observe the response of the political elite to this upsurge of popular democracy. Did they welcome the citizenry's eagerness to take responsibility for their lives? No, they feared it. They called it "a crisis of democracy", "an excess of democracy", that was making society "ungovernable" —i.e., no longer under *their* control.

I kid you not. These were the very words of an influential 1975 report by a blue ribbon group of social scientists to the Trilateral Commission. Titled "The Crisis of Democracy" their report took a hard look at what it considered a growing problem of governability in the major countries of North America, Europe and Japan—the Triad of advanced capitalism. Samuel P. Huntington, dean of political science in the U.S. and frequent consultant to federal government departments, analyzed the situation in the US. What Huntington saw was a kind of "democratic distemper" as people demanded more of government while at the same time challenging established authority. "People no longer felt the same compulsion to obey those whom they had previously considered superior to themselves in age, rank, status, expertise, character, or talents."[13] Government was "overloaded" by the popular demands placed on it. In a moment of unusual candor, Huntington said, "the effective operation of a democratic political system usually requires some measure of apathy and noninvolvement on the part of some individuals and groups."[14] When too many people participate too much, there is a "breakdown of democracy."

Huntington recognized that a little democracy can be a dangerous thing. With polyarchy the elite grants the people the right to vote. The danger is that that might lead them to think they also should be making the decisions. Huntington attributed the "distemper of democracy" to the periodic "creedal passion" that afflicts the electorate. That occurs when the people get carried away by their democratic values to the extent where they want to actually participate in decision making. Of course, that is a danger only to the elites who have reserved that role to themselves.

What the "breakdown of democracy" actually amounts to is a loss of social control by an elite no longer able to contain popular participation within the safe, controlled limits of electoral politics. The "crisis of democracy" is actually the crisis of polyarchy. As one critical Canadian commentator put it, "the whole discussion of governability... was of concern only to an elite uneasy about its declining position in society!"[15]

What Huntington and other defenders of polyarchy worried about as a "breakdown of democracy" was really the breakdown of elite social control. Polyarchy values stability as a fundamental social value, that is, as long as it is stable rule by an elite. As Huntington put it elsewhere, "The maintenance of democratic politics [i.e. polyarchy] and the reconstruction of the social order [i.e. popular social change] are fundamentally incompatible."[16] In other words, democracy is not about the popular will, where the people are directing the course of their common affairs, it is about containing that will under elite control. As we have seen, that is a concern that goes all the way back to the founding fathers of the American republic in the US.

That this is a perversion of the concept of democracy as popularly understood can be seen if we look at the relation between the state and civil society in a genuinely democratic society. *Civil society* consists of all those consensual social relationships citizens have with one another, from trade unions, political parties and voluntary associations to the family. Since de Tocqueville it has been recognized that a vital associational life is essential to a healthy democracy; it is this civil society that links government to the individual citizens and keeps it accountable. In effect, the state becomes an extension of civil society in the sense that it reflects its orientations. Ultimately power rests in civil society. That is what the sovereignty of the people means. That, at least, is the democratic ideal.

In polyarchy however, civil society becomes an extension of the state. That is, it is through its penetration and cooptation or even creation of the components of civil society that the elite garners the consent of the people to its rule and thereby achieves governability. This idea of the extended state is the key to Antonio Gramsci's understanding of hegemony. 'Hegemony' refers to the consensual domination by an elite whereby its rule is accepted as legitimate. Effective rule cannot be just "from above." It depends on structuring civil society down below so as to support the state. *Polyarchy then involves elite rule through an extension of the state into civil society. Popular democracy, on the other hand, involves an extension of an autonomous civil society into the state.*[17]

It is this understanding that has guided U.S. efforts to promote its kind of democracy around the world. Allying itself with friendly elites and patterning 'democracy' after its own political system, what the U.S. has been fostering worldwide is actually polyarchy. Over the last three decades a leading feature of U.S. policy in the Third World as well as in the former Second World of Eastern Europe and Russia has been aid for political development. This has involved extensive efforts to create and promote civil society. But this development of civil society has been geared to promoting leaders, organizations and values supportive of U.S. interests. It has done this as a means to forestall social change from popular social movements. As sociologist William I. Robinson has argued in his insightful book *Promoting Polyarchy*,

> US 'democracy promotion,' as it actually functions, sets about not just to secure and stabilize elite-based polyarchic systems but to have the United States and local elites thoroughly penetrate civil society, and *from therein* assure control over popular mobilization and mass movements."[18]

It is through this elite penetration of civil society that social stability is assured, abroad as well as at home. Polyarchy promotion might more accurately be described as democracy prevention, i.e. prevention of popular democracy.

Preventing Economic Democracy

One of the key things that polyarchic elites seek to protect from popular democracy is economic power. It is not just the political power and privileges of a governing elite that is to be protected; it is the property of the capitalist class whose interests they must serve. Why is this? It's not just that political figures require large sums from wealthy supporters to acquire elective office; this requirement has been deployed and maintained as a tactic to ensure elite control of the process. More fundamentally, it is because the interests of capital rule in a society where they own the financial and productive resources of society to which the well being of all others is linked. That's what it means to be a ruling class. The interests of capital rule and the interests of all other dependent classes can be met only if the interests of capital are met. That's why governing elites must act to protect and promote the interests of capital if they are to fulfill their function of preserving the social order. They have to protect corporate capital because it is too big to fail.

While there is this link between the political and the economic spheres in capitalism, at the same time they are separate spheres. Capitalists qua capitalists do not themselves usually govern. In this respect capitalism is different from previous social formations like feudalism. In feudalism economic and political power were combined in the same 'class', the nobility. In capitalism these are separated.

The separation of the economic sphere from the political sphere in capitalist society has far reaching implications. On the one hand, it has made possible the legal equality of all citizens regardless of race, gender, class or other social characteristics. This formal leveling individualizes citizens and detaches citizenship from any social or communal identity. That is what is democratic about it. But at the same time, it also disempowers citizens qua citizens from any real control over their economic fate insofar as it inhibits their systemic ability to counter capital's domination of the political system which permits it to shape law and policy to its advantage. In this way democracy is limited by the separation of the political and economic spheres. In feudal society these spheres were united. The political power of the nobility enabled them to extract value from the commoners who were excluded from political participation. By separating the economic sphere, capitalism is able to extend the rights of citizenship to commoners while at the same time denying them economic power. "Capitalism, then, made it possible to conceive of 'formal democracy', a form of civic equality which could coexist with social inequality and leave economic relations... in place."[19]

It is this separation that popular democracy threatens to breach. The interests of popular classes, once unleashed, are in conflict with those of capital. People seek higher wages, not lower. They seek free health care, not purchased health care through the insurance business; they seek free education, secure pensions and development of public infrastructure. All of these are excluded from the costs models of capital. Consequently, social movements are likely to use the political power they create against the economic power of capital to determine the priorities of the state. Even modest demands for limiting the negative effects of the market on people's lives in the name of social justice can appear as unacceptably radical to capital and the elites that represent it. This is seen as an excess of democracy.

What I have called the globalized state is the model toward which the state tends to evolve under conditions of neoliberal globalization. In its pure form a fully globalized state would be what Martinot calls an administrative state, i.e. one devoid of democratic politics. My argument is that as long as a nation, i.e. a people with a collective identity, still exists, and as long as a sub-global governing unit such as the state is needed to rule over a territory and its population, there is a constraint on such an evolution. A globalizing state either needs to establish a degree of legitimacy for the sake of governability or it will need to utilize instruments of coercion to maintain its rule over a subject population.

Why is that? It is because fundamentally the interests of transnational capital which neoliberalism promotes are contradictory to the interests of the populations of nations, even in their ethnic and class diversity and heterogeneity. This originally arises from the contradiction between capital and labor under capitalism. Only it is made more severe by the globalization of capital which severely limits the benefits that labor could win from capital so long as it was national in character. Once capital is no longer confined to a national economy, then the contradiction between it and the working class along with other popular classes (the petty bourgeoisie and even surviving elements of national capital) becomes more evident. American workers may complain about the export of their jobs to China or Mexico, American Congress people may rail against these countries or their citizens to score political points, but at the end of the day a realization will sink in that the corporations chose to go abroad to pursue their own interests, and manipulated the laws of states to make it possible. It is thus that a democratic politics encompassing an alliance of popular classes and groups around a shared national identity, the 99%, becomes possible. Essentially it amounts to a struggle for a democratic retrieval of the state from transnational capital, and refocusing it on domestic interests.

We Need to Change Our Political Institutions

But a retrieval of the state requires a transformation of the state. The institutional structure of the nation-state was designed to exclude the popular classes from governance. That is why democratic struggle cannot be limited to changing state personnel. It must also change its institutional structure, as we have seen in Venezuela and Cuba. The lesson in all this has been clearly expressed by the Zapatistas in Mexico who have emphasized that democratic politics is not possible within the political space of a globalized state, but requires a reconstituting of political institutions from within civil society.[20]

In the broad sweep of history the invention of the nation-state, at first in Europe and then imposed elsewhere by European colonialism, had opened the way conceptually for a democratization of politics. Its realization would require long historical struggles by popular classes, a process still underway today. But by attaching state institutions to national identities by promoting a sense of a collective identity on the national level (in addition to or irrespective of diverse identities of the different ethnic groups that inhabit the state territory), a collective agency was brought into political processes previously reserved for elites. This eventually impacted the concept of sovereignty. While initially conceived as residing in the state (as it had earlier resided in the monarch), the outcome of the revolution for independence by England's American colonies was that the new state was seen as the product of the People. And it was in that People—the new *American* nation—that sovereignty rested.

Of course, in fact elites continued to rule. The republican form of government constructed for the United States was designed to prevent popular democracy. Nevertheless, government derived its legitimacy from the consent of the governed. And so the political terrain, but not necessarily the political institutions, was opened up to the collective will of the nation. The Constitution constructed a managed democracy designed to protect elite rule from a democratic public. However, the legitimacy of the system required that the people *believe* that they rule. And so the elite told them that they did. As a result the political terrain became a contested terrain where, when popular forces struggled unsuccessfully to have their will represented in the counsels of that elite, democracy came to reside not so much in the political institutions themselves as in the popular struggles. Democracy is found not so much in the halls of Congress as in the streets.

It was thus that the nation-state opened the way to a deepened concept of democracy. The very concept of a nation presupposes the collective agency of that people. It is that collective agency that makes common action possible. Without it there is nothing but disconnected, powerless individuals in a seriality. It is the sense of mutual connection that facilitates elite rule through the agency of the state. Of course the collective agency that makes democracy possible seldom involves *all* of the nation. But the democratic ideal speaks in the name of the nation as a whole, articulating a common good. It is thus that mass social movements are born, to recapture what may be seen as having been lost. What may begin as an effort to promote a particular interest can grow into a massive social movement only if it is able to articulate values or interests that are universal for the society. This is the democratic politics of a nation. And it comes more often from popular classes than from the political elite.

Improving on Madison's design, the globalization of the state offers a new prophylactic to democracy. Now it is "the market" and "global competitiveness" and "the rules of free trade" that have been inserted to prevent democracy. The citizenry is told that they can no longer protect themselves from predatory practices of foreign corporations because their representatives entered into treaties that protect "investor rights" against the democratic will of the people, and enabled the free flow of capital, thereby facilitating capital and corporate flight. Workers are told that they must surrender hard won wage and benefit agreements so their employers can remain competitive in the world market, or so the company will not ship their jobs abroad to a low wage country. Austerity is imposed on the people in order to assure "investor confidence", a code word that conceals the fact that the vote of the wealthy in financial markets trumps the people's vote. It is against such betrayals of the national interest, it is against this treason by the state that democratic struggles must be directed.

A globalized state has a chronic legitimacy problem. In a nation-state with a polyarchic political system, elections can confer some legitimacy on the rulers. But when the state functions to promote the interests of transnational capital rather than those of its own people, then elections lose their meaning. What does it matter who you vote for, if all your representatives are compelled to tread the same path—no matter what they vowed to you prior to polling day?

Popular democracy must be more than protest against elite policies or disruption of the institutions through which they rule. Protest is a beginning of the formation of an autonomous civil society, a counter hegemony from below. But as long as the politico-legal structure of polyarchy remains in place, the power to make the big decisions will remain with the elite. Popular forces may succeed in driving elites to seek more secure locations in which to meet and 15 million people may protest worldwide against their wars, but they still control the institutional tools that give them the power to decide and impose their decisions on the rest of us. We can only affect their decisions at the margins, limiting time and place perhaps, but not altering their course. Especially popular social movements of protest may even win some policy changes (expanding the scope of official justice), but when those movements disband, as they always do eventually, their gains will likely be eroded over time.

Popular democracy must be more than this if it is to realize the values suggested by the original Greek word meaning the rule or power, *kratos*, of the people, *demos*. Democracy means people's power. It means participating in the decisions that affect ones life, as the New Left put it back in the 1960s. It is the vision of *popular participation in collective decision making about collective action for a common good*.

We do not yet have a theory of participatory democracy. But we do have valuable practice of it in various social movements. In popular struggles democracy is being constantly reinvented as we saw in the Occupy Wall Street general assemblies. As demonstrators chant "This is what democracy looks like!" they are affirming that it is the collective action of expressing a common will that is the essence of democracy. In addition to episodic protests, there are more institutionalized examples of participatory democracy. The participatory budgeting practiced in Porte Alegre in Brazil and the community councils in Venezuela are vehicles for community decision making on the use of local public funds. Similarly, the members assemblies of cooperatives are exercises in direct democracy.[21] But it is more difficult to link these democratic practices at the national level. Martinot's discussion of the role of mass organizations in national decision making in Cuba offers one model of institutionalized popular participation. But even then it is difficult to sustain a sense of meaningful participation when the popular input of 11 million persons finally gets synthesized in a single decision.

A sense of meaningful participation at the individual level is needed to sustain motivation for continuing participation. This is more easily sustained at a local level. A collective identity is fruitful in this regard. When individuals identify with a collective larger than self—be it a cooperative, a class, an ethnic group, a religion, a nation or whatever—then its action becomes viewed as my action. That collective is a part of who I am and so what it does is mine. It is then that collective autonomy empowers individual freedom.

It is through the collective action of social movements that today we have a sense that a more democratic world is possible. We have come to a consciousness of our interconnectedness, not just on the personal level but also on the social and even global levels. This gives us a common interest in the possibility of finding a common good. The individualized decisions that operate in the market fragment us into powerless consumers. The neoliberal program massifies us, making us passive objects of the polyarchic elite. The struggles for social justice of today's social movements are the birth pains of a new participatory democracy that will emerge from the womb of our present world with at least an alternative political culture expressed through alternative political structures. Everywhere participatory democracy is on the march as we the people take up the class war.

There have been democratic moments throughout the history of the US. The degree of democracy at any moment depends on the relative power of capital and the popular classes. For example, the power of capital was at a zenith in the 1920s until the economic system collapsed into a great depression. In desperation, social movements arose demanding that their government protect their interests in the name of social justice.

The political elite responded with the New Deal programs in hopes of saving capitalism from itself. That was a democratic moment In our history. That was the beginnings of an American social democracy. But capital was never altogether happy with its decline in class power under the social liberalism that predominated for nearly a half century. Thus when it encountered its limits in the stagflation of the 1970s, it sought to recover class power by a strategy of globalization and curtailment of the New Deal and Great Society programs. It was able to do so due to the absence of the countervailing power of social movements.

Now we have reached another turn of the screw as capitalism has arrived at another crisis born of its own contradictions. Are we at another turning point where a democratic upsurge of social movements will force a correction upon capital? And if so, will this one save the system from itself once again or will it pull up the roots of the problem, creating a new system that finally resolves the contradiction between capitalism and democracy that has marked the modern era? The answer is up to us. We must remember the words of Frederick Douglass: "Power concedes nothing without a demand. It never has and it never will."

Venceremos!

ENDNOTES

1   Sheldon S. Wolin, *Democracy Inc.: Managed Democracy and the Specter of Inverted Totalitarianism* (Princeton University Press, 2008)

2   Kevin Phillips, *Wealth and Democracy: A Political History of the American Rich* (New York: Broadway Books, 2002)

3   Howard Zinn, *A Peoples History of the United States: 1492 to Present* (New York: Harper, 2005 expanded edition).

4   Robert N. Bellah, Richard Madsen, William M. Sullivan, Ann Swidler, and Steven M. Tipton, *Habits of the Heart: Individualism and Commitment in American Life* (University of California Press, 1985 & 1996) p.256

5   November Issue

6   Wolin, supra endnote 1.

7   Joseph A. Schumpeter, *Capitalism, Socialism and Democracy* (Harper and Row, 1975), p. 285.

8   Cf. *Defying Corporations, Defining Democracy*, Dean Ritz, ed. (New York: Apex Press, 2001).

9   *The Lincoln Encyclopedia*, Archer H. Shaw, ed. (New York: Macmillan 1950). Cf. also http://www.ratical.org/corporations/Lincoln.html

10   Attributed to Thomas Jefferson, a critical history of this quote can be found at http://www.monticello.org/site/jefferson/private-banks-quotation

11   Students for a Democratic Society, *The Port Huron Statement*, 1964.

12   You can witness this process in action at http://www.youtube.com/watch?v=6dtD8RnGaRQ&feature=player_embedded

13   Michel Crozier, Samuel P. Huntington, Joji Watanuki, *The Crisis of Democracy: Report on the Governability of Democracies to the Trilateral Commission*, (New York: New York University Press, 1975), p. 75.

14   *Ibid.*, p. 114.

15   *Ibid.*, p. 206.

16   Samuel P. Huntington, "The Modest Meaning of Democracy," in Robert A. Pastor, *Democracy in the Americas: Stopping the Pendulum* (Teaneck, NJ: Holmes and Meier, 1989), p. 24.

17   Cf. William I. Robinson, *Promoting Polyarchy: Globalization, US Intervention, and Hegemony* (Oxford: Oxford University Press, 1996), p. 58

18   Robinson, *op. cit.*, p. 69.

19   Ellen Meiksins Wood, *Democracy Against Capitalism* (Cambridge: Cambridge University Press, 1995), pp. 208-213.

20   EZLN, "Sixth Declaration of the Lacandon Jungle", 2005 http://www.globaljusticecenter.org/2012/01/15/the-sixth-declaration/

21   Michael Lebowitz has argued persuasively for the importance of such processes in human development in *The Socialist Alternative: Real Human Development* (New York: Monthly Review Press, 2010). Cf. my review in *Socialism and Democracy*, Vol. 25, No. 2 (July 2011), pp. 188-191.

RESOURCES

BOOKS & ARTICLES

Samir Amin. *Accumulation on a World Scale: A Critique of the Theory of Underdevelopment*. (Monthly Review Press, 1974).

Anatole Anton, Milton Fisk, Nancy Holmstrom, eds. *Not For Sale: In Defense of Public Goods.* (Westview Press, 2000).

Benedict Anderson. *Imagined Communities: Reflections on the Origin and Spread of Nationalism*. (Verso, 1983 and 2006).

Juan José Arévalo, *The Shark and the Sardines*, trans. June Cobb and Raul Osegueda (L. Stuart, 1961).

Arnold August. Democracy in Cuba and the 1997-98 Elections. (Editorial Jose Marti, 1999).

Peter Bachrach. *The Theory of Democratic Elitism: A Critique.* (Little Brown, 1967).

Antonio Carmona Baez. *State Resistance to Globalisation in Cuba*. (Pluto Press, 2004).

Richard Barnet and Ronald Muller. *Global Reach: the Power of the Multinational Corporations*. (Simon and Schuster, 1974).

Carleton Beals. *Latin America: World in Revolution.* (Abelard-Schuman, 1963)

Jose Bell Lara. *Globalization and the Cuban Revolution.* (Editorial Jose Marti, 2002).

_____. *Cuba: Socialism Within Globalization.* (Editorial Jose Marti, 2008).

Berch Berberogulu. *Globalization of Capital and the Nation-State: Imperialism, Class Struggle, and the State in the Age of Global Capitalism.* (Rowman and Littlefield, 2003).

C. Fred Bergsten. *Toward an New International Economic Order.* (Lexington Books, 1975).

_____. *Managing International Economic Interdependence* (Lexington Books, 1977).

Fidel Castro. *The World Economic and Social Crisis*. (Cuban Council of State,

1983).

____. *Capitalism in Crisis: Globalization and World Politics Today.* (Ocean Press, 2000).

Graciela Chailloux Laffita, et. al. eds. *Globalization and Cuba-U.S. Conflict.* (Editorial Jose Marti, 1999).

Christopher Chase-Dunn. *Global Formation: Structures of the World-Economy.* (Basil Blackwell, 1989)

Noam Chomsky. *Profit Over People: Neoliberalism and Global Order.* (Seven Stories Press, 1999).

Armando Cristobal Perez. *El Estado-Nacion: Su Origen y Construccion: Un Tema de Metapolitologia.* (Editorial de Cienias Sociales, 2008).

Kevin Danaher. *Corporations are Gonna Get Your Mama: Globalization and the Downsizing of the American Dream.* (Common Courage Press, 1996).

Cliff DuRand. "The Exhaustion of Neoliberalism in Mexico", *Confronting Global Neoliberalism: Third World Resistance and Development Strategies,* Richard Westra, ed. (Clarity Press, 2010).

Jeff Faux. *Global Class War.* (John Wiley, 2006).

____. *The Service Economy: The Future of the Middle Class.* (John Wiley, 2012)

Milton Fisk. *The State and Justice: An Essay in Political Theory.* (Cambridge University Press, 1989).

Andre Gunder Frank. *Capitalism and Underdevelopment in Latin America.* (Monthly Review Press, 1969).

____. *Latin America: Underdevelopment or Revolution.* (Monthly Review Press, 1969).

____. *Lumpen-Bourgeoisie and Lumpen-Development: Dependency, Class, and Politics in Latin America.* (Monthly Review Press, 1972).

Thomas Frank. *One Market Under God: Extreme Capitalism, Market Populism, and the End of Economic Democracy* (Doubleday, 2000).

John Gerassi. *The Great Fear in Latin America.* (Collier Books, 1965).

Peter Gowan. *The Global Gamble: Washington's Faustian Bid for World Dominance,* Verso, 1999.

Duncan Green. *Silent Revolution: The Rise and Crisis of Market Economics in Latin America.* (Monthly Review Press, 2003).

Jerry Harris. *The Dialectics of Globalization: Economic and Political Conflict in a Transnational World.* (Cambridge Scholars Publishing, 2008).

____. *The Nation in the Global Era: Conflict and Transformation.* (Brill, 2009).

Michael Hardt and Antonio Negri. *Empire.* (Harvard University Press, 2000).

David Harvey. *The New Imperialism.* (Oxford University Press, 2003).

____. *A Brief History of Neoliberalism.* (Oxford University Press, 2005).

____. *The Limits of Capital.* (Verso: 2006).

____. *The Enigma of Capital and the Crises of Capitalism.* (Oxford University Press, 2010).

Helga Hernes. *Multinational Corporations.* (Gale Research, 1977).

Eric Hershberg & Fred Rosen, eds. *Latin America After Neoliberalism: Turning the Tide in the 21st Century?* (The New Press, 2006).

E.J. Hobsbaum. *Nations and Nationalism Since 1780.* (Cambridge University Press, 1990).

Neil Hood and Stephen Young. *The Economics of Multinational Enterprises.* (Longman, 1979).

Michael Hudson. *Global Fracture: The New International Economic Order.*

(Pluto Press, 1977).

_____, *Super Imperialism: The Origins and Fundamentals of US World Dominance.*(Pluto Press, 2003).

Marjorie Kelly. *The Divine Right of Capital: Dethroning the Corporate Aristocracy.* (Berrett-Koehler, 2001).

David C. Korten. *When Corporations Rule the World.* (Berrett-Koehler and Kumarian Press, 1995, 2001).

Stephen Lendman. *How Wall Street Fleeces America: Privatized Banking, Government Collusion and Class War.* (Clarity Press, 2011).

Arthur MacEwan. *Neo-liberalism or Democracy?* (Zed Books, 1999).

Fred Magdoff and Michael D. Yates. *The ABC's of the Economic Crisis: What Working People Need to Know* (Monthly Review Press, 2010).

Osvaldo Martinez. *Neo-Liberalism in Crisis.* (Editorial Jose Marti, 1999).

John McMurtry. *The Cancer Stage of Capitalism* (Pluto Press, 1999).

_____. *Value Wars: The Global Market Versus the Life Economy.* (Pluto Press, 2002).

István Mézáros. *Socialism or Barbarism: From the "American Century" to the Crossroads.* (Monthly Review Press, 2001).

Russell Mokhiber and Robert Weissman. *Corporate Predators: The Hunt for Mega-Profits and the Attack on Democracy.* (Common Courage, 1999).

Ted Nace. *Gangs of America: The Rise of Corporate Power and the Disabling of Democracy.* (Berrett-Koehler, 2003).

Leo Panitch and Ralph Miliband, eds. *The Socialist Register 1994: Between Globalism and Nationalism.* (Merlin Press, 1994).

Leo Panitch, ed. *The Socialist Register 1995: Why Not Capitalism.* (Merlin Press, 1995).

_____ and Colin Leys, eds. *The Socialist Register 1999: Global Capitalism versus Democracy.* (Merlin Press, 1999).

_____. *The Socialist Register 2001: Working Classes, Global Realities.* (Merlin Press and Monthly Review Press, 2001).

_____. *The Socialist Register 2002: A World of Contradictions.* (Merlin Press and Monthly Review Press, 2002).

_____. *The Socialist Register 2003: Fighting Identities: Race, Religion and Ethnonationalism. .* (Merlin Press and Monthly Review Press, 2003).

_____. *The Socialist Register 2004: The New Imperial Challenge.* (Merlin Press and Monthly Review Press, 2004).

_____. *The Socialist Register 2005: The Empire Reloaded.* (Merlin Press and Monthly Review Press, 2005).

_____. *The Socialist Register 2008: Global Flashpoints: Reactions to Imperialism and Neoliberalism.* (Merlin Press and Monthly Review Press, 2008).

Leo Panitch, Greg Albo and Vivek Chibber. Eds. *The Socialist Register 2011: The Crisis This Time.* (Merlin Press and Monthly Review Press, 2011).

_____. *The Socialist Register 2012: The Crisis and the Left. .* (Merlin Press and Monthly Review Press, 2012).

T.V. Paul, et.al., eds. *The Nation-State in Question.* (Princeton University Press, 2003).

Richard Peet. *The Unholy Trinity: the IMF, World Bank, and WTO.* (Zed Books, 2003).

John Perkins. *Confessions of an Economic Hit Man* (Plume, 2005).

James Petras and Henry Veltmeyer. *Social Movements and State Power: Argentina, Brazil, Bolivia, Ecuador.* (Pluto Press, 2005).
_____. *Global Depression and Regional Wars.* (Clarity Press, 2009).
Jack Rasmus. *The War At Home: The Corporate Offensive from Ronald Reagan to George W. Bush.* Kylos Productions, 2006.
_____. "The Trillion Dollar Income Shift, Part I, *Z Magazine,* Feb. 2007, 44-49.
_____. "The Trillion Dollar Income Shift, Part 2, *Z Magazine,* April 2007, 48-51.
William I. Robinson. *Promoting Polyarchy: Globalization, US Intervention, and Hegemony* (Cambridge University Press, 1996)
_____. *Transnational Conflicts: Central America, Social Change, and Globalization.* (Verso, 2003).
_____. *A Theory of Global Capitalism: Production, Class, and State in a Transnational World* (Johns Hopkins University Press, 2004).
_____. *Latin America and Global Capitalism: A Critical Globalization Perspective.* (Johns Hopkins University Press, 2008).
Dani Rodrik. *The Globalization Paradox: Democracy and the Future of the World Economy.* (W.W.Norton, 2011).
Peter Roman. *People's Power: Cuba's Experiment with Representative Government.* (Westview, 1999).
Isaac Saney. *Cuba: a Revolution in Motion.* (Zed Books, 2004).
Joseph A. Schumpeter. *Capitalism, Socialism and Democracy.* (Harper and Row, 1975).
Holly Sklar, ed. *Trilateralism: The Trilateral Commission and Elite Planning for World Management.* (South End Press, 1980).
Lewis D. Solomon. *Multinational Corporations and the Emerging World Order.* (Kennikat Press, 1984)
Joan Edelman Spero. *The Politics of International Economic Relations.* (St. Martin's, 1990).
Joseph Stiglitz. *Globalization and its Discontents.* (Norton, 2003).
William K. Tabb. *The Amoral Elephant: Globalization and the Struggle for Social Justice in the Twenty-First Century,* (Monthly Review Press, 2001).
_____, *Unequal Partners: A Primer on Globalization,* (The New Press, 2002).
_____. *Economic Governance in the Age of Globalization.* (Columbia University Press, 2004).
Michael Taylor and Nigel Thrift, in *The Multinational Corporations and the Restructuring of the World Economy.* (Croom Helm, 1986).
Henry Veltmeyer & Anthony O'Malley, eds. *Transcending Neoliberalism: Community-Based Development in Latin America.* (Kumarian Press, 2001).
Lori Wallach and Michelle Sforza. *Whose Trade Organization: Corporate Globalization and the Erosion of Democracy.* (Public Citizen, 1999).
Ellen Meiksins Wood. *Empire of Capital.* (Verso, 2003).
Richard Westra, ed. *Confronting Global Neoliberalism: Third World Resistance and Development Strategies.* (Clarity Press, 2010).
_____. *The Evil Axis of Finance: The US-Japan-China Stranglehold on the Global Future.* (Clarity Press, 2012).
World Bank. *World Development Report 1997: The State in a Changing World.* (Oxford University Press, 1997).

INTERNET AND MEDIA

www.AFGJ.org Alliance for Global Justice -- peoples think tank and organizing
site with focus on Latin America.

www.alternet.org/ AlterNet is a news mag & online community for "strategic
journalism." Confronts corporate media & right-wing disinformation,
so as to "funnel [visitors'] energy into change." Editors for submis-
sions on: Rights; Corporate Accountability; Democracy; Media;
Health; Iraq; Water; Immigration; Drugs; Sex.

www.americaspolicy.org Americas Program of IRC. Analysis, news, and information on Latin America and inter-American affairs.

www.autonomista.org Argentine Autonomista Project

www.brechtforum.org/economywatch The Brecht Forum

www.cepr.org Center for Economic and Policy Research is an independent,
nonpartisan think tank that was established to promote democratic
debate on the most important economic and social issues that affect
people's lives.

www.globaljusticecenter.org Center for Global Justice – research and learning
for a better world.

www.ciponline.org Center for International Policy– Advocating a U.S. foreign
policy based on cooperation, demilitarization and respect for human
rights.

www.commondreams.org building progressive community by daily posting of
articles on current events.

www.corpwatch.org holding corporations accountable

www.counterpunch.org/ "Counterpunch" ed by Alex Cockburn & Jeffrey St.
Clair. Called "America's best political newsletter," it attracts many
great writers.

www.epi.org Economic Policy Institute

http://fbc.binghampton.edu Fernand Braudel Center , directed by Immanuel
Wallerstein, the "father" of world systems theory.

www.fpif.org. Foreign Policy in Focus

http://forumonpublicdomain.ca Forum on Privatization and the Public Domain

www.globalresearch.ca Centre for Research on Globalization -- publishes news
articles, commentary, background research and analysis on a broad
range of issues, focussing on social, economic, strategic and environmental processes.

www.globalsouth.org An independent monthly e-journal for global interdependence

www.net4dem.org/mayglobal Global Studies Association

www.ips-dc.org Institute for Policy Studies, a progressive think tank in Washington DC that produces many policy reports, articles and books.

www.ifg.org International Forum on Globalization, an alliance of 60 organizations in 25 countries, Spanish and English

www.irc-online.org International Relations Center (formerly Interhemispheric
Resource Center), IRC. A nonprofit organization whose mission is to
provide information and analysis that increase social and economic
justice throughout the world.

www.leftforum.org/ Left Forum brings together organizers and intellectuals
from across the globe to share ideas for understanding and trans-

forming the world with an annual conference each spring in New York City.

www.monthlyreview.org Monthly Review – an independent socialist magazine. /mrzine also has many articles.

https://nacla.org/ The North American Congress on Latin America (NACLA) – in-depth analysis of Latin America and the Caribbean.

www.opendemocracy.org forums on social issues

www1.oecd.org dac/debt/ Organization for Economic Cooperation and Development

www.poclad.org Program on Corporations, Law and Democracy

www.radicalphilosophyassociation.org The Radical Philosophy Association, the parent organization of the Center for Global Justice, has some interesting papers in their Anti-Intervention Project page.

www.socialistproject.ca Canada's Socialist Project has video talks left streamed as well as theoretical articles.

www.sweatshopwatch.org news and action to eliminate sweatshop exploitation in the garment industry. Empowering workers by informing consumers.

www.tni.org Transnational Institute: a worldwide fellowship of committed scholar-activists.

www.truthdig.com. Progressive articles on current events up-dated daily.

www.truthout.org Progressive articles on current events up-dated daily.

www.unstats.un.org/unsd/ United Nations statistics

www.venezuelanalysis.com Current news and analysis on Venezuela and the Bolivarean revolution

www.wsws.org World Socialists website.

http://jwsr.ucr.edu e-Journal of World Systems Research

www.zcommunications.org/znet Progressive articles on current events up-dated daily.

BROADCAST MEDIA

http://www.democracynow.org/ Democracy Now: The War & Peace Report. Daily online global & US news. Amy Goodman & Juan Gonzalez hosts. Excellent source. Interviews both insiders & "outsiders." Great alternative to CNN.

http://english.aljazeera.net/ Al Jazeera English. Its global coverage is a real-world alternative to BBC. HQ in Doha, Qatar, bureaus in Kuala Lumpur, London & Washington. Run by former CBC head. US stories by Avi Lewis. Baghdad office accidentally shelled by US in 2003, 1 journalist dead. Strong on Mideast news.

http://rt.com RT (TV Network), previously known as Russia Today,is a government-funded global communications network based in the Russian Federation offering round-the-clock news bulletins, documentaries, talk shows, etc. Many well known progressive Western commentators appear on its various shows. RT offers ongoing coverage of Occupy Wall Street and other issues addressed by US commentators and activists.

CONTRIBUTORS

José Bell Lara, is professor at the Latin American Faculty of Social Sciences, University of Havana (FLACSO-Cuba). He has written *Globalisation and the Cuban Revolution* (2002) and *Cuban Socialism within Globalisation* (2007). Bell Lara is part of the international advisory board of the journal Critical Sociology.

Armando Cristóbal Pérez holds a doctorate in Political Science from the University of Havana. He has taught there as well as at the Higher Institute of International Relations. He has held diplomatic postings in Moscow and Madrid. He has been Executive Secretary of the National Union of Cuban Writers and Artists (UNEAC) as well as a founder and Vice President of the Cuban Society for Philosophical Research (SCIF). His recent publications include *Literatura y sociedad en Cuba (Ensayos literarios), Del acoso a la consagración. La Cuba del siglo XX en la novelística de Alejo Carpentier (Investigación literaria) , Las puertas del infierno también son verdes (cuentos), Un traspatio en el jardín (cuentos), El Estado Nación. Su origen y construcción (investigación y estudio de teoría política)* y *ena con Buda (*novela-thriller en proceso de edición)

Orlando Cruz Capote holds a Doctorate in Historical Science. He is a researcher at the Institute of Philosophy in Havana and its former scientific subdirectory from 2005-2008. He is Professor at the Higher Institute of International Relations Raúl Roa García and a member of the Nacional Union of Cuban Writers and Artists (UNEAC), as well as a founder of the Cuban Union of National History. For 35 years he has done historical, philosophical and political research. His recent publications include *Apuntes para la historia del movimiento juvenil cubano* (1987); *El Peligro Mayor* (1993); *Historia de la Revolución Cubana 1959-2000* (2001-Inédito); *Proyección Internacional de la Revolución Cubana hacia América Latina y el Caribe* (1959-1962); *El contexto* *histórico-político y filosófico del debate teórico internacional sobre la Identidad Nacional: Un estudio acerca de su re-conceptualización en Cuba y un balance historiográfico de lo publicado en el país entre 1989 y el 2005"* (2006); *Cuba: Nación y Raza en el siglo XX* (2010). He has written essays such as the problem of the Nation-state and continuing research on globalization and nationalism, participation and socialism and contemporary international relations.

Cliff DuRand is a Research Associate at the Center for Global Justice in Mexico, which he co-founded in 2004. He is also coordinator of Research Network in Cuba and has led trips annually to Cuba since 1990. A veteran of the 1960s social movements, he has worked to build institutions of the Left. In 1982 he co-founded the Radical Philosophy Association and the Progressive Action Center, long the "home" of the Left in Baltimore. For 40 years he was a professor of Social Philosophy at Morgan State University. His continuing research and activism focuses on globalization, participatory democracy and socialism.

Olga Fernandez Rios is a Researcher at the Institute of Philosophy in Havana and its former Director from 1988 to 1999. She was professor of Marxist studies and sociopolitical theory at the Central University in Villaclara and at the University of Havana. She has held diplomatic postings, first in the Cuban Mission at the UN in New York and for the last 10 years in the Cuban Interest Section in Washington DC and in the Cuban Embassy in Chile, in both places in charge of Academic Exchanges. She is a member of the Cuban Academy of Sciences. Her research interests focus on the theory and practice of democracy, state and political system. Among her publications are: "Formación y Desarrollo del Estado Socialista en Cuba"; "La terca actualidad del socialismo"; "Democracia: mito y realidad"; "Democracia y Justicia Social: romper el mito o buscar alternativas"; "Socialismo y Democracia en el pensamiento político de Che Guevara"; "Socialismo y Valores Éticos. Una reflexión a partir de El Socialismo y el Hombre en Cuba de Ernesto Che Guevara"; "Cuba: participación popular y sociedad"; and "El Socialismo en Cuba: Búsqueda y Descubrimiento".

Steve Martinot has been a human rights activist for most of his life, as union organizer, community organizer, and anti-war organizer, including Latin America solidarity work. He has worked as a machinist and truck driver, and taught literature and cultural studies at the University of Colorado and San Francisco State University. His latest book is *The Machinery of Whiteness* (Temple University Press, 2011). His two preceding books, also from Temple, are *The Rule of Racialization* and *Forms in the Abyss: a philosophical bridge between Sartre and Derrida*. He lives in Berkeley, CA, leads seminars on the structures of racialization in the US, and is active in a neighborhood assembly and participatory budget movement.

INDEX

16566333R00120

Made in the USA
Charleston, SC
28 December 2012